Maurice Leonard was born in Surrey, and studied drama at the Guild-hall School of Music and Drama. He currently works as a television producer, on such top-rating shows as *What's My Line*, *Whose Baby* and *Strike It Lucky* and was previously associated with Thames Television's long-running *This Is Your Life*, where he worked on the lives of such diverse subjects as Miss Bluebell, Arthur Askey, Dame Eva Turner and Kiri te Kanawa.

Maurice Leonard's previous titles include MADAME BLAVATSKY, THE MEDIUM and SLOBODSKAYA, a biography of the Russian soprano Oda Slobodskaya, under whom he studied singing. He has contributed articles to many journals and magazines, including *Music and Musicians* and *Records and Recording*.

Kathleen

The Life of Kathleen Ferrier
1912–1953
Foreword by Elisabeth Schwarzkopf

MAURICE LEONARD

Futura

A **Futura** Book

Copyright © Maurice Leonard 1988

First published in Great Britain in 1988 by
Hutchinson, an imprint of Century Hutchinson Ltd, London

This edition published in 1989 by
Futura Publications, a Division of
Macdonald & Co (Publishers) Ltd
London & Sydney

ISBN 0 7088 4319 0

Printed in Great Britain by
The Guernsey Press Co. Ltd, Guernsey, Channel Islands

Futura Publications
A Division of
Macdonald & Co (Publishers) Ltd
66-73 Shoe Lane
London EC4P 4AB

A member of Maxwell Pergamon Publishing Corporation plc

CONTENTS

She that comes late to the dance
More wildly, must dance, than the rest
Though the strings of the violins
Are a thousand knives in her breast.

A while there was the voice to cry,
A while there was the hand to touch
And if they did not understand
It may be that we asked too much.

FOREWORD

I sang in three cities with Kathleen Ferrier. First, in Manchester under the direction of Sir John Barbirolli in the *Messiah*; second, in Vienna, where we performed the *B Minor Mass* [Bach] and the *Missa Solemnis* [Beethoven] under the direction of Herbert von Karajan with the Wiener Philharmoniker and then (if my memory doesn't betray me) we subsequently went with those two events to La Scala, Milan.

To speak about the last performance first – it was one of the very few times I saw Herbert von Karajan burst into tears, when Kathleen sang the 'Agnus Dei'. I also remember going to lunch with her in a nearby restaurant – which now no longer exists – when she told me the most excruciatingly funny stories of her experiences within our profession. She had a huge laugh and people turned their heads towards us – no mean achievement considering the normal din in Italian restaurants!

Of the Vienna performance, I know of an unissued record and I am very proud that I can still listen to my voice mingling with hers.

But the greatest experience of all was when she stood on the platform in Manchester sending out her message as the contralto soloist in the *Messiah*. It seems to me now – and did then – that there was a prophet speaking through her singing, or some other such super-human person. I can only repeat what we would call in German a *Binsen-Wahrheit* [truism], which applies to her above all others: there are great singers but very few geniuses whom you recognise after hearing one note – Kathleen Ferrier was one such genius.

Elisabeth Legge Schwarzkopf

To Geoffrey Handley-Taylor, FRSL

PREFACE

When my sister, Kathleen Mary, was born in a small village in Lancashire, no one could have forseen that she was to become a world-famous singer. Yet, looking back, it seems clear that our family background, her early life, the impact of the Second World War and her own great gifts all contributed to the development of the person and the artist she became. *Kathleen* describes very clearly how it all happened, often in her own words: the ups and downs, the successes and failures that are an inevitable part of a singer's life. Her reactions are illuminating and sometimes extremely funny. Descriptions of concerts, reproductions of press notices and the comments of her colleagues and friends, all go to make up this touching picture of a unique artist.

Kathleen was always completely absorbed in whatever she sang. Although in solemn music such as Bach's *St Matthew Passion* and the *B Minor Mass*, in Elgar's *The Dream of Gerontius* or Brahms's *Four Serious Songs*, she expressed her deepest thoughts and feelings, in recitals she could convey a great variety of moods. She would come on to the platform, tall, beautiful, her eyes sparkling, her very appearance telling the audience that they were all going to enjoy themselves. Whether she sang sad or happy songs she held everyone enthralled.

At the height of her career Kathleen was stricken by cancer and the author tells how she faced it with incredible courage. I went to many of her concerts and she never showed the slightest sign that there was anything wrong with her. Singing was the one thing she wanted to do and she was determined to do it, come what may. Knowing how serious her condition was, I was always amazed that she could sing 'O Death, How Bitter' and the Rückert songs with such heart-breaking passion and sincerity. Now I think that perhaps it was her way of facing an intolerable situation.

From her earliest days Kathleen was a joy to me, and I consider myself very fortunate to have been her sister. Some of the love that she inspired has rubbed off on me, and over the years thousands of people have written to me about her and for many she has become a symbol of all that is good and brave.

Many of those people who value her records nowadays never heard her sing in person. Many were not even born when she was alive. So it seems strange that there is still so much interest in her and her work. Perhaps there are some obvious reasons for this. Her voice was a lovely natural contralto, immediately recognisable and full of warmth. Her words, whether in English, Italian, French or German, were always clear and she sang a wide variety of songs which appealed to many different tastes. She found in song the perfect way of expressing herself, her gaiety, her love of people, her spirituality. But there is something else . . . something that cannot be expressed in words, but only in music.

Maurice Leonard is one of those who is too young to have heard Kathleen singing in person, but he too has been captivated by her records. Realising his enthusiasm, I have been happy to let him have access to Kathleen's diaries, letters and press notices and I am sure that this biography will be welcomed by all those who want to know more about Kathleen Ferrier.

Winifred Ferrier

INTRODUCTION

I first remember hearing Kathleen sing when I was fourteen. Her death was announced that day and, in tribute, BBC radio played her recording of 'What Is Life'. Not such an inappropriate choice as it might seem as she had made what virtually amounted to a hit record out of that eighteenth-century Gluck aria, and it is now permanently associated with her. Kathleen's voice is instantly recognisable and could never be confused with anyone else's. But it was not just the gorgeous voice, it was the way she sang which was unique, and its effect on me was personal and moving.

Shortly afterwards an uncle and aunt came to visit. My uncle looked down in the mouth. He was upset, my aunt explained, because his 'girlfriend' had died. That 'girlfriend' was Kathleen, whom he had never met but regarded, as did many others, as a personal friend. Years later I told Winifred, Kathleen's sister, this story. She had heard similar anecdotes before: 'She was everyone's girlfriend,' she said. My family were no great musicologists – they enjoyed a good tune but, to them, Kathleen was something special.

When she sang all musical barriers disappeared, whether her audience consisted of great maestros like Bruno Walter and Herbert von Karajan, in the great concert halls of London, New York, Paris or Rome, or of a callow fourteen-year-old listening to the radio at home.

The aim of this book is to try, in some way, to repay Kathleen for what she has given me. When I started my research, one of the first calls I made was on her teacher Roy Henderson. I confessed to him that I had never seen Kathleen on stage and he tartly informed me, 'Then you only know a quarter of what she did. You had to *see* Kathleen to know what she was all about.' Doubtless, but some of us, by virtue of our tender years, must remain underprivileged. Hopefully, this biography will increase peoples' knowledge of her as a person.

I could not have written *Kathleen* without help from many people. First and foremost I must thank Winifred Ferrier, who gave me access to all Kathleen's personal and business letters, many of which have never been published, and to Kathleen's diaries. Winifred wrote her sister's biography in 1955, but since then much new material on Kathleen and, literally, dozens of letters which she had written to friends have come to hand. Several attempts have been made to write a more up-to-date book on Kathleen, but these have all been resisted by Winifred, as has an attempt to make a feature film of Kathleen's life. Winifred is very protective towards her sister's memory and it was only after a lengthy period following my initial approach, during which I had proved myself loyal to Kathleen, that cooperation was forthcoming. Since then the floodgates have opened. Winifred has not only been cooperative, she has given me a great deal of practical help and advice for which I am deeply grateful.

I would often work for hours at a time in Win's little dining room, where most of her files on Kathleen are stored. There, long into the night, I would immerse myself in Kathleen's diaries and letters. There were several framed photographs of Kathleen on the walls and behind where I sat, hanging from the door, was a heavy green brocade evening dress, which Winifred had made for her, and which Kathleen wore many times for recitals, notably during her American debut. The hem at the back is worn where it has brushed over the boards of numerous concert hall floors.

When I returned home I would often play Kathleen's records for a couple of hours or more and as soon as I woke up in the morning, I would put the records back on the gramophone. A day rarely passed when I did not write about her, listen to her records, read her letters or talk about her to those who had known her.

This research period stretched over three years, and was quite an adventure. Initially Win provided me with contacts by going through her address book and giving me the whereabouts of those of Kathleen's colleagues who were still alive. They, in turn, gave me other addresses, or directed me towards previously untried avenues of investigation, and so it went on until I had built up a formidable pile of anecdotes, memories and opinions.

I must also thank Bernie Hammond, Kathleen's former secretary and nurse, who lived with Kathleen during the last eighteen months of her life. Bernie's response to my initial enquiries was spikey and it was only after a protracted, and intense, cross-examination that she too agreed to help. Then she opened her heart to me and forwarded a 150-page document consisting of the copious diary she had kept for the period she had spent with Kathleen. None of this material has ever been published before.

I had a stroke of luck when interviewing Sadler's Wells Opera's principal soprano, Joan Cross. She had sung with Kathleen in Kathleen's first opera, and readily contributed her memories as well as providing me with a useful research tool by handing me, almost as soon as I had crossed the threshold of her Saxmundham cottage, a huge leather-bound scrap book full of cuttings of Kathleen. 'This was obviously meant for you,' she told me. Apparently, someone had given her the book, recently, knowing she had worked with Kathleen. It had been bought at a village jumble sale. Whoever the original compiler was, I am indebted to him or her, for it contains hundreds of clippings, many from small provincial papers, which were largely unavailable from the current newspaper clippings services I had already consulted.

Contralto Nancy Evans, was also helpful. As well as appearing at Glyndebourne together, she and Kathleen had toured extensively, sharing rooms. It is easy to see why the two women got on so well, for she too has a great sense of humour.

Another contralto, Gladys Parr, was also a joy. At ninety-one, she was deaf as a post, but full of memories and *joie de vivre*. We shrieked at each other until I was hoarse.

On the first occasion I called on Roy Henderson, who was then eighty-one, he was in the garden building a conservatory. Over tea, he gave me some cakes which he had baked himself to a recipe from Gerald Moore. His music room not only contained a framed photograph of Kathleen as Orpheus, but also the piano where they had worked together, notably on the role of the Angel in *The Dream of Gerontius*.

I am also indebted to John Newmark, of Montreal, who was Kathleen's accompanist over several years. He sent me many long, personal letters which Kathleen had written to him, again none of which had been published. He had intended using these in his own autobiography, but due to ill-health felt that he was unlikely to be able to make a start and gave them to me instead.

In addition to the above, I must thank certain other people and organisations, among them: John Amis; Helen Anderson; the late Dame Isobel Baillie; Blackburn District Library; the Rt Rev Cuthbert Bardsley; Lady Barbirolli; Alan Blyth; Paul Campion; Annie Chadwick; Benita Cress; Andrew Dalton, John Parry and Michael Letchford of Decca Records; Peter Diamand; Victoria Dunne; Peter Feuchtwanger; Michael Garady; Kitty Harvey; Fred Maroth of Educ Media Associates of America; Walter Foster of Canada; Leon Fontaine; Dr Howard Ferguson; James Ivor Griffiths, FRCS; Lord Harewood; Susannah Jacobson; John Laurie; Adele Leigh; Alison Milne; the late Gerald Moore; my editor, Kate Mosse of Century Hutchinson; K. A. Newton, FRCP, FRCR; Peter Orr; Catherine Parnall; Burnet Pavitt; Lin Pritt; Roy Purkess; Anne Ridyard; Hans Schneider; Donald Scholte; Elisabeth Schwarzkopf; Desmond Shawe-Taylor; Bernard Taylor; Gordon Thomson; Dame Eva Turner; Jo Vincent; the Bruno Walter Memorial Foundation; John Watson of EMI; the Trustees of the Tennessee Williams Estate; Wyn Wilson and William Wordsworth.

I

The Pianist

ONE

In her brief career, Kathleen Ferrier became one of the best loved of British singers. The transition from telephone operator in Blackburn, Lancashire, to internationally famous singer, in demand by the world's leading conductors and composers, was a magnificent achievement.

In 1953, the year of her death, she could have taken her choice from offers to sing in countries throughout the world. She was already booked for appearances in Africa, and for a coast-to-coast tour of America. Stravinsky had offered her the first performance of a new work, and Toscanini was hoping she would sing for him at La Scala. Herbert von Karajan was trying to induce her to appear in a new production of *Tristan und Isolde* at Bayreuth, and Benjamin Britten was so anxious for her to record his canticle *Abraham and Isaac* that engineers were sent to her bedside when she was too weak to go to a studio.

It was all to no avail. The cancer, against which she had fought so valiantly, finally gained its victory, killing her at the age of forty-one.

Kathleen Mary Ferrier had been in a great rush to get into the world. Indeed, the doctor who delivered her vainly called 'Hold back' to her mother as the flaxen-haired child slid into his hands. It was almost as though Kathleen knew she had a lot to get through in the short time allotted her.

Kathleen, or Kath as the family called her, was born at No 1 Bank Terrace, Higher Walton, Lancashire, on 22 April 1912. Mahler had died the previous year, and Benjamin Britten, with whom she was later to work so closely, was born the year after.

Apart from the speed of her delivery, no remarkable circumstances attended Kathleen's birth. She was the fourth child of William and Alice Ferrier. Their first child had been stillborn, and this may have made Alice overprotective of the surviving three. Her father William was headmaster of the local All Saints' School. While not a poor man, his salary was small, and so there was enough for the necessities of life but little left over for luxuries.

Alice was forty when she gave birth to Kathleen, and William forty-five, but the Ferriers had been hoping for another child, and no baby could have been more welcome. Winifred was the eldest, a capable girl, eight years Kathleen's senior. George was five years older than Kathleen, and already displaying an irresponsibility of temperament which would later cause him, and his family, a great deal of trouble.

William had been the son of a travelling tailor, a calm, steady lad who had taken full advantage of the teacher training college to which his father had scrimped to send him. He studied music theory, becoming an expert on the tonic sol-fa system, and his strong, bass voice made him popular at college concerts. When, aged eighteen, he gained his first position as a teacher, at St Thomas's School, Blackburn (the town in which he was born), he kept up his musical interests by singing with, and training, the church choir.

If there was artistic temperament in the Ferrier household, however, it stemmed from Alice. Intelligent and passionate, with a keen instinctive love of music, she had had little opportunity in her hard life to express herself, a frustration that manifested itself, at times, in aggressive, resentful outbursts.

Her father had started work in a mill at the age of nine. He married early and had two children, but was widowed by the time Alice was eight. This bereavement turned him morose. He neglected his family, leaving Alice to bring up her six-year-old brother, Jimmy, as best she could.

When Jimmy was twelve, Alice felt she could leave him on his own, so she found herself a job at St Thomas's School, helping to look after the infants. She loved this, but sadly her pleasure was shortlived. Her father remarried, had three more sons, and his wife, in business, with her own dressmaking shop to run, found the boys too much to cope with, so Alice had to give up her job and stay at home to look after her half-brothers.

While at St Thomas's, however, Alice, then fourteen, had cast a favourable eye on William. A good-looking youth of nineteen, he seemed to her attractively mature and level-headed. They struck up a friendship which continued and blossomed into a romance even after Alice had left the school. Eventually they became engaged.

Even though William supplemented his salary by teaching at evening classes, his earnings were so small that it was seven years before he and Alice could afford to marry. And even when they did get married, in 1900, Alice and William were obliged to live with William's widowed mother in a rented house in Blackburn.

Alice's mother-in-law was bed-ridden, and heavy, and while William was at work, Alice often had to lift her. She was used to hard work, and thought little of this at the time, but the strain took its toll and Alice attributed the stillbirth of her first son to this, and also the health problems she later developed.

With the arrival of Winifred and George there was considerable financial hardship. And when, in 1910, the rent of the house was raised from 5/9d per week to 6/3d the situation worsened significantly. William might have paid the new rent and meekly put up with things but not Alice. Determined to do the best possible for her children, she searched the area until she found a cheaper house, and there the family lived until she discovered she was pregnant again. With three children the new place would be too cramped, so larger accommodation was needed. It was Alice, again, who found No 1, Bank Terrace, Higher Walton, a small village situated between the thriving towns of Preston and Blackburn, where Kathleen was born.

By the time Kathleen was eighteen months old, the Ferriers had moved yet again, now to 57, Lynwood Road, Blackburn. The reason for this was Alice's desire to provide her children with the fullest possible lives. It was not only that the schools were better in Blackburn – the town itself, with its parish church, concert hall and numerous shops, offered far more than Higher Walton. And there was the Corporation Park just a few minutes away from Lynwood Road, where the children could run about safely in the open air. The move was made possible because, at Alice's instigation, William had applied for, and been awarded the headmastership of St Paul's School, Blackburn, a position which brought a rise in salary.

Kathleen showed an early interest in music. While still a toddler, when her cousin Trixie came for a visit, Kathleen ran to the piano to play for her, but could only manage one finger tunes. She burst into tears, crying, 'I want to play, but I can't play properly!'[1] Clearly her

[1] *The Life of Kathleen Ferrier*, Winifred Ferrier, Hamish Hamilton.

passionate desire for perfection had early beginnings.

Perhaps those tears also showed an obstinately determined will. She certainly demonstrated this a few years later, when some local boys tried to disrupt a little sale she and a friend had organised in aid of Dr Barnado's homes. She had been on the gate, collecting the halfpenny entrance fee, when the boys tried to get in without paying. Kathleen was big for her age, and loved a rough and tumble, and she was not going to allow the boys to upset her plans. She chased them far up the road.

In later years, Kathleen would tell people that she had been a plain child. She even convinced Sir John Barbirolli of this by delving into a box of photographs and producing several snaps of herself as an infant. She also told the critic, Neville Cardus, that her mother had looked hard at her one day and commented, 'I'm ill off about our Kath, she's going to be so plain.'[1]

Certainly the photographs tell us she was not conventionally pretty. Curly hair was then the fashion for children, and Kathleen's hair was straight. Plumpness was considered attractive and Kathleen was gawky. But if she was not beautiful, she was highly intelligent. Spurred by an elder brother and sister, she was able to read before she started school. She learned to recite poetry from memory and loved doing this for visitors, with no trace of self-consciousness. She was a born performer.

She started at St Silas's Elementary School when she was five, but did not stay more than a few months, as Alice had heard that its standards of hygiene were low. Ever concerned for her children, she withdrew Kathleen and placed her in Crosshill, the preparatory department of Blackburn High School. Crosshill was fee-charging, and in order to meet these fees Alice had to get a job.

In fact, she found two jobs. The first, in the daytime, was with the Army Recruiting Office, and the second took up four evenings a week, when she helped out William at a local play centre.

Actually, she was delighted to have the excuse to go out to work: housework bored her stiff, and she thoroughly enjoyed her jobs, particularly the one at the recruiting office. Her jobs were so time-

[1] *Kathleen Ferrier, A Memoir*, ed Neville Cardus, Hamish Hamilton.

consuming, however, that she felt obliged to spend all her non-employed hours looking after the family, and thus she was unable to join any of the nearby music societies. She resented this, as she loved music, regarding it almost as sacred. Such was her respect for it that when eventually the family acquired a wireless set no one was allowed to talk while music was being broadcast; it was either listened to or switched off.

Kathleen continued to amuse herself at the piano, and progressed from playing one finger tunes to using two fingers and a thumb. She played for a family friend who was so impressed that she bought her a copy of *Smallwood's Piano Tutor*. With the aid of this, and help from Alice, Kathleen learned to read music. Although Alice had not had music lessons, she had taught herself, and played the piano quite well. William, also, was always ready to help and advise her.

Winifred was already having piano lessons, and George was singing in a choir, so now something had to be done for Kathleen. Convinced that the child had pianistic talent, Alice took her to the best available teacher, Miss Frances E. Walker, who taught from her home, 131 Montague Street, in Blackburn.

Miss Walker was a local celebrity and much respected in the district – her pupils had gained a remarkable 500 LRAM and ARCM diplomas. Students came from all over the North-West to study under her keen ear and hawk-like eye.

She has been described by a former pupil, as 'a dumpy woman with fierce, beady, little eyes'. Her hands were broad, with short fingers, but she could play magnificently, and had been taught by the famous Tobias Matthay. There were two grand pianos crammed into her tiny studio and another, a full-sized concert grand, in her lounge. Dedicated to her art, when Alice arrived with Kathleen in hand, Miss Walker made it plain that she was not prepared to accept a beginner.

But she met her match in Alice, who was not to be put off so easily. Just listen to my daughter, she begged Miss Walker. Miss Walker relented and was agreeably surprised. She was dubious about Kathleen's unorthodox fingering, but she took her on.

Kathleen's talent flowered under Miss Walker's guidance and it soon became evident that Alice's belief in her daughter had not been misplaced. Winifred has kept a full diary of Kathleen's career and, according to her files, in 1924, when Kathleen was twelve, she entered the Lytham St Anne's Festival and came fourth out of forty-three entrants. Her examination pieces included Bach's *Prelude in E Minor* and Schafer's *At Eventide*, the adjudicator was Dr C. H. Moody. A year later, again at the Lytham St Anne's Festival, she came second out of a class of twenty-six, her pieces including *En Bateau* by Debussy, and Julius Harrison was adjudicating.

Kathleen became a familiar sight in Montague Street, the tall girl with the bobbed, flaxen hair, swinging her music case as she walked to Miss Walker's.

But, while Kathleen was showing such promise, George was proving a difficult child. By the age of fourteen he had grown to the startling height of 6 ft 8 inches and this made him the butt of a lot of teasing from his schoolmates. This seemed to affect his behaviour which, at times, could be disconcertingly uncontrolled and irresponsible.

As well as her music, Kathleen enjoyed school. Doris Ormerod, who taught Kathleen when she was in the Lower Fourth Grade, remembers her as 'intelligent, worthwhile and what I'd call a real character, but not an academic by any means'. Miss Ormerod also recalls that Kathleen was in the choir, but permission for this was only granted on the understanding that she did not sing out. Her voice was too loud, and there was an unacceptable huskiness about it. 'We all knew she was musical,' continued Miss Ormerod, 'she came from a musical family, but none of us had any idea she was brilliant.'

Kathleen was so good at games that at one time it was hoped she might become a games mistress. Doris Coulthard, a fellow pupil at her school, recalled, 'She was a real tom-boy, marvellous at netball and all the sports. She walked on her hands beautifully, and did the most perfect cartwheels I've ever seen.'

She acted in the school plays, and one of her roles was Bottom in *A Midsummer-Night's Dream*. Due to her height, Kathleen was often cast as a man. She was also a clever mimic and her inspiration for much of this came from the many mill girls in the area. She travelled on the trams with them and was intrigued by the way they used their lips, communicating with each other down the length of the vehicles without making a sound. This skill had developed as a response to the noise of the mill machinery, which made normal conversation impossible.

Kathleen was always delighted when her uncle George, William's brother, came for a visit. He was a jovial man and could easily be persuaded to give a fruity vocal rendition of 'Lily of Laguna', to which he did a little dance.

She was also pleased to see her uncle Jim, Alice's brother. Uncle Jim had spent most of his life on Africa's Gold Coast – the 'White Man's Grave', as it was then known – and the children loved him to gather them up and tell blood-curdling stories of his encounters with elephants, snakes and the like. And so, often as not, did William, who had had no chance to travel but was fascinated by anything to do with foreign parts.

Alice, however, was horrified one weekend when Uncle Jim drank an entire bottle of whisky, which he had brought with him. Although this may well have been normal practice in Africa it was certainly not the custom in the Ferrier household. But Alice was not distressed so much by the immorality as by the cost: five shillings a bottle.

By now William was a member of the Blackburn St Cecilia Vocal Union, a local choir with a fine reputation, and regularly took part in performances of *Messiah* and *Elijah*, so the Ferrier children were brought up in the tradition of English choral music and Kathleen never lost her love for it. In her professional life she would sing the *Messiah* more than any other work.

In addition to the St Cecilia Vocal Union, William, Winifred and Kathleen later joined Dr Herman Brearly's Contest Choir. The choir took part in many competitions and on one memorable occasion were invited by the famous Glasgow Orpheus Choir to join them for a festival.

The Hallé Orchestra came regularly to Blackburn to take part in oratorios and to give concerts, and when this happened the whole Ferrier household turned out in force. Kathleen took such delight in these events, and was also showing so much promise as a pianist, that her family felt she ought to go to a music college when she left school. That, however, did not happen and, indirectly, her brother George was to blame.

By now, George was in Canada. He had been in scrapes all his life, so when an emigration scheme was offered under the auspices of the Salvation Army it had seemed sensible for him to take advantage of it.

But he remained a continual worry to his parents. They feared he might get into serious trouble in Canada, and that they would then be required to finance his return to England. He was their only son so, no matter how great the sacrifice, they knew that if the call came they must respond – but there was no possibility of saving the cash for his fare home if Kathleen stayed at school, let alone went on to music college. To aggravate the situation, William was about to retire, and the family would then have to manage on a drastically reduced income.

Aware they might be jeopardising Kathleen's future, the Ferriers still could see no alternative other than to remove her from school. Winifred felt particularly guilty, since she herself had stayed on at school until she was eighteen, and then gone on to teacher training college. But she was powerless to help: although she was now a teacher, she had to repay a loan from the education committee, and this left her only barely enough on which to live. Kathleen was the most composed of all. She accepted the decision without protest.

The same could not be said for Kathleen's headmistress, Miss Gardner, who voiced her objections to Alice in the strongest terms. Miss Gardner felt that a bright, popular girl like Kathleen should have every chance in life. Alice, who probably privately agreed with her, did not waver in her decision and neither did she mention her concern over George, which was, after all, a private, family matter. She firmly informed the headmistress that she had found Kathleen a job as a trainee at the St John's Telephone Exchange in Blackburn, at a salary of 8/3d (41½p) a week.

When Miss Gardner heard *that* she was even more indignant. But Alice over-rode all objections, pointing out that the job was safe and carried a pension, something not to be scoffed at in those days.

Another, more subtle, change was taking place in Kathleen's situation, one of which she was probably only vaguely aware. Her uncle Bert noticed it first. He had been on a visit from Birmingham and, when the time came for him to leave, Kathleen and Winifred walked with him to the bus station. After he had said goodbye to Kathleen, he turned to Winifred and remarked, 'Do you know, I think our Kath's going to be beautiful.'

At fourteen, she was not only leaving school behind but childhood as well.

TWO

Kathleen started work with the Post Office in August 1926, four months after her fourteenth birthday. At that time switchboard telephone operators scribbled down telegrams in pencil on dockets as they were telephoned in. Kathleen's job was to take these dockets to the typing pool and, later, to collect the typed forms and put them in envelopes. These were then sent by chute to the despatch department two flights below. Sometimes, if she discovered that she had made a mistake, but the chute had already been despatched, she would race downstairs to intercept it before anyone else could get to it. It was her proud boast that she could always beat that chute.

As she gained confidence, so her friendly, out-going personality asserted itself. She introduced her colleagues to her much applauded skill of turning cartwheels and walking on her hands and, a co-worker recalls, was reprimanded when caught by her supervisor, 'A little decorum, if you *please*, Miss Ferrier,' he demanded.

She was soon put in charge of the telegram delivery boys. Roughly the same age as she, these were a rowdy bunch and she later confessed to *The Gramophone* magazine that they 'led her an awful dance'.

Kathleen's spare time was also fully occupied. Being good at tennis, she joined the Exchange team and became an enthusiastic member. True to the Ferrier tradition, she joined a choir, the James Street Congregational Church Choir, and she was also a keen girl guide. A Miss Cope, now living in Sussex, remembers Kathleen taking part in the camp fire sing-songs and lustily joining in the chorus of 'On Ilkley Moor Bar t'At'.

Sometimes, when she visited her cousins Trixie, Dorothy and Margaret, there would be other sing-songs, but these were much more disciplined – both Alice and William insisted that all the items, even the comedy songs, were sung with a strict regard for musical values.

Shortly after joining the telephone exchange Kathleen took part in the Blackpool Festival. The adjudicator was Granville Hill, music critic for the *Manchester Guardian*, who reported of her piano playing that 'the phrasing was delicate and appropriate. The touch was dainty in the staccato passages, but more firmness of outline was necessary.'

Kathleen's studies with Miss Walker intensified. She had already, in the December of 1925, passed her finals for the Associated Boards of the Royal Academy of Music and the Royal College of Music. She continued to enter competitions and festivals, and when the dates of these conflicted with her work shifts she would pay other girls to stand in for her.

In the June of 1928, when she was sixteen, she again played in the Lytham St Anne's Festival. Her pieces included Haydn's *Sonata in D Major, No 7* and *Little Shepherd* by Debussy. The adjudicator, J. F. Dunhill, placed her second out of twenty-seven entrants.

But now a far more exciting prospect appeared on the horizon. That same summer, the *Daily Express* announced, in a fanfare of publicity, that it was holding a national competition for under seventeen-year- olds, to discover the most promising young British pianist. Run in conjunction with several piano manufacturers, the prizes inevitably included many desirable upright and grand pianos.

To discourage less serious students, an entrance fee of 2/6d (12½p) was charged. Despite this, a not inconsiderable amount at the time, over 20,000 aspiring pianists entered. These were divided up according to geographical areas, and Kathleen was one of the twenty accepted for her own local area contest, which was to take place at the Memorial Hall, Manchester, on 21 November. The prize was to be an upright Cramer piano, valued at £250, and a chance to take part in the finals at the Wigmore Hall, London, later in the year. Kathleen's name appeared in a national newspaper for the first time, as she was listed with other hopefuls.

From then on, Miss Walker's sole aim was for Kathleen to master the test pieces – Morgan's *Le Bal Poudré*, Rowley's *The Rambling Sailor* and Swinstead's *Serenata*. As the day of the contest drew nearer, Miss Walker tried to calm Kathleen's nerves with the sound advice: 'If *you* feel nervous, then so will all the others, and many will be more nervous than you.' Sensible words, no doubt, but of little comfort to an anxious sixteen-year-old.

So, on 21 November, Kathleen made her first visit to Manchester. The Memorial Hall is just a stone's throw from the Free Trade Hall, where she was later to have so many triumphs with Sir John Barbirolli and the Hallé. Sadly, of course, no premonition of this filtered through to her. As she sat nervously awaiting her turn in the Memorial Hall's green room, listening to the other contestants she wondered instead why she had subjected herself to this ordeal, a thought which was increasingly to occur throughout her career.

The result was a near thing, and two of the entrants had to be recalled to repeat their performances three nerve-racking times, which seems unnecessarily brutal. But finally the judges, Dr Harvey Grace and G. O. O'Connor Morris, agreed and the announcement was made that Kathleen was the winner. A fine Cramer upright piano was to be hers, but not before it had stood for several weeks, with an explanatory placard, in the window of a music shop in Blackburn.

Kathleen had not long to rest on her laurels, since the finals were to be held at the Wigmore Hall on 1 December, which gave her just nine days in which to prepare. In London she would be competing against the other sixty-six local area winners and she had a new repertoire to study.

All expenses for the London trip were covered by the *Daily Express*. This was to be Kathleen's first visit to the capital, and as she had to stay two nights in London, her mother had hoped to accompany her. Disappointingly, at the last moment Alice fell ill. But Winifred, who was between jobs at school, gladly stepped into the breach.

They took the train south, on 30 November. Winifred recalls Kathleen's delight in the taxi, courtesy of the *Daily Express*, which conveyed them from Euston to the Russell Hotel, where they were staying. Both of them, however, were over-awed by the hotel's magnificence. They thought they must have come to the wrong place: could there be another, more modest, Russell Hotel?

This fear laid to rest, they were shown to their room, where they spent a perplexing few minutes trying to find the light switch for the toilet, which was dark and windowless. By accident they discovered that the light came on automatically when the door was closed. This was a great relief. 'We laughed until we cried over that,' recalls Winifred.

Pianos were provided at the hotel, on which the contestants could practise, and Kathleen spent her first evening in London rehearsing.

Next morning the sisters took another taxi, this time to the Wigmore Hall. But now even the novelty of the taxi ride could not cheer up Kathleen. Winifred had never seen her so fraught. She did not relax during the day, and as she stepped onto the platform she was visibly shaking.

Among the contestants were three others of particular interest. One was Frederick Stone, who was to become one of the most distinguished accompanists in the country, and who would later accompany Kathleen at many recitals. The two others were Phyllis Sellick and Cyril Smith who went on to earn fame both as soloists and piano duetists. Phyllis Sellick still recalls the tension of that bleak, December day: 'It was pretty awful, everyone sitting and awaiting their turn to take the dreadful walk across the stage, to play in front of the judges. I particularly remember the piano we used, it was a Steinway grand. I'd never played on such a wonderful instrument and neither, I am sure, had Kathleen.'

But the piano did not help Kathleen, and she had her first sour taste of failure when her name was not included among the six finalists. Ironically, on that same day the *Blackburn Times* had published its congratulations on her pass at the Regional Final, and had extended its hopes for her success in London. The piece would make bitter reading when she returned home the following day.

That evening, Kathleen and Winifred went to Drury Lane Theatre, to see Paul Robeson in *Showboat*. Something in Robeson's singing, triggered Kathleen's pent emotions and she burst into tears.

She continued sobbing even after the show, and all the way back on the bus to the Russell Hotel. There she found a telegram awaiting her from Miss Walker: 'Never mind, love, you did your best.' This kindness, from her formidable teacher, produced even more tears.

Next morning the taxi, again paid for by the *Daily Express*, arrived to take them back to Euston Station. Just to add a finishing touch to their humiliation they dropped their battered suitcase noisily down a flight of steps at the hotel. People turned to stare, and they left stiff with embarrassment.

It was a depressed pair that returned to Blackburn, in sad contrast with the optimistic young women who had departed two days previously.

Kathleen was not of the disposition to mope, but even if she had been she would have received scant sympathy from her family. 'Work it off!' was Alice's answer to most of life's disappointments. And at least Kathleen now had the new Cramer piano. As for Miss Walker, as far as she was concerned the past was the past, and Kathleen must now concentrate on the next step in her pianistic career, the ARCM Diploma. This would be taken in 1929 and was the bridge to the LRAM (Licentiateship of the Royal Academy of Music), which followed two years later.

The ARCM examination was held in London and Kathleen made the journey with a party of students, under the personal supervision of Miss Walker herself. 'She was an absolute dragon, never letting us out of her sight for a minute,' recalls Joyce Crow, another of Miss Walker's students.

Kathleen was thrilled to be going to London again and hoped this time to see some of the sights she had neither had the time nor the inclination to take in on her previous visit. But this was still not be be. No sooner had they arrived at Euston than all the students were whisked off to Chappell's rehearsal rooms, and made to practise there for the rest of the day.

They stayed the night in a small hotel behind the British Museum, Joyce Crow recalls, two girls to a room, and Kathleen took her examination the following morning, returning to Blackburn that afternoon. This time, however, her trip was successful and she passed the ARCM.

Living about ten minutes' walk from the Ferriers, were two professional singers, Tom and Annie Barker. He was a bass and she, singing under her maiden name of Chadwick, was a soprano who had trained in Italy alongside Britain's uncontested Queen of Oratorio, Dame Isobel Baillie. The Barkers were in demand for concert parties, and Kathleen played the piano for them when they rehearsed, competently handling their often complicated arrangements.

One Sunday they had two illustrious guests, the famous Covent Garden baritone, Dennis Noble and Isobel Baillie. Naturally, Annie invited her young friend, but on the great day Kathleen sat transfixed, too shy to contribute to the conversation. All the same, it was an afternoon she never forgot.

Annie and Tom now teamed up with three other artists to form a quintet, which they called The Sevilles. These were tenor Ernest Allen, contralto Jennie Renton and comedian Albert Hodgson. As well as providing comic relief, Hodgson acted as accompanist. The Sevilles were a popular attraction at local halls, but eventually Hodgson complained that it was too much to expect him to play the piano as well as perform his own act. He persuaded Annie to ask Kathleen to be the accompanist. She willingly accepted.

In common with many professionals, the group seldom met except to perform. At their next booking, for which Allen had not attended a rehearsal, the tenor was horrified when, after being introduced to the seventeen-year-old Kathleen, he was told she would be accompanying him. After Kathleen's death, reporter Frank Dugdale wrote of this occasion in the *Lancashire Evening Post*, basing his piece on an interview he had had with Ernest Allen:

'She looks young – will she be all right?' he [Allen] asked Anne Chadwick in a whisper.

'Oh, she'll be all right,' was the reply.

'Does she know our items?' Ernest persisted.

'If she doesn't, she soon will!' was all he was told.

That night Ernest was opening with Leoncavallo's 'Tis the day', and he had had a few pianists who had not invariably succeeded with the tricky accompaniment. He took the music across to Kathleen Ferrier.

'Have you played this?' he asked.

She hadn't but she'd heard it. 'I think I shall be able to manage it,' she said, and Ernest Allen went on to the stage wondering what he was in for. But not for long.

'She played the opening so brilliantly that I never had a qualm about the rest, and I don't think I ever sang the song better,' he told me.

It was the same with every item they put before her. 'Kathleen was the best accompanist we ever had, but we couldn't get her to sing,' Ernest Allen said.

The party used to sing 'Love is meant to make us glad' from *Merrie England*. This is set for five voices but The Sevilles sang it as a quartet, with a certain amount of 'fifth voice' added when one of the four had a moment with a note of his or her own.

'We used to say, "Kathleen will put in the fifth part", and it became one of our stock jokes among ourselves,' Ernest Allen said. 'She would giggle when we said it, but she never joined in. Anne Chadwick got her singing once or twice, but not in public.'

A supper was usually served to the artists after the show and, although Kathleen did not receive a fee, she thought this a marvellous bargain for her services – particularly because, during the supper, Annie would regale the company with anecdotes of her stage experiences. Kathleen never lost her relish for backstage stories. She thrived on the theatrical atmosphere of those concert parties, and loved the thrill of eating late into the night. Probably it was no later than ten o'clock.

Dugdale continued in his article:

Years later, when she was a famous singer, Kathleen Ferrier was met at Preston station by Ernest Allen who, as conductor of Clitheroe Wesley Choir, had engaged her to sing in the *Messiah*.

Of course, they talked about the old days as they drove to Clitheroe. When they spoke of Jennie Renton, Kathleen said this: 'You know, Ernest, I'm sure Jennie had the loveliest contralto voice I've ever heard!'

And she meant it. Kathleen Ferrier was like that. 'She never had a trace of swank and she never forgot a friend,' Ernest Allen said.

She had been booked through agents for this Clitheroe engagement, of course, but she gave Allen a cheque for the same amount as her fee. Staying with Mr and Mrs Allen, Kathleen lit the fire, answered the phone, helped with the washing up.

'You've no idea how grand it is to be among folk you really know,' she said.

Word soon spread about Kathleen's excellence as an accompanist, and other groups invited her to play for them, and she never turned down a booking.

She played for The Raleigh Quartet, one of the members of which was Audrey Brierly, daughter of Dr Brierly, conductor of the St Cecilia Vocal Union. And it is Audrey Brierly who mentions for the first time

Kathleen's longing to be a singer, and remembers that by this time she had sufficiently conquered her nerves to join in the choruses from the piano.

Kathleen's life slipped into a pattern. After she had finished work at the Exchange, she would rush to that evening's engagement, change her frock in some dusty back room and, as there was no time for anything to eat would go hungry until after the performance. She received no payment, but there was no question of her being exploited at these performances. The Barkers themselves received only token fees, and sometimes worked for nothing. It was accepted that making music was sufficient reward in itself.

Her first professional engagement as a soloist was on 10 March 1929, at a Celebrity Concert at Blackburn's King George's Hall. Coming on in the first half, she played Mendelssohn's *Andante* and *Rondo Capriccioso*. 'Polished and sensitive' was the verdict of the *Blackburn Times*. Topping the bill was the distinguished soprano Lilian Stiles Allen, who invariably brought the house down with her moving performance of Gounod's 'Ave Maria'. Watching Madame Stiles Allen in action was a great lesson to Kathleen.

Despite Kathleen's success at the King George's Hall, she had to wait a full year before she was invited to participate in a further Celebrity Concert. This time she performed at the Queen's Hall, Blackburn, where the star was the Australian baritone, Peter Dawson. She was billed as 'One of Blackburn's Famous Pianists'.

There was another success in 1930, when she entered the Liverpool Festival in May and won the first prize and Gold Medal by playing Brahms's *Scherzo in E Flat Minor*. And then, in the June of the same year, she was promoted to telephonist at the Exchange, with a salary of 19/– a week, and took her place at the switchboard, proud to be one of the operators, the *crème de la crème* of the Exchange, and no longer a mere probationer.

That same month she entered the Lytham St Annes Festival and won the competition for under nineteen-year-olds, with Beethoven's F Major Sonata.

As a result of winning both the Lytham and Liverpool Festivals, she was invited by the BBC Manchester to give a short radio recital. She played Brahms's *Scherzo in E Flat Minor*, and a dance, arranged by Percy Grainger, entitled 'Shepherd's Hey'.

As the recital was transmitted live at noon, Kathleen had to pay one of her colleagues to stand in for her at the Exchange and since she was an amateur, and therefore not entitled to a fee from the BBC, she actually lost money due to the broadcast. But what did that matter, compared to the glory?

Kathleen made her third trip to London on 14 May 1931, and gained her LRAM Diploma. With this achieved, she could practise less and spend more time with The Sevilles. After a great deal of thought she plucked up the courage to ask Annie Chadwick to give her some singing lessons.

At that time, Annie, like everyone else, believed that Kathleen's voice was in no way outstanding. But she understood Kathleen's longing to be a part of things, so she agreed to teach her.

By all accounts, Annie was a good singer. Many who had heard her believed that she could have had a national career if she had wanted, but the stresses of the big time were not for Annie, who liked to take things easy. But she was sound vocally, and it was she who gave Kathleen her first lessons in technique, based on the method of her teacher in Italy, plus any tips she had picked up along the way. 'I started her off,' says Annie proudly.

It was of course some months before Kathleen dared to sing in public as a soloist and in the meantime she continued to compete in festivals as a pianist.

Miss Ormerod, her former teacher at Blackburn High School, asked if she would play the piano on Old Girls' Day, and Kathleen agreed at once. Most of the old girls knew she belonged to a chorus and, as she was playing, one of them whispered to her neighbour, 'You can tell she's a singer, look at the size of her mouth.' This was told to Kathleen and she repeated the story for the rest of her life.

It became known that Kathleen was taking lessons from Annie and, as a result, she was invited by Harold Marsden, a local solicitor and guest conductor with the James Street Congregational Church Choir, to sing the small mezzo role in the trio, 'Lift Thine Eyes' from *Elijah*.

Kathleen accepted but then had an attack of nerves. Trying out the music at home, she groaned, 'I shall never be a singer'. But after the performance, on 21 December 1931 the *Blackburn Times* noted, 'Miss Ferrier sang pleasingly.' Her natural musicianship, coupled with her experience in front of audiences, had seen her through, and she was only too delighted to accept when Mr Marsden offered her other small roles.

1931 ended on a note of triumph when she played Beethoven's *Moonlight Sonata* at a concert organised by Miss Walker. The *Blackburn Times* reported that Kathleen 'gave the outstanding performance of the evening'.

She was booked for another Celebrity Concert, at the King George's Hall, this time as accompanist to the entire company. The cast included singers Essie Ackland and Harold Noble, and violinist Louis Godovsky, all established favourites. The experience she gained by working with three such talented but highly individual artists was invaluable.

Now that Kathleen was winning competitions she was frequently called upon to make short acceptance speeches. Being a perfectionist, she decided to take elocution lessons: in 1932 it was quite unacceptable for anyone who hoped to be taken seriously not to speak 'properly'.

Her elocution teacher was Miss Ida Shaw, who taught from her home in the Preston New Road, which she grandiosely termed 'The School of Dramatic Art'.

Miss Shaw was fascinated by all aspects of the theatre and, in addition to teaching elocution, she wrote and produced plays and pageants. She had written a pageant for the girl guides, entitled *The Old Order and the New*, the theme of which was the 'contrast between medieval and established spiritual values'. The municipal officers of Blackburn did not balk at this exalted theme, and the pageant was performed for three consecutive nights at the Northgate Public Lecture Hall.

Kathleen, who had never relinquished her association with the girl guides, was asked by Miss Shaw to play the part of King Arthur. She was an excellent choice for the part, being tall and possessing a low voice. Wearing chain mail, breastplate, and a home-made beard, she made a handsome and romantic young king. The first two nights went splendidly.

Unfortunately, complications arose on the final night. In the middle of the third act a member of the six hundred-strong audience moved the stage curtains to get a better view. They rested on the footlights and began to smoulder; as the preceding scene had been set in a dungeon, with carbon sticks giving off a suitably smoky atmosphere, no one noticed until the curtains actually burst into flames, and set fire to the scenery.

People screamed and rushed for the exits. It was Kathleen who saved the situation. She was centre stage at the time and, acting on impulse, strode downstage and announced in loud calm tones, 'There is nothing to worry about'. Things immediately calmed and cast members ran for the fire hoses, which put out the fire.

But once the fire hydrants had been turned on there seemed no way of turning them off, and in a short space of time, the hall was awash. There was further disruption when the fire brigade arrived and as fireman slithered among the exiting, sodden audience the remainder of the show was abandoned.

Happily, no one was seriously injured, and Kathleen was the heroine of the evening. 'Thank God it happened on the last night and not the first,' she told the reporter from the *Blackburn Times*.

Already, as leading lady, she had an eye for the essentials.

THREE

Kathleen had a pleasant surprise on her twenty-first birthday, when her fellow telephone operators presented her with a bouquet for which they had made a collection while she was off duty. She was deeply touched.

By now, Uncle Bert's prediction had come true and she had developed into an attractive young woman. She had plenty of boyfriends, was keen on dancing and knew all the hit songs of the day, in most of which she was word perfect (she was never to lose her love of dance music), but it was not until she was twenty-one that she began to keep company with any one man in particular. Bert Wilson was a slightly-built, pleasant-looking bank clerk who lived with his parents in Chorley. He was a good tennis player, athletic, and as keen on dancing as Kathleen. His father Robert was a Justice of the Peace and chairman of the Withnell Urban District Council. The Wilsons were a solid, middle-class family.

Unfortunately, soon after Kathleen met Bert he was transferred to the Lytham branch of his bank, a few miles from Blackpool. They missed each other dreadfully, and when a posting became available to the Blackpool Telephone Exchange Kathleen eagerly seized the opportunity.

She took digs in Bispham, north Blackpool. This seemed adult and exciting at first, but Bert still boarded with his parents back in Chorley so she found she was left with many lonely hours on her hands. To cheer her up, Winifred took her on holiday to the Lake District. This worked wonders and, with the fickleness of youth, she teamed up with a young man who owned a motor-cycle. In truth, she was interested more in his machine than in him, and took every opportunity to ride pillion, roaring through the country lanes with her hair streaming out behind.

Winifred tried to interest Kathleen in mountain climbing but, after very briefly trying it, she denounced it as 'a mug's game' and returned to the motor-bike.

Back in Blackpool again, Kathleen became friendly with another operator, Marion Parr, who lived with her mother. Mrs Parr was musical and invited Kathleen to use her piano whenever she liked, although Mrs Parr made no secret that her real love now was singing.

She thrived in the artistic atmosphere at the Parrs, and also on Mrs Parr's cooking. She was fond of her food and claimed that Mrs Parr's apple pie was the best in the world. She grew close to the family, gave up her solitary room in Bispham and came to lodge with them. Marion Parr (now Sandilands), vividly remembers those days when she worked and lived with Kathleen.

When Kathleen was not with the Parrs she was with Bert. She was captain of the exchange table tennis team, and he would go with her to tournaments, loudly cheering her on. They also joined a cycling club and Kathleen bought a bicycle on HP, paying 2/6d a week. The cycle was also useful for visits home to Blackburn.

Sometimes she took Bert home with her, and Alice and William both liked him. Mr and Mrs Wilson were just as keen on Kathleen so, after a few months, it seemed reasonable for the couple to become engaged. Both sets of parents were delighted but Winifred had reservations, feeling that Bert took her sister too much for granted. Annie Chadwick, too, felt they were unsuited. Regrettably for Kathleen's future happiness, however, neither woman spoke up at the time.

Later in 1933 the Post Office was introducing a new service for its telephone subscribers: this was TIM, the talking clock. A female voice, with clear enunciation, was required for this service and employees were invited to apply.

Together with Mary Ball, another operator, Kathleen and her friend Marion eagerly put down their names. There were to be regional heats with the winners going to London for the final audition.

For the Blackpool heat all contestants had to say: 'At the third stroke it will be 10.45 and 30 seconds.' Both Kathleen and Mary failed, Kathleen on the shameful grounds that she had inserted an extra aspirate into the sentence. So much for Miss Ida Shaw's elocution lessons. Marion, however, did well and went on to pass further tests held at Preston and Manchester, qualifying her for the London audition.

Kathleen bore her disappointment well, and transferred her enthusiasm to supporting Marion. 'Kathleen rejoiced over my success as though it were her own,' Marion Parr recalls. When Marion arrived at her London hotel she found a telegram awaiting her: 'All the best Claude, from Cuthbert and Clarence.'

These were the names Kathleen, Marion and Muriel Rothwell (another friend) used when they took part in concert parties at the Exchange socials. They had formed a trio of male impersonators and, dressed in toppers and tails, performed songs in the style of the famous Western Brothers. Kathleen, as Clarence, doubled as the pianist.

Despite this support, Marion was not to triumph as TIM. That distinction went to a Miss Cain, a London girl. Marion telephoned Kathleen with the sad news immediately after the audition, and confessed she felt she had let down the side. The following morning, as Marion was about to leave to catch her train, she received a letter from Kathleen, who had written immediately after the telephone call: 'You have not let the office down. Rubbish! Don't worry! You've brought the office into the limelight. . . . You've done splendidly. Anyway, it's all in a lifetime.'

When Marion got back to the Exchange, Kathleen threw her arms about her and told her it had been a foregone conclusion that a Londoner would get the job anyway.

Kathleen soon had another competition to worry about. Spurred on by Mrs Parr, she enrolled in the 1935 Blackpool Festival, competing as a singer. The competition would not take place until October but she put her name down in May, allowing plenty of time to practise the required pieces.

Winifred tells us that 'Kathleen had always wanted to sing, but never thought her voice was good enough'. This was the reason for her earlier reluctance – Kathleen was a perfectionist, unwilling to undertake anything she doubted her ability to do well. But now, with several small parts to her credit and Mrs Parr's encouragement, she was beginning to reassess the situation. And if the time had really come for a fresh approach, she was determined to set about it properly.

With her move to Blackpool, her lessons with Annie Chadwick had inevitably tailed off, but Kathleen now decided to study singing again, on a regular basis, and she had a teacher in mind.

Thomas Duerdon was married to Kathleen's cousin Margaret; he was also choirmaster of St John's Church, Blackburn. He had a solid local reputation as a musician, and a great deal of experience of singers. Kathleen considered him the ideal person, and he was more than willing to teach her. Although the lessons would have to take place in Blackburn, Kathleen was quite happy to make the journey once a week on her bicycle.

In June, however, she had to interrupt her lessons when she was made a temporary Post Office Demonstrator. This involved travelling throughout the region with mobile exhibitions, inducing potential subscribers to try out telephones and discover the many services available to them.

Kathleen felt perfectly at home meeting the public, and enjoyed the break in her routine, but the interlude soon came to an end and she was back at her usual place on the switchboard, and her weekly lesson with Duerdon.

Plans for her marriage were going ahead, meanwhile, and thanks to his position at the bank, Bert had managed to secure a company house for them at Warton, near Lytham. Kathleen and Marion would often cycle over to Fort Rose, as it was called, to prepare it for Kathleen's future married life.

To all appearances she was just another happy young bride-to-be, but inwardly she was dreading the day. She felt that, despite her affection for Bert, and their common interests, marriage should offer something *more*. As always, she kept her feelings to herself but, years later, she confided to Winifred that she had felt trapped by circumstances, yet could see no way of calling off the marriage. Both families had become so involved with the wedding plans that she could not bear the thought of all the fuss if they were cancelled. So she simply went along with them, and hoped for the best.

She was also hoping for the best at the Blackpool Festival, which was now fast approaching. She felt that Duerdon had improved her voice tremendously, clearing her tone and urging her to pay attention to line and diction.

It was to no avail. The adjudicator, Sir Richard Terry, did not even mention her in his summary. This failure seemed to endorse her fears that she was not cut out to be a serious singer. Better to restrict her singing to enjoying herself with Claude and Cuthbert.

Some fifteen years later, when she was probably Britain's greatest singing star, Sir Richard Terry came to congratulate her after a performance, not realising that the much-fêted diva was in fact the same performer he had so cursorily rejected at Blackpool. He was not left in ignorance for long, for Kathleen took amused pleasure in reminding him of the occasion. In fairness to Terry, there can have been little comparison between Kathleen's singing at twenty-three and what it was to become at the height of her career.

As far as her wedding guests were concerned, she did not let the results of the festival cloud a lovely day. The ceremony took place on 19 November 1935, at Hillside Methodist Church. Kathleen wore a white chiffon dress and carried a bouquet of scarlet roses. The three bridesmaids (Winifred, Bert's sister Florence and Kathleen's cousin Beatrice) wore scarlet dresses and carried white bouquets. William gave her away while Alice fidgeted nervously with her bronze chrysanthemums. The *Blackburn Times* carried news of the event under a four-column heading, 'Wedding of Miss Kathleen Ferrier'. Her piano-playing had already made her a local celebrity. Another reason why it would have been difficult quietly to cancel the wedding.

Among the wedding presents was an oak standard lamp from the girls at the telephone exchange. She felt sad when she looked at it, for it marked the end of her old life. The Post Office had a ruling that married women could not be employed and so, with the announcement of her wedding, she had automatically had to terminate her employment. She had worked for the Post Office for nine years and her starting wage of 8/3d had risen to £2.3s.0d; she had enjoyed the work and made lots of friends. She wondered how she would fill the time now that she was married.

After the reception, at Withnell Fold Concert Hall, the *Blackburn Times* tells us that, 'Mr and Mrs Wilson left for the honeymoon in London and the South. The bride travelled in a brown coat and hat, trimmed with Persian lamb.'

They were staying with Winifred at her flat in Edgware, where she had moved to be close to the school she was now teaching at. Who knows what Kathleen's emotions were as she made her way south, knowing that – despite everyone's good wishes – she did not love her new husband.

Years later Kathleen confessed to Winifred that she had dreaded every night of her honeymoon. Whatever had been her expectations of marriage they were clearly disappointed and, after a period of enforced separation while Bert was in the army, the marriage was eventually dissolved in 1947, on the grounds that Bert had been unable to consummate it. Both, however, kept up appearances at the time, and even their friends were not aware that there were problems. She and Bert made the best of their marriage, such as it was; there were no barbed comments, and their disagreements seemed few. Occasionally, their frustrations boiled over, and once Kathleen pleaded with Bert, 'Why don't you make more fuss of me?' She received the cold response, 'You don't run after a bus once you've caught it.'

Although not cut out for the job, Kathleen set conscientiously about becoming a housewife, and soon invited Marion and other friends to tea. On the first occasion, she proudly baked them rock cakes in her new cooker. 'That's exactly what they were like,' recalls Marion Parr, 'hard as rock.' Her cooking improved, of course, but there was always a hit-and-miss element about her dishes.

Time seemed to hang heavily on her hands during the day, and she missed the companionship of the Exchange. In order to fill her time, she started to give piano lessons and was soon teaching ten children a week at a fee of 2/– a lesson. A source of diversion in the evenings was the Lytham Vocal Society, to which both the Wilsons belonged, cycling to Lytham every Tuesday for rehearsals.

Among the singers was a woman called Margaret Dakin, who worked at the bank with Bert. After practice, Margaret would invite them home and they would have more music. Kathleen played duets with Margaret's sister and would often round off the evening with a couple of her comedy songs, of which by now she had a plentiful stock.

Margaret was impressed by Kathleen's voice and urged her to audition for solo parts with the Society, but she laughed it off. Her failure at the Festival still stung. But when Margaret's mother asked her to sing for the Mothers' Union she felt, after having received so much hospitality, that she could not refuse. She chose 'Bless This House', which she sang to her own accompaniment. This proved to be the biggest singing success she had ever had. The mothers clapped enthusiastically, and the surprised, but gratified, Kathleen provided a few comedy songs as an encore.

But Kathleen had no time to make a return appearance for, no sooner had the Wilsons settled at Fort Rose than they had to move. Bert was promoted to manager, which was welcome news, but his new branch was many miles away, in Silloth, Cumbria.

Although Silloth (which in 1936 had a population of just 3,000) had none of the bustle of Blackpool, it had other attractions. Situated close to the Cumbrian capital of Carlisle, it had a harbour where ships docked from all over the world, and behind the town the view from the golf course, across the Solway Firth to Scotland, provided a backdrop of spectacular mountain scenery.

Bank House was a pretty, two-storey building; its rooms pervaded with the scent of the nearby pine forests. The bank premises occupied the ground floor and the living accommodation was above. When lunch was ready, Kathleen would announce the event by dancing a heavy tattoo on the floor.

She and Bert soon involved themselves in the social life of the town, and joined the choral and the amateur dramatic societies, accepting any parts offered. Once, when they were short of men, Kathleen obliged and strode on stage with her hair screwed up under a cloth cap. She made props, baked pies for social functions and helped with anything required. She played tennis, swam in the sea, and took a keen interest in golf, becoming very good, and very determined. Sometimes, if she played a bad shot, she would hurl the club along the fairway after the ball. When she later played golf with Roy Henderson he was to say, 'She could hit a ball as hard and as straight as any man.'

She resumed giving piano lessons but with rather less enthusiasm. She loved children, and became a godmother several times over, but lacked a teacher's patience. A natural musician, she found it tiresome to have to instil basics into those less gifted. Sometimes, if she found a child particularly irksome she would walk to the window and make pained faces to her friend, Eleanor Coyd, who worked in the dress shop across the way.

She was resident piano and organ accompanist to the Silloth Choral Society and accompanied, free of charge, any local singer who asked. The bass, Jack Holliday, made an appearance in Silloth and Kathleen accompanied him. 'After the concert she invited me home,' he recalled, 'and it was there that I first heard *her* sing. No doubt many claim they were responsible for her taking up singing seriously, but I think I had as much to do with it as anyone.'

It seemed, with the move to Silloth, she had gained confidence in her voice. Probably her success with the Mothers' Union helped. Another reason was that here she was accepted as a singer in her own right, rather than as a pianist simply being indulged. Her voice, also, was maturing; it had taken its time, as is often the case with contraltos.

When the 1937 Carlisle Festival was announced she put down her name for the Open Piano Class. But when Bert bet her a shilling she would not dare to enter the singing contest, she took him up.

The Festival lasted a week, during which Kathleen passed through to the finals in both classes. The instrumental finals were first and she was required to play two pieces, *Sarabande* by Thiman, and Arensky's *Study in F Sharp*.

Kathleen was first on the bill, an unfortunate position: not only had she no other performer upon which to gauge herself, but the audience had not had time to warm up. Despite this, she was the winner, and the *Carlisle Journal* for 23 March 1937, carried a report of adjudicator (the Royal Academy of Music teacher and music publisher), Maurice Jacobson's remarks: '. . . she set a high standard. . . and gave them an elastic, supple and most romantic performance; judged on its own merits, a rattling good performance. "I can't criticise her technique," he said, "because, technically, it was most competent; colouring and pedalling so good."'

Such praise at a festival was rare, and clearly she outclassed all the other competitors. Her triumph, however, was soured by complaints from some of the entrants, who claimed it was unfair for a LRAM to enter the Festival since her qualifications made her virtually a professional. This had not occurred to Kathleen and, upon reflection, she realised there was some truth in the accusation.

This unpleasantness made the vocal finals even more important. Whatever else, no one could accuse her of being a professional singer!

There were two adjudicators; Maurice Jacobson again, and Yeoman Dodds. Kathleen sang Roger Quilter's 'To Daisies' and possibly this expressive setting of Herrick's words particularly suited her voice. Certainly the adjudicators thought so. Jacobson was as fulsome in his praise of her singing as he had been of her playing. The *Carlisle Journal* again recorded his comments: '. . . Mrs Wilson, of Silloth, had a very, very beautiful voice indeed, one of the finest voices they had had.' Elsewhere in the editorial the events of the Festival were summarised: 'The most striking individual success. . . was that of Mrs Kathleen F. Wilson. . . . In addition to winning the premier vocal award. . . she also took first place in the open pianoforte class. Mrs Wilson, announced as champion, was presented with a silver rose bowl amid applause by the Secretary of the Festival.'

Kathleen treasured the rose bowl and after her death Winifred returned it to Carlisle where it is presented each year to the winner of the lieder class at the Festival.

II

The Singer

FOUR

After the Carlisle Festival, Kathleen was offered several engagements, the most exciting being a performance of *Messiah* at the Brow Street Methodist Church, Maryport, with the famous tenor, Trefor Jones. She also accepted the contralto part in *Elijah* to be given early in 1938. This, however, was not her first appearance as a professional. She had already sung at a Harvest Festival in a church in Aspatria with a tenor, Joe Wallace, where they had both been paid 7/6d (37½p). She had no car, so Joe had picked her up and driven her to Aspatria.

'She was dying to have a go,' Joe remembers. 'She told me she had spent hours practising. We laughed a lot on the way to the church, but when I heard her sing I was impressed. A sound like that comes just once in a lifetime.'

Kathleen had a new friend now, Wyn Hetherington, who also sometimes drove her to engagements. Kathleen confided to Wyn that her main worry about singing was breath control, which she felt was lacking in her technique. She hoped it would not let her down. Wyn had a three year-old son, Peter. He was with Kathleen one day while she was sewing a button on to his father's coat. 'Clever Kaff,' he said when she showed him the finished job. The soubriquet stuck and, after that, she often called herself Kaff, and signed her letters KK (Klever Kaff).

In November 1938, she took part in the Workington Festival, where she sang Vaughan Williams's 'Silent Noon'. There seems to have been some unsteadiness in her tone but 'Silloth's Champion Vocalist', as the *West Cumberland Times* dubbed her, still came first and won a gold cup.

The adjudicators were J. E. Hutchinson and J. F. Stanton. As Dr Stanton presented the trophy he described her voice as having 'true contralto texture'. The *West Cumberland Times* reported that, as Kathleen accepted the trophy, she told an amused audience, 'I must rush home to mother, won't she be proud of me?' Alice and William were visiting at the time.

Her next booking in December 1938 was at the Workington Opera

House where she appeared in a variety show. It was called *Artists You Might Never Have Heard*, and she shared the bill with performing dogs, comedians, impressionists and acrobats. William and Alice were in the audience this time, Alice nervous as always, while William just sat back and beamed, as he usually did when Kathleen appeared. Also in the audience were BBC radio producer Cecil McGivern and W. S. Newell, a journalist for the *Whitehaven News*. McGivern recruited talent for the BBC variety show *Hark Forrard*, which Newell presented.

Wearing a simple, white dress, Kathleen sang 'Curly Headed Babby'. McGivern later described her performance as 'electrifying', and Newell wrote in the *News* that he was 'at once struck by . . . the sheer artistry of her singing'.

After the show, McGivern booked her for the next edition of *Hark Forrard*, which was to be on 23 February 1939. Before this, however, she won a gold medal at the Millom Festival, by singing Hugo Wolf's 'Verborgenheit', in English. Adjudicator Maurice d'Oisley announced: 'Her voice . . . makes me imagine I am being stroked.'

At a rehearsal for *Hark Forrard*, in the Whitehaven Empress Ballroom, she sang 'At the End of a Perfect Day' accompanied by the Cleater Moor Male Voice Choir. She was asked to sing this song many times in her career, invariably with a male voice choir, and she would refer to it, all in one breath, as 'At the End of a Perfect Day with a Male Voice Choir'.

By now, Kathleen had amassed quite a few newspaper cuttings and had pasted them into a school exercise book. Among them is a cutting, from an unnamed newspaper, probably the *Whitehaven News*, in which Newell briefly recalls that Empress Ballroom rehearsal. 'We discovered that the key [for 'At the End of a Perfect Day'] was about three tones higher than the ordinary contralto range but Kathleen made a great show. Eventually we rewrote the whole thing [for her].'

All the Ferriers were excited at the prospect of the forthcoming broadcast, but probably Alice most of all. Sadly, she didn't live to hear it. Her health, never good, now deteriorated rapidly, and she died from complications arising from a strangulated hernia. Alice's death, at sixty-six, was a terrible blow to the family, for she had been a true matriarch, the architect of their lives. Kathleen was well aware that she might not have been making the broadcast at all, but for Alice's determination to arrange music lessons for her.

Hark Forrard was broadcast live from Newcastle in the evening, at the peak listening time of eight-thirty. The broadcast proved popular, and an unattributed review in Kathleen's scrapbook reads: 'Mrs Kathleen Wilson, making her first appearance on the air as a vocalist, scored an immediate success. Much of her large audience, in all parts of the country, enjoyed her singing of "Cumberland Way" and "Curly Headed Babby". Her rendering of "At The End of a Perfect Day", accompanied by the choir, will long be remembered.'

As Newcastle is eighty miles from Silloth, the BBC had organised a coach to pick up Kathleen and the choir, and take them to the studios. This worked well. On the return journey, however, the driver kindly agreed to drop off the choir members, one by one, at convenient locations, so that by the time he got around to delivering Kathleen it was four in the morning. Not that she minded – although half-frozen to death because the coach was unheated, she was still in a daze of excitement.

In the April of 1939, she again entered the Carlisle Festival and won the coveted *Cumberland News* trophy for the best soloist. She sang Richard Strauss's 'All Souls' Day'. *The Cumberland News* reported this as 'a most wonderful rendering of a terribly difficult song.' The adjudicators were Dr Armstrong Gibbs and Dr J. E. Hutchinson. In his summation, Dr Hutchinson remarked that her voice was 'soul satisfying' and 'stood out like a beacon'. After the festival, Hutchinson chatted to the reporter from the *Cumberland News* and added, 'I said this morning she had a tremendous lot of promise. Afterwards I was told she was a married woman, but I still say there are possibilities which are rather marvellous . . . Mrs Wilson is a real contralto with a most artistic conception of the song . . . we had no hesitation in awarding the prize to the contralto.'

BBC Newcastle invited her to make further broadcasts and although there was no question of refusing, transport was a constant problem. Her husband could not take time off from work to drive her, and she could not expect the BBC to pay for a taxi. Limousines were sent for only the biggest stars. Eventually her father solved the problem by buying Kathleen a little Morris car.

She loved the car, and as its registration number started with the letters JT, she christened it John Thomas. In those days it was not necessary to take a driving test, so she simply bought a licence from the post office, and after some kangaroo starts and jerky practice around the local lanes, used the car to take her to all her engagements. John Thomas could be temperamental however, and once, when Kathleen was driving Winifred down South Road, he suddenly stopped. Kathleen, who knew nothing about cars but was always prepared to have a go, lifted the bonnet and began tinkering with a screwdriver. To her amazement he started at once, no doubt terrified that she'd do him a serious injury!

After Alice's death, William did not want to live alone in Blackburn, so he went to stay with Winifred in her flat in Edgware. This arrangement soon proved impractical. The flat was too small for two, and besides, Winifred was not happy leaving her father alone all day while she was at work: he was a gregarious man and had always been used to company. So a family conference was held and, despite their own personal difficulties, Kathleen and Bert suggested that he came to live with them.

They did their best to keep the strains of their marriage from William, and it is possible that they succeeded – certainly if he did glean that something was wrong he never mentioned it. But by now their relationship, never good, had deteriorated badly. In particular, Bert objected to the amount of time Kathleen spent pursuing her career. He complained to Margaret Dakin that he was becoming known as Mr Kathleen Wilson, a state of affairs he found very hard to accept.

Within a short time, meanwhile, William was pottering about Silloth as if he had lived there all his life, and he soon got to know more of its history than many who had. He spent hours at the docks, watching the cargoes being unloaded, and delighted in showing visitors around. A great conversationalist, he would chat to anyone who would listen to him.

He took great interest, too, in Kathleen's singing, and would transpose music for her. He was an excellent copyist and often suggested songs for her. Kathleen found this a great help as there was a shortage of interesting music in the standard contralto repertoire. He also supported her determination now to take singing lessons in earnest. Remembering how impressed Dr J. E. Hutchinson had been with her singing, she wrote asking him if he would consider accepting her as a pupil. He invited her to his home in Newcastle to discuss the matter. But it was a two-hour trip at least from Silloth to Newcastle and as she drove John Thomas eastwards that first day she realised that on a regular basis the round journey made the whole project quite impossible. Even apart from the time required, she would be arriving for lessons too tired to benefit from them.

Ironically, it was the war, which had broken out in September that year, which resolved the situation. So far, Silloth had experienced few ill effects from the conflict, but it was a different story in Newcastle, with its concentration of heavy industry, and the city was a regular target for German bombers.

Due to this, many schools had been evacuated and Newcastle Central High School, where Hutchinson taught music, had gone to Keswick. To continue with his pupils, Hutchinson made the journey there once a week, breaking his journey for the night in Carlisle, where he taught privately at the home of local soprano, Ena Mitchell. Carlisle was a mere half-an-hour's drive from Silloth and he was happy to include Kathleen among his private pupils. It was an arrangement that suited Kathleen perfectly. She would not ask Bert to pay for her lessons, but financed them by once again taking in piano students.

Hutchinson was a well-known teacher who had been a pupil of Alberto Visetti, a singer much in vogue in London during the 1920s and among whose students were two outstanding soloists, the soprano Agnes Nicholls, who, in 1906, created the role of the Blessed Virgin in Elgar's *The Kingdom*; and the contralto Louise Kirkby-Lunn, of whom no less an expert than Sir Henry Wood had written: 'a singer with whom I never found fault in so much as a quaver'.

Kathleen's lessons became the high point of her life. She always arrived with more music than she could hope to get through but in consequence, as Hutchinson became more involved with her, the lessons extended from half an hour to several hours at a stretch. As she had suspected, since breath control is the foundation upon which all technique is based, work was particularly needed on hers, and Hutchinson concentrated on this until she could produce a steady, unbroken stream of sound.

Kathleen was uncomfortable with some of the notes at the break in her voice, where she changed from middle to chest register, as she felt they lacked colour. This fault was ingrained, and took hours of practice to correct. She was never satisfied with her progress and often, even after a long session, would beg Hutchinson, 'Let's try out my break again, love.'

Hutchinson introduced her to the 'Laudamus Te' from Bach's *B Minor Mass*, and the part of the Angel from Elgar's *The Dream of Gerontius*, and as her technique improved she became able to sing Bach, Handel and early Italian arias with a true bel canto sound.

He soon recognised that she had a short range of just two octaves, and never attempted to stretch it, content to work between G below middle C to high G.

Gradually, and with growing wonder, both Kathleen and Hutchinson became aware that something rare was taking place in Ena Mitchell's front room. It seemed that Kathleen possessed a gift, which, even at that stage, was clearly far beyond the ordinary.

FIVE

It is difficult to guess what might have happened to the Wilsons'
marriage if the war had not intervened, giving them a chance to think
things out separately. As events turned out, when Bert was conscripted
into the army in 1940 it was, in effect, the end of their marriage. They
saw each other a couple of times thereafter, when Bert was on leave, but
soon drifted irretrievably apart. In 1947 they agreed that an annulment
would be best for both of them. Although the plaintiff, Kathleen took
pains to point out that Bert was not to blame, and that the marriage had
simply been a mistake from the start.

From then on Kathleen rarely mentioned her marriage and in later
years few people knew it had ever taken place. Bert later married Wyn
Hetherington, whose first husband had died. Kathleen gave them her
blessing and, if she was in the area, would visit them. 'Bert and I often
talked about her,' says Mrs Wilson. 'We remained in touch until Kath
died. There was never any unpleasantness, everyone behaved in a
civilised manner and it was all handled smoothly.' Wyn and Bert had a
happy marriage until Bert's death, of cancer, in 1966.

Shortly after Bert's call-up, Kathleen reverted to her maiden name.
She claimed this was for no other reason than that Ferrier had a better
professional ring to it, but the change also symbolised her freedom, and
was the outward emblem of her new life. Despite her loyalty to Bert,[1]
Kathleen had suffered emotionally during her marriage. She never
confided in strangers and rarely to friends, but both Annie Chadwick
and Winifred were well aware of the misery she had gone through.

Shortly after Bert's conscription, Kathleen and her father were given
notice to quit Bank House. The new manager now needed the premises.
It was difficult to find somewhere else to live as there was an aerodrome

---

[1] And his to her. For whatever Bert's private feelings, it seems he spoke
nothing but well of Kathleen. Certainly no interviews give evidence to the
contrary.

near Silloth and RAF personnel had taken all available accommodation.

Winifred was able to solve the problem. Due to the uncertainties of the war she felt she now wanted to be with her family, and she looked for a teaching position in Carlisle. Jobs were easy to get due to the number of men who had been conscripted. She quickly found a position, and was able to take over the house of another teacher who had been called up. Kathleen and William moved in with her.

There was not a lot of space in the house on Windermere Road – and the kitchen was so tiny that Kathleen used to complain that to get to the oven she had to open the back door. Yet Carlisle suited her: she could walk to Ena Mitchell's for the lessons with Dr Hutchinson around which her life was now so happily centred. She practised singing for hours but also, in order to pull her weight domestically, she undertook to do the shopping and the housework.

Air-raid warnings were common, and she learned how to imitate the sound. A Silloth friend recalls, 'She demonstrated this at a party by standing outside the back door and howling for all the world like a siren. Several people were fooled.'

Another trick she mastered was shinning to the top of a lamp-post. It astounded passers-by.

In the early months of 1941 she met tenor John McKenna, who was appearing at Carlisle. He recommended she audition for Eve Kisch, a flautist who was acting as director of the North Western Counties division of CEMA, the Council for the Encouragement of Music and the Arts. The aim of CEMA was to organise troupes of artists to tour troop camps, works canteens, offices and factories, and bring entertainment to those who had little opportunity of visiting theatres. Usually of a high standard, the CEMA concerts were very popular, and attracted large audiences.

'She bore it well,' said Kathleen of her audition with Eve Kisch. She did indeed; she offered Kathleen a contract on the spot.

When the excitement subsided, she worried that she was acting selfishly. The CEMA bookings meant that she would be unable to look after her father, thus placing an unfair burden on Winifred. But one look at Kathleen's face convinced Winifred and William that if she were stopped it would break her heart, so they brushed her worries aside. In any event, they were as excited as she was. Hutchinson also gave her his encouragement, knowing that there is no better training for a performer than singing to an audience.

Thereafter, she travelled extensively with CEMA, as far north as Scotland and as far south as Warwickshire, appearing in church halls, warehouses, barns, function rooms and anywhere where it was possible to put a piano. Sometimes Eve Kisch would travel with her and Kathleen would sing to music arranged for piano, flute and voice. Sometimes the flute would be replaced by a trumpet, or oboe, depending on the instrumentalists available. Kathleen often scored the arrangements for these trios herself. Maurice Jacobson, the pianist and music teacher who had adjudicated at the 1937 Carlisle Festival, was also on the CEMA list of entertainers, and he frequently appeared with her as her accompanist. Her programmes usually included Handel, Purcell, Schubert (in English), a few operatic arias such as 'Softly Awakes My Heart', songs by Vaughan Williams or Frank Bridge, and folk songs.

She appeared in Hanley, with the Etruscan Choral Society under its conductor Harry Vincent, and received the first standing ovation of her career. This touched her deeply: she never forgot the warmth of that Hanley audience. Indeed, when after the war the ECS purchased, by public subscription, a small hall – even though by that time she had a prodigious reputation in music, in demand all over Britain, and the hall could only seat 120 – she readily agreed when Vincent asked her to sing at the inaugural concert, and she refused to accept a fee. She continued to sing regularly at the Etruscan Philharmonic Hall and always waived fees. The hall is now renamed the Kathleen Ferrier Hall.

One of the great musical partnerships of the war, and immediate post-war years, was that between Kathleen Ferrier and Isobel Baillie. They had already met at Annie Chadwick's tea party, but they first sang together at a Hallé performance of *Messiah* at the Empire Theatre, Chester-le-Street on 7 December 1941.[1]

[1] In her biography *Never Sing Louder than Lovely* (Hutchinson), Baillie gives 21 December as the date of her first appearance with Kathleen. Kathleen's diary records her debut with Baillie as 7 December 1941. On both occasions the work was *Messiah*.

Interest was obviously centred on Baillie, but Kathleen too received favourable mention in the local paper. She sang a further *Messiah* with Baillie on 21 December at Lytham. This was a much grander affair and she responded to the occasion with enthusiasm. 'That was my first *real Messiah*,' she excitedly told Baillie . 'It will not be your last,' was the response.[1]

Both performances had been conducted by Alfred Barker, leader of the Hallé, who had engaged Kathleen at a fee of £3.3s.0d. per performance. In Lytham Kathleen was staying at the same boarding house as Barker and she confided in him that night that she would love to make singing a full-time career. Barker told her that if she was serious about a singing career then she would probably have to move to London. It was obviously an evening for candour, since he added that he felt her singing lacked commitment and that she also needed lessons in deportment. It could have been depressing to have been the subject of such criticism, particularly after her fine performance, but she accepted that Barker's comments were prompted by a genuine desire to help.

At a CEMA concert in Newcastle, Kathleen was booked to sing with diminutive baritone Mark Raphael. Raphael recalls that she was a good four inches taller than he and they made an improbable pair as they stood side by side. Matters were improved by placing Raphael downstage and Kathleen upstage. They then appeared to be the same height to the audience. Although no one else who worked with her at this time commented on her having anything more than the usual flutters about going on stage, Raphael commented: 'I would never have said, at that time, that she could have had a great career. She was far too nervous.'

In the February of 1941 she took part in a concert in Penrith, where a silver collection was taken in aid of Warship Week, during which, predictably, she was asked to sing 'Rule Britannia' and 'Land of Hope and Glory'. In March she undertook a three-day tour with composer Michael Head, whose songs she included in her programme. Maurice Jacobson was, again, her accompanist and she described his playing as 'a perfect joy'.

She also found it a joy when she was introduced to Malcolm Sargent,

[1] *Never Sing Louder than Lovely*.

one of the country's most celebrated conductors. Alfred Barker presented her to Sargent after a Hallé concert with the words: 'This girl has a *voice*'.[1] Sargent, who met hundreds of singers, expressed a few polite words, then presumably forgot about her. But she wrote to him soon after, reminding him of the occasion, and asking if she could audition for him. After some delay he agreed, and she sang for him at a private audition in the ballroom of the Midland Hotel, Manchester.

Sargent was guarded. He told her she could have a great future, but he echoed Barker's advice that she should go to London if she hoped to be taken seriously.

Kathleen left the hotel depressed, believing she had let herself down. But eight days later, on 29 May 1942, she received a letter from Sargent: he had arranged for her to audition for John Tillett, of Ibbs and Tillett, one of the most important concert agencies in the world.

A few days later a letter followed from Mr Tillett, informing her that he would be pleased to hear her on 9 July, in London, at the Wigmore Hall.

Although a period of intense study obviously followed Tillett's letter, there were still many CEMA concert bookings to honour, and she also became involved in the Holidays at Home scheme. In response to the wartime restrictions that made holidays away from home impractical, various cities participated in a programme encouraging people to make the best of holidays in their home towns. To this end concerts were given in public places. Newcastle subscribed to this scheme, and Kathleen was booked, with the Newcastle String Orchestra, for a Serenade Concert in Exhibition Park. A marquee was erected and, as the weather was pleasant, the evening was a great success.

Not so successful though, were Kathleen's dealings with Tom Harrison, the Midlands representative for CEMA.[2] Harrison was a bold thinker, but his ideas did not always work out as planned. On this occasion he was setting up a series of concerts for factory workers, and had booked Kathleen to appear with the Ruth Pearl String Quartet. But he was having a hard time with several of the organisers, who

[1] *The Life of Kathleen Ferrier*.
[2] The anecdotes concerning Harrison are based on an interview published in the *Birmingham Post* on 23 January 1954.

doubted the wisdom of introducing a contralto to a factory audience. It was thought too up-market.

The music critic, Eric Blom, became involved and attended rehearsals. Listening to Kathleen for a few minutes, he told Harrison 'She'll do'. And he was proved right: the factory workers welcomed Kathleen and the Quartet enthusiastically. The *Birmingham Post* published Blom's glowing review, which so pleased Kathleen that she carried it in her handbag for weeks.

But then, inspired by this triumph, Harrison planned another, more ambitious event. He arranged for a concert to take place on the River Trent. Kathleen was again to appear with the Ruth Pearl String Quartet which would be augmented by flautist John Francis. They would be placed in a punt, which would majestically glide down the river, past the audience. The theory was that the music would be heard softly at first, then would gradually get louder as the punt drifted into view.

Unfortunately, the principle of Harrison's enterprise was not fully appreciated by his team. Rather than risk the punt drifting lethargically on the current, out of control, an outboard motor was fitted. But no one knew how to control its speed so, instead of the pastoral sequence intended, the punt chugged briskly into view and just as briskly out of view again. Kathleen spent the entire recital being shunted to and fro in front of a mystified audience. To add to the mystification, there was a strong wind which rendered most of the music inaudible.[1]

Undaunted by this fiasco, in June Harrison arranged another open-air concert for her, at Wednesbury, where she would be singing from a bandstand. By this time, Kathleen was a little disenchanted with Holidays at Home. The vagaries of the climate usually provided rain or wind, or both, and no audience was going to stand around for hours, shivering and drenched, no matter how gifted the performer. But she let Harrison talk her into Wednesbury and, true to form, the wind howled and the rain poured while she sang Handel's 'Art Thou Troubled?'. Someone erected a makeshift shelter for her, but she was soaked to the skin, and there was virtually no audience.

The mayor, however, with an umbrella protecting his robes of office,

[1] This anecdote recounted by John Francis.

had to remain. He was hideously embarrassed and rounded on Harrison afterwards: 'A girl with a voice like that oughtn't to be singing in a park!' Kathleen agreed with him and vowed to Harrison that this would be positively her last performance in the open air. A few days later she went down with a severe cold.

To try to compensate, the Mayor of Wednesbury invited Kathleen back, to give a concert in the Town Hall, and she accepted. Since he had particularly enjoyed 'Art Thou Troubled?' he was disappointed when he received advance notice of her programme, to see that the aria was not included. Harrison explained that as Miss Ferrier had sung it on her previous visit to Wednesbury she thought an alternative item might be preferred. Even so, the mayor was insistent that not everyone had heard her sing 'Art Thou Troubled?', and that they should have the opportunity. Kathleen agreed.

The date of Kathleen's audition with John Tillett, 9 July, finally dawned. Wigmore Hall did not hold the pleasantest of memories for her, since it was here that she had failed the *Daily Express* competition finals. Winifred went with Kathleen, and tucked herself away in the stalls, while Kathleen sat on the stage awaiting Mr Tillett, who was very late. He probably had little interest in hearing Kathleen, but Sargent had requested he do so, and the wishes of so eminent a client could not be ignored.

When Mr Tillett arrived, with an accompanist, Kathleen sang a few songs for him but, as with Sargent, she was uneasy, convinced the empty hall was deadening her voice. Mr Tillett, however, was accustomed to assessing talent and, even in those unpromising conditions, he had no hesitation in welcoming her as a client. She knew at once that this was one of the most significant steps in her career. Ibbs and Tillett were at the centre of the concert world.

On the way home the sisters excitedly made plans for the future. Kathleen had given considerable thought to Sargent's advice that she move to London and now, after Mr Tillett's encouragement, she was ready to do so. Winifred gave her every support, and agreed to accompany her, knowing she could easily get a teaching post in London; thus she would be able to help Kathleen out financially, if she did not at first earn enough to live on. They would rent a flat big enough to accommodate all three of them for, naturally, William would be coming too.

With this plan in mind, Kathleen resumed work with CEMA. By now CEMA had increased her fee, which had started at three guineas, to eighteen guineas a week, which Kathleen thought generous and which was undeniably a vast improvement on the £2.3s a week she had earned at the telephone exchange. That August, she appeared at Rotherham, Cockermouth, Lancaster, York and Liverpool. At Rotherham she was presented with a blue and white Spode tea service, which she arranged proudly on the kitchen dresser back home. In Liverpool, she sang with the Leslie Bridgewater Salon Orchestra. 'It is just plain, honest singing, without any frills,' wrote the reviewer for the *Liverpool Evening Express*, 'but with the effortless charm of the artist. She is a great contralto.'

The great contralto displayed very little charm, effortless or otherwise, when she read in the same review: 'She is worthy to be mentioned as a possible successor to Clara Butt.' 'I don't sound a bit like Clara Butt!' she complained to Winifred. But as her fame increased she was frequently to find herself compared with Butt, something which never failed to irritate her.

On 7 September 1942, she left for a five-day CEMA tour with W. S. Newell. In Wigton, one of their venues, no audience at all had arrived by the time the concert was due to start. Newell later recounted the experience for the *Whitehaven News* of 26 October 1950:

> I still have vivid memories of a Sunday afternoon during the war, when I took a party of local artists to entertain troops stationed near Wigton. We arrived at Wigton Drill Hall only to find that the troops had been confined to camp. However we had gone to Wigton to give a concert and a concert we were determined to give. We stood in the streets and asked passers-by to come in; eventually we had an audience composed of a few troops, some civilians and not a few children. It was a small audience, the room was so cold that Kathleen came onto the stage still wearing her outdoor clothes, but she sang to that audience just as she would have sung had she been on the stage at the Albert Hall with a crowded auditorium. That was a performance which I shall never forget and one that I rank as one of Kathleen Ferrier's best ever.

Worse than no audience is a hostile audience such as awaited her at the Castle Cinema, Egremont. The audience decided Handel and

Schubert were not for them and fighting and hooliganism broke out. Twenty-odd youths stomped around the auditorium, shouting and making cat-calls. Kathleen was terrified, but did not show it, and stoically continued singing.[1]

Plans for the move to London were given a boost when Winifred received a letter asking her to go back to her old school in the new year. Finding somewhere to live fell into place equally painlessly. During one of her engagements, Kathleen had worked with the pianist J. Wight Henderson. She told him of her plans and he put her in touch with a Mrs Dreda Boyd who lived in Frognal Mansions, a block of flats in Hampstead. Through Mrs Boyd, Kathleen took Flat No 2, at a rent of £150 a year, an amount which she considered utterly scandalous. However, the flat was big enough for three, and she agreed that they would move in on Christmas Eve.

[1] Undated and unspecified published interview with Newell. Date and location verified by Kathleen's diary.

SIX

On 5 October 1942, Kathleen started a three-week tour of factories in the Manchester area. At a rubber dinghy factory she was intrigued by the twenty-five inch zips used on the dinghies, so the foreman slipped one into her handbag, to take home. She knitted a sweater to fit it, zips being scarce in wartime and much too precious to waste.

Kathleen had been receiving good press notices from local papers, but knew that her next major appearance, a recital at Houldesworth Hall, Manchester, would be covered by a national paper, the *Manchester Guardian*. She was preparing a publicity leaflet at the time, and hoped to include in it a favourable review. A shock awaited her. The critic, Granville Hill, praised her voice, but took her to task for her diction:

> Miss Ferrier must always be careful to get her words clear. We have written that her singing can reveal fine tone shading but this does not mean that such a result is invariably achieved. During two or three songs yesterday, the words lost savour and character and then a sense of monotony was noticed in the actual tonal effect. The haziness in diction was not frequent yesterday, but Miss Ferrier is too good an artist to let it go uncorrected.[1]

Kathleen took Hill's words to heart. She was to have her favourites among the critics, and those of whom she was less fond. She dubbed Edward Sackville-West as Sackville-Pest and Desmond Shawe-Taylor as Shawe-Failure. There was also a manager whose Christian name was Basil; she found him somewhat lack-lustre, and named him Dazzle. These names were not malicious, they were simply plays on words, like her other favourites, 'Softly Awakes My Tart' and 'Bad Mess of Bedlam'.[2]

Perversely, now that the move to London was arranged, Kathleen

[1] *Manchester Guardian*, 21 October 1942
[2] 'Softly Awakes My Heart' by Saint Saëns, and 'Mad Bess of Bedlam' by Purcell.

was busier than ever in the north. The family decided to split up for a few weeks, and Winifred came to London to supervise arrangements while William stayed with friends in Lancashire. Kathleen remained in Carlisle.

Between 25 November and 12 December 1942 she appeared at Cockermouth, Stanley, Crewe, Holmes Chapel, Winsfold, Great Sanghall, Chester, Newcastle, Malton, Runswick Bay, Crook, Durham, Sunderland and Hackness. She arrived at the latter destination fifty minutes late, having lost her way in the black-out.

On the 14 December she gave a recital at Millom. Her accompanist was Violet Carson, at that time a little-known pianist and folk singer, but who was to become world famous as Ena Sharples, the battle-axe of Granada Television's *Coronation Street*.

She sang again in *Messiah* in Edinburgh on 20 December, where she stayed a couple of nights with Alexander and Rosalind Maitland, a wealthy and artistically knowledgeable married couple with whom she had become friends. Members of the Maitland family had known the sculptor Rodin: Mrs Maitland and her mother had visited Rodin's studio to buy some sculpture. Rosalind wanted *The Kiss* but her mother said, 'No, dear, it is much too exciting to live with,'[1] so they bought instead a Mother and Child, which now reposes in the Scottish National Gallery. Mrs Maitland's other distinction was that, as a child, she had once lunched with Brahms. This piece of information was a deathly party-stopper.

While at the Maitland's, Kathleen came across the score of Brahms's *Four Serious Songs* (Vier Ernste Gesänge) and, trying them out, found them intensely moving. The songs, based on biblical texts, are Brahms's last published work, and are a celebration of Christian forgiveness over the harsher judgments of the Old Testament. Kathleen spent hours at the piano, enthralled by them.

She could not, however, spend as much time learning them as she would have liked because she had to leave Edinburgh for an *Elijah* at Runcorn on 23 December, her first booking from John Tillett. Her diary for the date carries the entry: 'Engagement from Ibbs & Tillett – Whoopee!!' She felt she had to be at her best for this.

[1] Anecdote supplied by Winifred Ferrier.

The baritone for *Elijah* was Roy Henderson, another of Tillett's clients, whose career had encompassed both Glyndebourne and Covent Garden. Kathleen had great respect for him. Tillett had told Henderson that he would be singing with a 'new girl' and that he would value his opinion of her.

After the performance Henderson had had to report that he was unimpressed. 'It was a good voice,' he remembered, 'but too dark. And she kept her nose buried in the score the whole time, terrified to look up. I told her she should learn her words and throw away the book.'

The next day, Christmas Eve, Kathleen travelled to London with Henderson, as she was due to move into Frognal Mansions. On the train she told him she hoped she would be able to get enough engagements to afford to stay in London as she was 'desperate' to be a professional singer.[1]

That Christmas Day the Ferrier sisters went to bed early. The flat seemed a barn of a place after their tiny house in Silloth and, as the weather was bitterly cold, they spent most of the day stoking the stove to keep warm, and fitting all the windows with blackout curtains.[2]

As Kathleen snuggled in bed that night, she wondered if she had made the right decision by moving to London. Her career was foremost in her mind, but there was another, more sinister reason. She believed hospitals in London were superior to those in the north and, although she was in excellent health, she had a neurotic horror of contracting cancer.

Occasionally she had a pain in her breast. This had started shortly after she was married, when Bert had accidentally caught her a blow with his elbow. She had paid little attention to it at the time, but the ache persisted and, like many others, Kathleen believed that a blow to the breast could cause cancer. As a girl in Blackburn, she had known an old lady who had died of the disease and the memory of her ravaged body haunted her.[3] So dread gripped her mind each time she felt the pain.

On Boxing Day, however, she and Winifred went to a performance of

[1] Interview with Roy Henderson.
[2] As a preventative measure against bombing during World War II, all windows had to be made lightproof.
[3] Interview with Winifred Ferrier.

Messiah at the Royal Albert Hall. This was Kathleen's first visit to the hall, and she was stunned by the size of the auditorium. 'What a place to fill!' she gasped. She was not the first to be intimidated by the size of the Albert Hall, no less a figure than Wagner had experienced a similar sensation when he had visited London as a conductor.[1]

Kathleen's first London recital was on 28 December 1942, at a lunch-time concert at the National Gallery, one of a series of such concerts organised by Dame Myra Hess.[2] Maurice Jacobson was her accompanist and his wife, Susannah, the page turner. 'Kathleen was an excellent musician,' Mrs Jacobson recalled, 'but there was no real feeling for her words.' A similar judgment to Roy Henderson's. . . .

Kathleen herself described this, her first London concert, in a letter to Eleanor Coyd: 'Oh, boy! Did my knees knock! But I got through without running off in the middle or swallowing in the wrong place. Myra Hess was very nice and encouraging. There was a huge crowd there and it was a bit of a facer, so I was glad when it was safely over.' In her diary she merely noted, 'Went off well, crowds there.'

By now, several people, whose opinions she respected, had told her that her interpretation was lacking in emotional conviction. Part of the trouble was that she had been brought up in a culture that scorned outward display. As Winifred remarked, 'In the north you don't give vent to your feelings. Kath dismissed things that worried or moved her with a joke.'

Recalling how impressed she had been with Roy Henderson, she decided to ask his help. Henderson taught at the Royal Academy of Music and she presented herself there one morning, unannounced, and explained she would like to see him on a personal matter. She was asked to wait in the canteen where he usually took his coffee break. When he arrived she reintroduced herself, and said abruptly, 'Please will you

---

[1] '. . . he succumbed there and then to a severe attack of Albert Hall stage fright – an illness familiar to nearly every artist on stepping for the first time upon the platform of that gigantic amphitheatre.' *Thirty Years of Musical Life in London* Herman Klein, Heinemann, 1903.

[2] Kathleen's programme consisted mainly of lieder by Brahms, Schubert and Worf, (Sung in English), plus Armstrong Gibbs's song 'By a Bier Side' and the folk song 'Love is a Bable'.

give me some lessons?"[1] He agreed, and they arranged to start working together, at Henderson's home, from 9 March 1943. It was impossible to fit in lessons before then as Kathleen was booked more or less solidly with CEMA engagements.

She was determined to establish as many firm London contacts as possible. After attending a concert conducted by Reginald Jacques, she had no hesitation in bounding over and congratulating him. Dreda Boyd, who was with her, was impressed by her courage. In fact, Kathleen was not as forward as Mrs Boyd had thought; she had met Jacques before.

Kathleen was enjoying London. She familiarised herself with its geography and became fascinated by the Underground system, using it whenever possible. She knew exactly which trains would take her where, and refined this to such an art that she even knew which end of the train to get into in order, at the end of her journey, to alight at the nearest point to the escalator, which she would invariably rush up, two steps at a time. She never had time to dawdle.

London seemed full of famous people. She went to the theatre whenever she had the money, seeing Joan Hammond in *La Traviata* and a performance of Noël Coward's *Blithe Spirit*. At the latter, she noticed actor John Clements in the audience. Her happiness was complete when, at an art gallery, she saw Jessie Matthews escorted by C. B. Cochran. 'Seeing the celebrities, begorra,' she wrote to friends in Silloth. 'It was grand.'

By now she was travelling regularly and extensively throughout Britain, and beginning to feel the strain, particularly if she accepted a non-CEMA booking, which meant she could expect no help with her travel arrangements. The wartime trains were crowded and unheated, even in the middle of winter, and often there were delays which could stretch into hours. She frequently had to make journeys sitting on her suitcase because all the seats were taken, and dining on sandwiches she had brought from home, as there were no buffet cars. She was never sure what hour of the night she might reach her destination and, once

[1] Interview with Henderson. For those interested in Henderson as a singer there is among his recorded works a song cycle by Butterworth of Houseman's *A Shropshire Lad*. Originally recorded on 78s, it was dubbed onto an LP (Decca ECM 834) and is well worth tracking down.

there, taxis were rarely available to take her to her hotel. As black-out precautions were in operation, she had to find her own way through unlit streets, striking a match to read the street names.

The hotels themselves, inadequately heated because of fuel shortages, were pretty inhospitable. It was common for the bedding to be damp. Food was rationed, and the dining rooms, with their meagre menus, closed early, making no provision for late diners, so that often Kathleen could get nothing to eat after a performance. It took all the charm she could muster, to persuade the cook to leave her a salad or sandwich.

Despite these difficulties, Kathleen was enjoying herself. Full of energy, she breezed through the obstacles and derived great satisfaction from actually earning her living as a singer.

In London, she auditioned for the Promenade Concerts but was turned down. She wrote to the BBC, listing her northern broadcasts, but was curtly informed there was nothing suitable for her. Despite these setbacks, she felt she was making progress, as her lessons with Henderson were going well.

Initially, like Hutchinson, Henderson concentrated on Kathleen's breath control. Most teachers have their own system, and Henderson states he modified what Hutchinson had instilled into her, superimposing a method he termed Continental, much favoured by the older school of teachers. He gave her exercises to strengthen her diaphragm, helping her to sustain the longest phrases or the strongest notes. Kathleen would stand with her back to the wall, while Henderson pressed her abdomen forcing her muscles to resist him.

Diaphragmic control is an essential part of vocal training. Enrico Caruso was so proud of his technique that he would demonstrate it by propelling a grand piano across the room with a series of jerks from his diaphragm, a practice which his operatic colleague, Dame Nellie Melba, thought unnecessarily vulgar. Such strictures did not hamper the Russian soprano Nina Koshetz who, her pupil Kathryn Grayson recalls, would lie on the floor and, solely using her diaphragm, raise and lower a pile of encyclopaedias which had been placed upon her.

These theatricalities were not in Kathleen's repertoire, but in later years, she would explain to her dressmaker that any dress she wore at a recital, must allow for at least a three-inch expansion of the diaphragm.

Soon after their studies began Henderson had come to appreciate the enormous potential of Kathleen's voice, but he also realised great care was needed in its handling: 'It was an instrument,' he recalls, 'with which I would have to be wary, as I did not want to tamper with its unique timbre.'

Apart from the natural hardiness of the voice, one of the reasons for its uniqueness of sound was entirely due to the bounty of nature. Kathleen's throat cavity was enormous: 'One could have shot a fair-sized apple right to the back without obstruction,' Henderson commented.

On the debit side, Henderson found the voice too monochrome, and the upper range constricted: 'At anything above high E the notes would tend to lack quality and, at times, go off pitch. There was an F which, I felt, was the upper limit, but this could only be supported by extra exhalation.'

She knew little of the physiology of singing, and Henderson advised her not to worry about this, nor to read books on the subject as they would only confuse her.

Once her technique had a solid foundation he became coach rather than teacher, and provided guidance on interpretation and repertoire. They worked on a regular basis until 1947, after which Kathleen continued to take lessons whenever she felt the need. She always valued his advice and, throughout her life, he was her 'Prof'.

Later, after the television film *Blow the Winds Southerly* had been screened, its director, John Drummond, learned that her former teacher, Dr Hutchinson, had been upset because so much emphasis had been placed on Roy Henderson's training. Whereas he did not wish to detract from Henderson's work, he nevertheless felt that his own contribution to Kathleen's progress was equally significant.

There are those however who believe that Kathleen's uniquely glorious sound was entirely the result of natural endowment rather than of voice lessons. One such is soprano Helen Anderson, a former CEMA colleague who performed many times on the same bill as Kathleen:

When I first heard her in 1941/2, which was before she began to study with Roy Henderson, her voice was all there and just as beautiful as it ever was.

Of course, Roy Henderson helped her a lot with repertoire but he did not make her voice. Dr Hutchinson always said that he did not make her voice either, he just helped her to even it up.

Perhaps the other thing to stress is the wonderful effect she had on her audiences in those early CEMA concerts. Usually nobody had ever heard of her, but they all sensed that here was a winner and rose to her with enormous enthusiasm, so that it was a real thrill to take part in concerts with her. It was partly voice and partly the warmth of her personality which communicated so strongly to her audiences. She so loved singing to people that they instinctively loved her back.

The critic Alan Blyth, endorses this magnetic effect Kathleen had on her audiences:

It is true that her voice was so much part of her personality that the sound on its own gives a listener today only about a quarter of the impression that it did when you could see as well as hear her. In person, she had a combination of dignity and radiance that made her performances in the *St Matthew Passion*, *Messiah* and *The Dream of Gerontius* so urgent and appealing; it was a kind of inner joy expressed through the medium of her voice. In recital, of course, the seriousness could turn to fun in a trice, and then she would lighten her tone and nimbly dart through 'Kitty me love' or some other trifle, leaving the seriousness of oratorio or Brahms far behind.

Although not an opera fan, Kathleen had been working on 'What Is Life' ('Che Faro') from Gluck's *Orfeo ed Euridice*, and sang this for the first time, in public, at a concert in Crewe on 10 March 1943, the day after the start of her studies with Henderson. A few months later Tom Harrison heard her sing it at a concert in the Black Country in aid of the Miners' Welfare Fund. He told her she was born to sing *Orfeo* and she replied that curiously enough it was the only opera in which she had any great interest.

On 13 March 1943 she was booked for a recital at Lewes. Her accompanist was none other than that doyen of accompanists, Gerald Moore. Although she travelled on the same train as Moore, she did not introduce herself. And when the train arrived at the station, she waited in her carriage until she saw him alight, then followed, keeping out of sight. When Kathleen later confessed this anecdote to Moore, he attributed it to shyness, but in fact it was more probably a suitable sense of modesty. After all, Moore was a distinguished musician, while Kathleen was still largely unknown.

Moore congratulated her after the recital and, encouraged, she asked if he had any influence with the BBC and, if so, could he put in a good word for her there? She also asked him to give a good report of her to her teacher, whom he knew.

Although Moore had liked her singing, he had reservations about her platform manner, which he considered *gauche*. He mentioned this to Henderson, who took the matter in hand. 'She used to lope on like a tomboy,' he recalls, 'and I taught her to take her time and walk on with dignity.' In her down to earth way, Kathleen joked to Winifred, 'He says I'm not to come on as though I'm saying "Here's my nose, my arse will follow," but rather, "Here's my fanny, my face will follow."' Henderson continued, 'I gave her a concert stance, the right foot in front, slightly pointed, and the left foot about fourteen inches behind, placed at a slight angle. This looked elegant and gave an even distribution to the body weight, so that her breathing was not disrupted by shifting of position. I also encouraged her to leave her hands motionless at her sides, unless deliberately making a gesture, and these were kept to a minimum.'

Shortly after the Lewes concert Kathleen started a tour of Scotland which proved disastrous to her health. She went down with pneumonia and was rushed to the Northern Nursing Home in Aberdeen. All performances had to be cancelled. She dashed off a reassuring note home:

> Hello loves,
> Ain't I a twerp? I was feeling right as rain then started to shiver and ache in every bone . . . I came in an ambulance, all posh! They'd a job to lift me!! Then was left in the care of the nurses here, perfect gems, and the doctor's been twice a day. My temps normal again now, though taking M & B tablets that Churchill had and am being washed more than I've ever been washed in my life before! I've even negotiated the bedpan and haven't done anything over the edge! Can't say when I'll be home yet, but will let you know.
> Loads of love, Kath.

Despite the cheerful letter the pneumonia had weakened her. Maurice Jacobson, who was with her as accompanist, somehow managed to scrounge a couple of bars of chocolate which he hoped might strengthen her. She was anxious to be back on top form as, on 17 May, she was to undertake the most prestigious booking, so far, of her career. She was to appear at Westminster Abbey in *Messiah*, under the conductorship of Reginald Jacques. Her fellow soloists were Isobel Baillie, William Parsons and a new tenor, Peter Pears.

To hasten her recovery, she went on a short holiday to Brindley Heath, Surrey, with William and Winifred. The weather was fine and she rapidly regained her strength, walking miles each day. She bought a recorder and practised 'Down by the Salley Gardens', which she had recently learnt, and was including in her programmes.

She returned to Frognal Mansions on 2 May, to receive the comforting news that Ibbs and Tillett had secured several worthwhile bookings for her while she had been away. On May 12 she empowered the firm to act as her sole agents for Great Britain and Ireland, at a commission of ten per cent.

Under Jacques's baton, the Westminster Abbey *Messiah* was a great success. *The Times*, in its review, considered the work 'rejuvenated'. All the soloists were singled out for praise, and Kathleen and Pears had the satisfaction of reading that, together with 'those two established Handelians', Baillie and Parsons, they had 'established their rights to be of that now not very numerous company'.

In the opinion of Neville Cardus, the Westminster Abbey *Messiah* was when Kathleen first made 'a serious appeal to musicians'.

III

The Diva

SEVEN

Most of Kathleen's bookings were still in the north, and in the June of 1943 she made appearances in Manchester, Chester, Liverpool and Stoke. At all of these she included 'Down by the Salley Gardens' which the *Liverpool Evening Express* found 'a gem of sincerity'. Not so glowing though, was the paper's criticism of her accompanist. Ruth Gibbs, poor woman, was dismissed as 'uncommonly dull'.

Henderson was constantly encouraging Kathleen to be less inhibited on stage. He caught exactly the mood he was after, one evening, when he had had dinner with the Ferriers. Winifred and Kathleen were washing up and, in a fit of high spirits, Kathleen threw the dishes across the kitchen, one by one, to Winifred, who was taken by surprise and only just managed to catch them. This, he explained, was the sort of spontaneity he wished her to incorporate into her singing.

The staff of J. Curwen and Sons Ltd, the music publishers of whom Maurice Jacobson was the chairman, had also experienced Kathleen's high spirits. She often called into the office, where there was a piano, to try out songs. Jacobson's assistant, Kenneth Roberton, remembers: 'She was always very lively and down to earth. I associate her with a little rhyme she taught me and which she used to recite in a broad Lancashire accent:

> In a field by 'Uddersfield,
> There stood a cow that would not yield,
> The reason why she would not yield?
> She did not like 'er udders feeled.

Another rhyme, in which she delighted, started with the quatrain:

> I wish I were a fascinating bitch,
> I'd never be poor, I'd always be rich.
> I'd live in a house with a little red light,
> And sleep all day, and work all night.

There were others, even less respectable.

As Kenneth Roberton had never heard her sing, and his only encounters with her so far had been when they exchanged bawdy jokes, he now made a point of attending one of her recitals. As had others, he found it hard to associate the joker with this almost spiritual being on stage. 'It was just a song recital,' he says, 'and I went with my wife. We were so caught up by her enchantment that we walked all the way home, about two miles, and didn't even bother to catch a bus. We didn't talk much, we just didn't want to break her spell.' Winifred felt the same, 'When she sang,' she said, 'she seemed to move on a more exalted plane, I could almost see it happening. In those days I used to find it terribly difficult to believe that this was the same down-to-earth, mischievous person I knew at home.'

Henderson was always looking for suitable halls in which Kathleen could give recitals and, with this in mind, he introduced her to Cuthbert Bardsley, then Provost of Southwark Cathedral and later Bishop of Croydon. Bardsley readily gave his consent for her to sing in the Cathedral, and went out of his way to be helpful. An engaging, handsome man, she took to him at once. Later, she returned to Southwark Cathedral for many performances of Elgar's *The Apostles* and *The Kingdom*.

Elgar's *The Dream of Gerontius* fascinated her, and she very much wanted to sing the part of the Angel. She had been introduced to the oratorio years before by her father who had taken her to a performance when she was a girl. When William was in the St Cecilia Vocal Union they had tackled it and found it very difficult – so different from *Messiah*. The choir had called it 'Gerry's Nightmare', to his amusement. Hutchinson had taught her the aria 'My Work is Done' but Henderson felt it too early yet for her to attempt the role in public. She accepted his judgment.

She was also eager to sing Verdi's *Requiem*, but again Henderson advised not, this time on the grounds of the unsuitability of the work for her voice. Later she was to agree with him, that her voice was the wrong colour and the tessitura of the *Requiem* too high. At the peak of her career she received an offer from La Scala, Milan, to sing the *Requiem*, and unhesitatingly turned it down, but not without a pang: 'It breaks my bleeding heart,' she said regretfully.[1]

[1] Letter to Winifred.

On 19 September, Henderson had the ideal opportunity to assess his pupil's progress as they were booked to appear together in *Elijah* at the Theatre Royal, Nottingham. The *Nottingham Journal* reported 'her richness of tone was a real delight'. This time Henderson agreed.

Ibbs and Tillett booked her for a 'miscellaneous' concert in Maestag, Wales. Among the other artists were violinist Marie Wilson, and that somewhat intimidating Sadler's Wells prima donna, Joan Cross. 'We were booked to sing everything under the sun,' she recalls, 'and ended up with the quartet from *Rigoletto*.'

It was a difficult day from the outset. At the rehearsal room Miss Cross denounced the pianist as 'hopeless'. When they arrived at the theatre there was another pianist 'tinkering with the keys', and they were told this was to be their accompanist for the evening. 'Under no circumstances!' thundered Miss Cross. 'He will destroy the perform- ance.' She had spent years touring and claimed to know instinctively that 'he was not up to the job'.

By now it was time for the curtain to rise, but Miss Cross refused to make her entrance until yet another pianist was engaged. Kathleen cringed at this behaviour; the nearest she had ever come to a display of temperament was when she had refused to sing at any more open-air concerts.

'She was mortified,' Miss Cross recalled. 'She really thought I'd gone too far. Eventually they located another pianist, a splendid lady with whom I'd worked before, but we stood around for ever waiting for her to arrive. Meanwhile, the concert had to start and Kath accompanied Marie Wilson beautifully.'

Joan Cross made a vivid impression on Kathleen and was later to figure prominently in her career.

At another concert in Wales, Kathleen deputised for Mary Jarred, who had been taken ill. Topping the bill was the great Covent Garden Turandot, Eva Turner. They had not met, but Dame Eva knew of Kathleen through her friend, Anne Ridyard, who had heard her in *Messiah* a few weeks previously. 'Have you heard of Kathleen Ferrier?' Miss Ridyard had enquired. 'No', was the response. 'By Jove, you will,' Miss Ridyard told her.

The spectre of Clara Butt continued to haunt Kathleen. After a performance of *Elijah*, the *Nuneaton Observer* commented: 'The extra- ordinary beauty of her "O Rest in the Lord" indicates her as a coming

Clara Butt.' The *Hinkley Times* countered: 'She has what Clara Butt never did have, a grand voice trained over its whole range.' This was monstrously unfair to Butt, who had been a magnificent singer, but the point that irritated Kathleen was that she in no way resembled Dame Clara either in voice or in style of singing.

On 28 November 1943, at Dover, she sang her first performance of Schumann's *Frauenliebe und Leben* in German, and Maurice Jacobson, who spoke the language fluently, helped her with the pronunciation. 'Went off fairly well,' she wrote in her diary, adding, 'Two sirens, not counting me,' a reference to Purcell's 'Blest Pair of Sirens', which she also sang.

Some months later she broadcast *Frauenliebe und Leben* and received a congratulatory letter from Jacobson, to which she replied:

> I had been thinking so much about you just before I received your letter – there must have been a bit of thought transference – but then, I always think of Dover and how I must have put you, and the audience, through it on that particular night! But you broke the back for me, and of all my German songs, and I am eternally grateful to you, because I love to sing them. It gave me the *warmest* pleasure to read your praise, bless you! I *do* love this cycle – sentimental or no – and it is lovely to know that you were moved by the broadcast.

On 5 December she appeared in Bristol. Oboist Leon Goossens was also on the bill. She liked Goossens and enjoyed the anecdote he told of travelling home after a provincial performance. As he waited for his train he had a cup of tea in the buffet. 'Have you been playing?' the tea lady asked him. He nodded, delighted she had recognised him. 'And did you score a goal?' she continued. There had been a football match the same day.

By now the BBC was beginning to take an interest in Kathleen, and offers trickled in. Usually she was asked to sing works she did not know, and had to learn specially for the single performance. She swore it was done deliberately. Dvořák's *Requiem* was one such case, which was broadcast on 8 December.

She ended the year with a performance of *Messiah* at the Albert Hall. Despite her fears, her voice had no difficulty in filling the enormous auditorium.

Kathleen started the new year as she had ended the old, with a performance of *Messiah*. This was at Bournemouth and Roy Henderson conducted. Then, on 9 January 1944 she was at Bromley for Bach's *Christmas Oratorio*. The tenor was Jan van der Gucht, with whom she enjoyed singing, even though he was so short he made her seem unattractively tall. This difference in stature became a source of many jokes between them, and on a later occasion, after they had both sung in *The Dream of Gerontius*, he presented her with a sketch he had drawn – a tiny Gerontius sheltering beneath the vast wings of a towering Angel.

As her next engagement was not for a few days Kathleen spent the interval helping Winifred paint a paper frieze for her pupils at school. This pleasant diversion was interrupted by a call from Ibbs and Tillett. The contralto, Astra Desmond, had been taken ill and was unable to honour her engagement the following day at Southwark Cathedral for a performance of *The Kingdom*. Could Kathleen step into the breach? Kathleen was delighted to help out – particularly as the venue was Southwark Cathedral – since she knew the part well and the extra fee would be welcome.

Isobel Baillie was the soprano. Vastly senior to Kathleen in terms of experience, she was 'like a mother hen to her',[1] to use Baillie's own phrase. She passed on various tips to Kathleen, many of which were helpful, but not all were received with the deference she felt due to them. Sometimes, too, Isobel's tips were in fact blunt comments, nothing to do with singing, as when she loudly enquired of Kathleen, 'Your feet are so big, I suppose you have to have your shoes made to measure?'

It was a trying time for Isobel. She had been a top oratorio draw for years, and now a young singer had arrived who was threatening to usurp her position. Isobel was also concerned about her voice – although, naturally, she would never have publicly admitted it. The soprano is constantly exploiting her upper register, and this can tarnish as a result, causing certain notes to sound forced or 'pinched'. This had happened with Isobel. Of course, her artistry compensated. She still sang brilliantly, and it would have been a deprivation for audiences had she chosen to give up oratorio simply because of difficulties with one or

[1] *Never Sing Louder than Lovely.*

two taxing notes. But the worry was there, the constant question of how long she would be able to continue.

With the hardiness of youth, Kathleen felt she should have retired earlier, but in spite of these difficulties, the two singers rubbed along well enough. Certainly audiences found little to fault when they sang together, and their performances of *Messiah* reached standards seldom heard before or since.

As Astra Desmond's illness seemed protracted, Kathleen was again asked to deputise for her on 15 February at a recital at Manchester's Houldesworth Hall, which was to be simultaneously broadcast.

Sixteen months before, in the *Manchester Guardian*, Granville Hill had advised her to pay more attention to her diction. Now, however, he wrote:

> Throughout the programme yesterday the soloist showed that she possesses . . . gifts of expression which are of a rare kind. The freshness of her style and her abilities in the matter of characterisation proved that Miss Ferrier brings to her music a keen intelligence. In quiet sustained passages she keeps her words clear without disturbing the legato. And in vigorous, rhythmic songs the smart bite of the consonants adds piquancy.

'Tuppence to speak to me, now,' was Kathleen's comment after reading this.

Even so, at times she received so much advice, and from such a variety of sources, that she could easily have become confused. The Australian soprano, Joan Hammond, advised her to take up opera. They had appeared together in a miscellaneous concert, and Kathleen had sung, with Jan van der Gucht, the duet 'Home to Our Mountains' from *Il Trovatore*.

On the other hand, contralto Gladys Parr advised her *not* to sing in opera: 'She would almost certainly have lost something of the quality of her voice – you must have an "edge" for opera, and I always hoped she would never get that edge to her voice, it would have spoiled it.'

But it seemed that Kathleen had already made up her mind in which direction her course lay. She told Joan Hammond she would feel foolish in opera, dressed up as someone else. This opinion was strengthened after she and Winifred went to a performance of *Madame Butterfly* at the

Golders Green Hippodrome. The opera was in English and when Pinkerton sang 'Fetch me a whisky and soda', they started to giggle, so much so that they had to leave. The more operas Kathleen saw, the less inclined she was to sing in them.

Yet, she sportingly agreed to sing the Flower Duet from *Madame Butterfly* with soprano Noel Eadie. They were in a concert together, the duet was Miss Eadie's speciality, and she would have been unable to perform it had Kathleen refused.

She also agreed, against her better judgment, to sing *Carmen* in a concert performance to be given at Stourbridge Town Hall. She found she could not take the opera seriously and, at home, would stick a rose between her teeth and burlesque the part. As the performance date approached, her laughter grew less and she entertained the gravest regrets that she had ever agreed to sing it. After the performance, the reviewer for the *Worcester County Express* was kindly, but suggested: 'Miss Ferrier's grave and beautiful contralto is more suited to oratorio than light opera.' She never touched *Carmen* or any of its arias again, although she was offered the part at various times throughout her career. She was also frequently asked, throughout her life, why she never sang the part. She responded to one such enquiry, 'Well, I'm a bit of a witch, but not a bad enough witch – unfortunately.'[1]

25 March was a red-letter day as she sang for the first time under Malcolm Sargent's baton. The performance, which took place in Liverpool, was Bach's *B Minor Mass*.

The following day she was reunited with Joan Cross, in Stockport, for a broadcast recital of Debussy's *La Demoiselle Elue*. This rarely-performed work is scored for orchestra, female choir, soprano and contralto. Debussy's experiments in harmony make his music difficult to sing, and the result is not to everyone's taste, yet this production aroused great interest. An audience of over two thousand turned up at the Centenary Concert Hall for the performance.

March had been a mixed month musically. Kathleen ended it as untypically as she had started it, with another opera. She played Elizabeth I in a concert version of Sir Edward German's *Merrie England*, at the Empire Theatre, Burnley. She was 'as good a contralto as Burnley has heard for years', stated the northern edition of the *Daily*

[1] Anecdote from Bernie Hammond.

Telegraph. Certainly, she preferred the character of Elizabeth I to that of Carmen.

On 30 June 1944, she was invited by Columbia Gramophone Co Ltd to test the recordability of her voice. Gerald Moore, who was a Columbia artist, would be her accompanist. Not every voice was suitable for the limited techniques of the time and some voices, magnificent in the concert hall, sounded somewhat less so when reproduced on record. Kathleen had a 'big' voice, and big voices could be subject to blast or turn out hard-edged. Contraltos, in particular, could develop a hoot on record that was not there on the concert platform.

Kathleen recorded four items, all in English, 'What Is Life', two Brahms lieder, and 'My Work is Done' from *The Dream of Gerontius*.

'What is Life' is the least successful of the four. Her acclaimed poignancy seems to have deserted her, and one can understand the charges made against her, in her early career, that she put little of herself into the interpretation. Also missing are the final top Fs of the aria, and this distorts it, leaving no proper finish.

Kathleen was frightened of those Fs. Henderson was working to consolidate her top notes but, at that stage, she preferred to avoid them, particularly in such an exposed environment as a recording studio.

The Brahms lieder ('Feinsliebchen' and 'Constancy') fare better, but of greater interest is the *Gerontius* aria. J. B. Steane writes in *The Grand Tradition* that 'Ferrier is one of those in whom we feel singing to be an expression of the spirit'. Critics were already remarking on this quality, and 'My Work is Done' embodies it, even though the accompaniment is piano and not orchestra.

Her maturity in this oratorio was still to come, under the guidance of Sir John Barbirolli, and yet this isolated aria is already so special on the record that one cannot help envying those who heard her sing it seven or eight years later. With the exception of *Orpheus*, Barbirolli considered *Gerontius* to be her finest work. It was one of the great regrets of her life that she never recorded it.[1]

---

[1] These test pressings were never meant to be issued, but were simply an exercise to investigate the recording potential of her voice. They remained unissued during her life and, undoubtedly, would have remained unissued for ever if Kathleen had had her way. But, in 1978, EMI made them available to the public on an LP entitled *Great British Mezzo-Sopranos and Contraltos* (HLM 7145).

The Columbia assessment was that since her voice was not ideal as a recording instrument, great care would have to be taken in the placement of microphones to avoid distortion. This did not unduly disturb her for, although recordings had been in existence for half a century, Kathleen was not greatly impressed with those she had heard, regarding them as something of a novelty and not to be compared in importance with a live performance.

That July she went to a performance of Rossini's *The Barber of Seville*, which she considered 'gorgeous' but an even greater thrill came when she found herself sitting next to Benjamin Britten, to whom she did not have the courage to speak.

That same month, on 13 July 1944, she appeared with the Gloucester Orchestral Society, and the men of the Gloucester Cathedral Choral Society, and sang a work new to her, Brahms's beautiful *Alto Rhapsody*.

She returned to the Etruscan Hall to take part in a concert. Her fellow artists were Peter Pears and Maurice Jacobson. The evening was divided into two parts: in the first, she and Pears performed songs and duets with a piano accompaniment; then, after the interval, Jacobson conducted his new composition, *The Lady of Shalott*, scored for tenor, piano, choir and orchestra. As Jacobson was conducting he could not undertake the complicated piano part, so Kathleen took his place. The members of the orchestra arrived during the interval, many on bicycles, with their instruments strapped to their backs, not an unusual occurrence, as they were mostly amateurs, working men whose enthusiasm and expertise in music bound them together.

Some weeks previous to the Etruscan Hall concert, Kathleen and Winifred had been on holiday, to the Lake District, with the Jacobsons. Susannah Jacobson recalls Kathleen concentrating on Brahms's *Four Serious Songs*. 'She sang them softly to herself, time and again, as we walked through the countryside,' says Mrs Jacobson. Kathleen was due to give the radio premiere of the songs in their orchestrated form that August.

As chairman of Curwens, Maurice Jacobson was able to introduce Kathleen to much music. He gave her 'Blow the Wind Southerly', a little known folk song. The effect when she sang it unaccompanied was so charming that thereafter she always performed it that way.

Michael Jacobson, Maurice's son, also worked at Curwens, and he and Kathleen became friends. She burst into his office one day, after sharing a taxi with an elderly man she knew, who had the irritating habit of jabbing her with his forefinger when talking. 'I don't like him,' she hissed at Michael. 'He's always trying to poke me in the back of a taxi.'

Michael also recalls his father telling him of another occasion when he and Kathleen were to give a recital on the Isle of Dogs. On their arrival they found that the canteen in which they were due to appear had been bombed. As they stood uneasily outside in the street, someone pushed an old upright piano out from a pub, leaving it under some nearby arches and Kathleen and Jacobson gave their concert there.

At about this time Kathleen did a tour of American camps, and composed the following for Winifred:

> *In a Field, All by Myself*
>
> Hello chum,
> I'm on me tum
> To pen this letter
> To My elder and better.
> It's time you were writing,
> My o' streak of lightning.
> One concert a day
> With these Yanks is OK.
> Taken by Jeeps
> In a series of leaps
> From one camp to another,
> And, listen here, brother.
> Fed on chicken and fruit
> O, ain't I a brute.
> But food in the tum
> Does away with the glum
> Long faced creature called Katie
> And makes her all matey.
> And life's a great pleasure,
> Mi darling, Mi treasure.
> So TTFN[1]
> I'll be writing agen.

[1] TTFN was from a popular radio show and meant 'Ta-ta for now'.

True to form, the BBC next invited her to broadcast a programme of songs all of which were unknown to her, and had to be specially learnt for the occasion. These included Chaminade's 'The Silver Ring', Leoni's 'The Leaves in the Wind' and Alicia Needham's 'Irish Lullaby'. Such was the success of this recital that she was asked to learn five more 'new' songs for another broadcast in a few weeks' time.

This meant she had to suspend work on the *Four Serious Songs*. They now occupied most of her practice time. The songs present enormous technical difficulties: a full tone is required throughout a vocal line that spans two octaves, and much of the music lies awkwardly for the voice, either at the bottom of the register or where the break occurs. Interpretatively, they are also full of pitfalls, their mood varying from bitterness to a noble sense of oneness with God.

Malcolm Sargent was equally enthusiastic about the *Four Serious Songs*. Brahms had written them for piano accompaniment but Sargent transcribed them for orchestra. Starting the transcriptions in 1943, he worked on them at the bedside vigil of his daughter, Pamela, who was dying of cancer. Kathleen believed Sargent had woven much of his personal tragedy into the orchestrations.

In order to concentrate on the songs without interruption, and take a respite from the flying bombs which at that time were regularly exploding in London, she and Winifred went to stay with Margot Pacey, an old friend who had worked for CEMA as an accompanist. She lived in Durham with her husband and six-week-old son, Johnnie.

Margot accompanied Kathleen as she worked on the *Four Serious Songs*. The third song of the cycle, 'O Death, How Bitter', affected Kathleen deeply; often she choked with emotion as she sang it, and sometimes, both she and Margot would be in tears. When this happened she would immediately stop singing, prod Margot in the back, and burst into one of her saucy songs, urging Margot to join in. Then, when they were in command of their emotions, they would continue.

Although the first performance of the four orchestrated Brahms songs was given by Nancy Evans at the Liverpool Philharmonic Hall on 10 August 1944, with Sargent conducting, Kathleen made the first broadcast of them on 26 August 1944. To prepare her for this, Sargent suggested Kathleen should come to Liverpool for the Evans concert.

After the performance, he introduced the two contraltos. 'He thought it quite amusing,' recalls Nancy Evans. 'Two singers with the same sort of voice and similar repertoires. I remember his smile as he was introducing us.'

Nancy and Kathleen hit it off at once and remained friends until Kathleen's death. Nancy was to help Kathleen in many ways, of some of which she was quite unaware, particularly towards the end of her life.

EIGHT

Despite their mixed response to the test pressings, the Columbia Gramophone Company was soon seduced by Kathleen's growing reputation. They invited her back to their studios to record two songs, which were issued on a single twelve-inch 78rpm record. The songs, 'O Praise the Lord' and 'I Will Lay Me Down in Peace' are by the eighteenth-century English composer Maurice Greene, and were selected by Kathleen, after consultation with Walter Legge, Columbia's Artistic Director.

Greene was not the most commercial choice of composer for a recording debut, as his songs were not generally well known and not much could be expected in terms of popular demand. Yet the critics received them kindly. Thomas Heinitz hoped the record would be 'the forerunner of things to come', and Scott Goddard, who later reviewed much of her work, called it 'a charming thing, admirably interpreted'.

Kathleen herself was not so charmed. There was excitement when the record arrived, but as soon as she heard it she was disappointed. Despite Columbia's reassurances, her voice sounded hard-edged. She put the record aside, not to be played.

She later discovered that, despite many tests, she had been placed too near her microphone. Those were experimental days (as they still are). Listening to the Greene songs today in LP form, however, that hardness of tone has disappeared. Modern techniques have repaired the original fault.

Far more important than the record, as far as Kathleen was concerned, was her first appearance in *The Dream of Gerontius* which took place in Leeds, with the Leeds Philharmonic Orchestra, on 18 November 1944. She and Henderson had painstakingly gone through every note of the score together, moulding each phrase so that, to quote Henderson, 'It appealed not only to the ear but to the heart, the mind, the soul and the eye. I wanted to make this work her own.'[1]

[1] *Kathleen Ferrier, A Memoir.*

Despite all the preparation, Kathleen had a fear of forgetting her words: this had happened in other works on a few occasions and left scars. The worst instance had been in Silloth, when she had been singing 'Where e'er You Walk'. She forgot the phrase 'All things flourish where e'er you turn your eyes', and the only substitution that sprang to mind was 'All things flourish where e'er they eat the grass'. Worse was to come for, in true Handelian fashion, the phrase had then to be repeated several times.

As a result of this she much preferred to sing from a score, no matter how familiar the work. But for this, her first *Gerontius*, Henderson had insisted she must sing from memory. She had accepted this, but as the date approached, she began to have reservations. Noticing how nervous she was at rehearsal, a member of the cast innocently suggested she might feel better if she used the score. A more damaging remark could not have been made, and she immediately sang the wrong words. She burst into tears and told Henderson she thought he was wrong to make her perform without the words in front of her. But he did not relent and, when she became persistent, he hid the score. She had no alternative but to make her entrance without it, and she must have been in terror. But she got through and her performance was described as 'outstanding'. She never used a score for the work again. Thereafter, the Angel became one of her most successful roles.[1]

The same could not be said for another of Elgar's compositions, *Sea Pictures*. This cycle, originally written for Butt, was a popular item in the contralto repertoire, but Kathleen felt little empathy for it. Nevertheless, it was *Sea Pictures* which provided the springboard for her first meeting with Sir John Barbirolli. The encounter, which took place on 8 December 1944, was unpropitious, and held little promise of a future partnership. Kathleen had been brought to Barbirolli's attention by certain members of the Hallé Orchestra, who had played for her during broadcasts. On the recommendation of these musicians he had booked her for a performance of *Sea Pictures* and viewed it as being in the nature of an audition.[2]

She arrived at the rehearsal full of foreboding, to find Barbirolli in an

---

[1] Information provided by Roy Henderson during an interview.
[2] Information provided by Lady Barbirolli.

unfriendly mood. The concert was in the City Hall, Sheffield, which he detested, likening the acoustics to playing in a bale of cotton wool. He barely acknowledged Kathleen's presence as she nervously nodded to him. She had put on a white, concertina-pleated dress[1] which she thought suited her, but clearly, as far as Barbirolli was concerned, she could have been wearing a sack.

She was horrified when, just as she started to sing, he tore his score from the desk and hurled it, narrowly missing her. It was actually meant for a musician seated behind, but she was not to know that. His temper did not improve during the day, and she was so nervous at the performance that she did not sing well. Barbirolli dismissed it as 'competent and cold-blooded'. She felt she would not be working with the famous JB again, and, with a shudder, wrote the whole thing off to experience.

Although she was sensible enough not to blame the white dress, stage clothes did often pose a problem for her during the war, as clothing was strictly rationed and choices were very limited. She had once suffered the embarrassment of arriving for an oratorio in a dress identical to that worn by the soprano. Soon afterwards Winifred, who was a good needlewoman, managed to find some green silk furnishing material, which needed no clothing coupons, and made her an evening dress from that. This proved a boon as the material did not crease and was ideal for packing when Kathleen toured. She wore it for years.

She had also become friendly with a clothes designer, John Turner. Through his connections he could sometimes acquire material on the black market, which he would make up for her. Turner, and his partner Leon Fontaine, often helped her choose clothes, and they accompanied her on one occasion when she needed a hat. She deliberately tried on hats in which she looked dreadful, to make them laugh. In the end even the shop assistant succumbed to Kathleen's infectious good humour.

Kathleen usually preferred a tailored look to her clothes, but whatever the style of her stage dresses she was insistent that her breathing should not be constricted and that they must not be too low cut. Turner bore these stipulations in mind and designed her dresses with a stole-style top which covered her bust, allowed freedom for her

[1] Information from Winifred Ferrier.

ribcage and left her arms and shoulders bare, which she liked.

Fontaine recalls she also had a fondness for the voluminous skirts of the day, 'I can see her still, twirling around at a fitting and saying "Look at our Kath now".' She joked with Fontaine that another reason for the full skirts was that they were an 'insurance policy' against thieving musicians. She could keep her handbag under her skirts while she was singing, the handle looped round the heel of her shoe. 'You can't trust these orchestral players an inch,' she said.

She once telephoned Turner for help when she was at the Albert Hall for a performance with Sargent. She had brought a black velvet cloak with her, which she intended to wear, but noticed, at the last minute, that the velvet pile had rubbed off in one place, leaving a white mark. Turner brought some Indian ink to the green room to dab over the bald patch. Unfortunately the top had came off the bottle en route and when he put his hand in his pocket it came out covered in ink. He nearly dropped the offending bottle on to the carpet but Fontaine dived forward and rescued it, splattering ink over his shirt front instead. By now the ink was running down Turner's leg, so Sargent produced a penknife and suggested cutting the ink-soaked pocket out of the trousers. Sir Henry Wood's widow was also in the green room. She gingerly held the end of the pocket for Sargent to cut, but it slipped from her grasp and as she grabbed to retrieve it, Sargent accidently stabbed her with the knife. . . .

Kathleen delighted in relaying these anecdotes to Winifred and William but sometimes, inevitably, it was they who were the butt of her jokes. For example, William liked to sing 'Annie Laurie', but when she accompanied him she would subtly change key in the middle. 'It used to drive him mad,' she told friends. She would also play the National Anthem, wait till people had started to sing and then, again, modulate discreetly upwards or downwards.

William had a keen ear, and was quite up to following changes of key in the middle of a song himself, if forewarned. When Kathleen practised the piano, he could tell at once if she struck a false note, and would call a stentorious 'Wrong!' from his armchair. As Kathleen progressed to contemporary works he would still correct her, but she often had to contradict him and explain that, improbable as it sounded, that was how the music really was written.

As 1944 rushed to a close Kathleen could face the future with optimism. She already had twelve bookings for January compared with the three she had had for the same month the previous year. Twelve performances a month were sufficient, for most were single performances in cities many miles apart, and the travelling often took a day each way.

There was a single dark aspect to her life. She still occasionally noticed a pain in her chest, now spreading down one arm. This was not persistent, but it nagged at her, preying on her mind.

Columbia invited her to make another record and, although she had reservations, she accepted. The recording industry was just starting a boom that, within a few years, was to see a gramophone in nearly every British home, and she had begun to realise the importance of gramophone records.

She chose two arias by Handel, both as little known as the Greene songs of her previous choice. 'Spring is Coming' and 'Come to me, Soothing Sleep' are from *Ottone*, one of the more obscure of Handel's mostly obscure forty-six operas. *Ottone* was an enormous success for the Italian prima-donna Francesca Cuzzoni, in 1723, but little has been heard of it since. When reviewing the record, however, the influential *Gramophone* magazine was 'grateful . . . for being given this lovely music'.

Nevertheless, Kathleen was still not happy about her contract with the Columbia Gramophone Company. Although the Handel arias were better produced than the Greene songs, she was beginning to feel she had joined the wrong team. Decca, a rival company, seemed far more technically advanced.

There was another reason why she wished to leave Columbia. She was somewhat disenchanted with its artistic director, Walter Legge. Legge had a vast knowledge of music and an enthusiasm for singers, so much so that he married two, Nancy Evans and Elisabeth Schwarzkopf. The latter pays tribute to the enormous influence he had in shaping her brilliant career, and Gerald Moore has written that, sometimes, after a Schwarzkopf recital it would be Legge who was exhausted!

He offered his advice to Kathleen during recording sessions, frequently stopping her performance to make suggestions. She always knew her music impeccably and was, in any case, receiving coaching from Roy Henderson, and in view of the misplacing of the microphones on her first record release, she would have preferred him to have concentrated on the technical problems rather than the artistic.

Legge also appreciated a handsome woman, as evinced by his choice of wives. Kathleen felt that, sometimes, his attention wandered away from the artistic into more fundamental areas, which were equally unwelcome to her. Henderson remembers her arriving for a lesson one day after she had shared a taxi with Legge. She did not say what had happened in the taxi but, whatever it was, she did not like it.

She complained to Henderson. He was a Decca artist, and told her, 'Why put up with it, come to Decca.' He took her to the Decca offices at Albert Embankment and introduced her. The result was an immediate contract, and as an inducement she was promised a complete recording of *Messiah*, something very dear to her heart.

In the meantime, there were contractual obligations to Columbia. To fulfil these she chose to sing five little-known duets with Isobel Baillie: 'Sound the Trumpet', 'Shepherd, Leave Decoying' and 'Let Us Wander' by Purcell and 'I Would that My Love' and 'Greeting' by Mendelssohn. According to Dame Isobel, Kathleen chose this unusual repertoire as she did not wish to record anything for Columbia which Decca, with its superior engineers, might wish to do later. On 21 September 1945, with Gerald Moore at the piano, the two divas immortalised their partnership on record.

When the records were released there was some discussion in the musical press as to whether the Purcell items presented the singers at their best, but as to the Mendelssohn, opinion was unanimous:

[They] are perfectly sung by voices that blend and with minds that are agreed upon style.

The Times

Their voices soar together like birds.

The Star

Crinolines and candlelight, a high backed pianoforte with a red satin front. Mendelssohn's music certainly evokes the atmosphere of the typical Victorian drawing room; but these duets are not merely period pieces, they have a perennial charm due to the pure spirit of lyricism which lives in them. One could almost sense the pleasure of the singers in having so grateful a vocal line to sing, and that pleasure they most certainly communicate to us. They are perfectly matched, this pair, and with Gerald Moore at the piano, an excellent recording, the performance is most refreshing and enjoyable. A more delightful disc has not come my way for a very long time.

The Gramophone

On 17 March 1945, Kathleen sang the *St Matthew Passion* at Southwark Cathedral, and also the following day at the Albert Hall, under the conductorship of Reginald Jacques. At the latter performance, as the weather was mild, she and Winifred took a picnic into nearby Kensington Gardens to eat in the interval. Jan van der Gucht was in the audience and they invited him to join them. For some reason he had not been engaged to sing over the busy Easter period and was disconsolate about it. 'I'm the most passionate tenor in London,' he complained, 'but today I haven't got a Passion.'[1] Kathleen loved the *St Matthew Passion* almost as much as *Messiah*. She must have been on particularly good form for this performance, as the reviewer for *The Times* of 19 March 1945, wrote, 'Bach, who loved the contralto voice, would surely have approved Miss Kathleen Ferrier's noble singing of the meditative arias.'

As is the case with many who start life with little money, Kathleen found it difficult to indulge herself financially, even though she was, by now, earning a comfortable living. She commanded between twelve and twenty-five guineas a performance – at a time when a decent mink coat, for example, could be bought for as little as a hundred pounds. Yet she bought her first fur coat secondhand, and then only to help out a friend who needed cash. Once it was hers she was mortified at what she had spent, and rushed to Winifred crying, 'I've done a terrible thing. Tell me I need a new coat. I do need a new coat, don't I?'

Once, when singing in Manchester, she saw a handbag that she liked in a shop window and went back several times to look at it. The next morning she read a good review of her recital in the paper and decided

[1] Information from Winifred Ferrier.

she had earned a treat – but even so she had to go to the shop and make the purchase immediately, otherwise she would have changed her mind.

While in Manchester, she had another engagement at the Free Trade Hall and, as she had plenty of time, caught a bus rather than take her usual taxi. There was a lot of congestion near the hall due, in fact, to the audience for her concert and, as she was about to alight, the conductor told her, 'If you're thinking of going to the concert, love, you'd better forget it. You'll never get in, the place is packed.'

After this, she gave a concert in Stoke, travelling there with her accompanist that day, Phyllis Spurr. She had worked with Phyllis before and found her a quiet and congenial travelling companion. One of Phyllis's greatest assets was that she would not try to engage Kathleen in conversation on the way to a recital. Apart from the strain to her voice, Kathleen liked to collect her thoughts on the way to a performance.

Now Kathleen auditioned again for the Proms, and this time was successful. Her Prom debut, which was broadcast, took place on 15 September 1945 when she sang 'L'Air des Adieux' from Tchaikovsky's opera *The Maid of Orleans*.

Before a performance, Kathleen would often take a spoonful of honey, it was her favourite recipe for the well-being of the voice. She believed it sweetened the tone.

Her voice would be needing all the help it could get on 7 November as the BBC had booked her for the British premiere of *On the Field of Kulikobo*, a massive symphony cantata by the Soviet composer Yuri Shaporin. The BBC Symphony Orchestra would be conducted by Albert Coates, and her fellow soloists were Laelia Finneberg, Frank Titterton and Roderick Jones. The work was to be broadcast simultaneously in Britain and the USSR.

Shaporin's music reflects his dedication to the ideology of the Soviet Union. Born in the Ukraine in 1889, he lived in Russia until his death in 1966. A previous work, celebrating the triumph of the Bolsheviks, was scored for orchestra, brass band, choir and piano. He later composed the opera *The Decemberists*, based on events leading to the Russian uprising of 1825.[1]

It was enterprising of the BBC to mount such an ambitious work as *On the Field of Kulikobo*[2] but to Kathleen it seemed a long way from *Messiah*. There appear to be no existing reviews of this broadcast, either in Britain or Russia. Winifred, however, was at the Maida Vale Studios for the performance. Her verdict was: 'There was no need to broadcast it in Russia, it was so loud I'm sure it could have been heard from England.' Whatever the merits or demerits of the symphony cantata, it has slipped into obscurity in the West. Possibly the prohibitive cost of producing it has contributed in some measure to this.

Kathleen was back on home ground on 9 December for a *Messiah* in Manchester at the 7,000-seater hall in Belle Vue. Her fellow artists were Isobel Baillie, Peter Pears and Norman Walker, and the Hallé was conducted by Sargent. The huge choir was drawn from three cities. There was some criticism at the use of so vast a choir, but Sargent pointed out that the first performance of *Messiah* had combined two cathedral choirs and that in every other performance in which Handel had been involved, he had made full use of the maximum available resources. 'On artistic grounds a performance with a thousand voices needs no apology,' Sargent thundered and, indeed, in a future performance he augmented the choir to precisely that number.

Kathleen gave seventeen performances of *Messiah* that December. She sang it from Blackpool to as far north as Dunfermline. In

[1] The Russian soprano Galina Vishnevskaya was engaged by the Bolshoi during the lengthy preparations for *The Decemberists*, which received its premiere at the Bolshoi in 1953. In her autobiography *Galina* (Hodder & Stoughton, 1985) she relates: 'They [government officials] wanted the opera to convey that the aristocrats who, in December of 1825, demonstrated and were massacred on Senate Square were actually revolutionaries – working class. Innumerable "commissions" from the Central Committee saw *The Decemberists* before it was allowed to be presented to the public. The staging was done over a period of several years, and in the process history was reshaped in every way. Lies oozed from every chink in the production. There is "sacred art" for you!' The *Oxford Dictionary of Opera* notes: '[*The Decemberists*] . . . has won approval in Russia for its heroic sentiments and "optimistic" musical style.'
[2] There is a BBC recording in existence.

Dunfermline the conductor was James Moodie. Maurice Jacobson, who was now accompanying her in recitals, advised him, 'Book her before she goes sky high, for she's going rapidly to the top.'

NINE

In the winter of 1945, Benjamin Britten started work on a new chamber opera, *The Rape of Lucretia*, which was to be premiered at the reopening of Glyndebourne in 1946. The libretto, by Ronald Duncan, was based on André Obey's play *Le Viol de Lucrèce* which, in turn, had been based on Shakespeare's poem *The Rape of Lucretia*.

Glyndebourne is a unique opera house. Situated near Lewes, Sussex, it was the estate of the late John Christie, in the grounds of which a small but exquisite theatre had been built for the purpose of giving operatic productions of the highest calibre. This venture was founded in 1934, and its inspiration was Christie's wife, the soprano Audrey Mildmay.

With the outbreak of war in 1939, Glyndebourne opera had closed, but the list of singers who had by that time appeared there includes names which are now legendary, such as Margherita Grandi, Dino Borgioli, Willi Domgraf-Fassbaender, Heddle Nash, Mariano Stabile and Ina Souez.

The reorganisation of the new company was a difficult and, at times, painful process, as some of the more established names had to be dropped in favour of exciting new talents that had come to the fore.[1]

Carl Ebert, one of the old coterie, was reinstated as artistic director; Rudolf Bing was general manager and Sir Thomas Beecham was conductor. Beecham, an enormous force in opera, had the added advantage of having at his disposal the vast resources of the Beechams' Pills empire. He refused to accept a salary for his post, but this munificence was not altruistic – rather, it had been inspired by a fit of

[1] Ina Souez was a case in point. Ageing and neglected after the war, this enterprising soprano reinstated her singing career by appearing, to much acclaim, with the popular American band, Spike Jones and His City Slickers. Although her repertoire had changed, obviously her artistry and spirit were still unassailable.

pique, directed against Messrs Boosey and Hawkes, the new proprietors of the Royal Opera House, Covent Garden, who had employed Karl Rankl as musical director, a position Beecham felt he might have better filled. He felt snubbed, and determined to use his talents to benefit the alternative Glyndebourne Company.

To this end Beecham and Ebert had started auditioning prospective artists. Kathleen was as unenthusiastic about opera as ever, but Henderson, who had appeared at Glyndebourne, introduced her to Bing, and strongly advised her to create as good an impression as possible on this powerful regime.

Beecham's stay with the company did not last long. Both he and Christie were egomaniacs and, predictably, did not see eye to eye. Matters reached a head when their wives became acrimoniously involved, and Beecham tendered his resignation. Ernest Ansermet was engaged in his place to conduct *The Rape of Lucretia*.

The opera relates the story of Lucretia, who is raped by Tarquinius, while her husband, Collatinus, is at war. Unable to bear this shame she kills herself. In the style of Greek tragedy, a Male and Female Chorus (represented by Britten as one tenor and one soprano), comment on the action.

As the part of Lucretia began to take shape, Britten and Duncan realised that certain special qualities would be required from the singer. Duncan later wrote in *Opera* magazine:

> I can remember the feeling of apprehension that came over us whenever we thought of the problem of casting it. I recall how insistent Britten was, when I was writing this libretto, that I should make Lucretia 'essentially pure and chaste' and how, when agreeing to this conception, I remarked somewhat cynically that by emphasizing these qualities we were creating a character which would make it particularly difficult for the modern singer to portray.

Britten had conceived Lucretia's music in the contralto/mezzo range, and it was Britten's friend, Peter Pears (who was already cast as Male Chorus), who suggested Kathleen might be right for the part. Britten recalled how impressed he had been with Kathleen in the 1943 Westminster Abbey *Messiah* and made an appointment to meet her with Duncan, at his London flat. Recalling that meeting Duncan continued in *Opera*:

Britten handed her his manuscript. She sat on the piano stool, and without any accompaniment began to sing the 'Flower Song'.

I am not a musician. I know less than nothing about vocal technique. There is only one word to describe the effect of that voice. It melted me with the tenderness of its tone. Britten smiled. Another of his hunches had come off.

She put the manuscript down, certain that we were disappointed. . . . She did not know that even while she was going down the stairs we were improvising a war dance of pleasure. We felt so confident of her ability to portray this essential purity of character that we decided there and then to exploit this potentiality even further. Britten suggested that when I came to writing the last scene, which was to contain Lucretia's confession, I should 'make it a dramatic piece, to stand almost wholly on its own, with the minimum help of noises from me'. And that's what we did, knowing that Kathleen had never sung in opera before, relying confidently on her natural simplicity and dignity, which was the precise quality we wanted, and something no stage technique could ever achieve.

Kathleen was stunned when she received Britten's invitation to create the role of Lucretia. Aware of the kudos Britten's name carried, and the reputation of Glyndebourne, it seemed a marvellous opportunity. But accompanying her exhilaration was a commensurate amount of fear. She felt sure that Britten's music would be difficult to learn. More deterring, however, was the knowledge that the part called for an accomplished actress, and that she had no theatrical training and no natural aptitude for acting. She would be working with such seasoned operatic professionals as Joan Cross and Owen Brannigan, and was convinced that she would make a fool of herself.

There could, however, be no question of refusing the part, and as there was a long rehearsal period she could only hope for the best. She was cheered, when she began to study the music, to discover that it was a lot less difficult to learn than she had anticipated.

Another source of cheer, although removed from *The Rape of Lucretia*, came from the unexpected quarter of Sir John Barbirolli, who invited her to sing in a performance of *The Dream of Gerontius*. After her dismal performance in *Sea Pictures*, Kathleen was sure she had burnt her boats with Barbirolli but, apparently, this was not the case. It was not that her performance had been better than she had thought – quite the reverse, Barbirolli had dismissed it and later had added that he had been 'dashed, even distressed' by it – but so many musicians had insisted that his assessment of Kathleen had been unjust that he had been persuaded to give her another chance. The performance was to take place at Sheffield City Hall, the scene of their previous encounter.

At ease with the role of the Angel, Kathleen was full of confidence and determined to make the most of this chance to redeem her reputation with one of the country's foremost conductors. She put everything she had into the part and Barbirolli was delighted with her. He told her she was the finest Angel he had heard, yet felt she could become even better, that there was even *more* potential. He said he would make it his ambition to bring out these latent qualities.[1]

She became his protegée. He took a personal interest in her music and did his utmost to nurture her talent. He gave her the pet name of Katie, and delighted in her candour, her humour and her beauty. She returned his admiration many times over.

After the Barbirolli *Gerontius*, Kathleen broadcast a recital of Mozart songs (her only essay into Mozart), and thereafter concentrated exclusively on *Lucretia*.

She arrived at Glyndebourne full of apprehension, but was heartened by the exquisite surroundings. The roses were in bloom and the garden was full of colour and perfume. There seemed to be birds everywhere.

As *The Rape of Lucretia* was the only opera of the season it was thought that it might prove unduly strenuous for the cast, so it was decided to select a second cast – not understudies – who could give alternate performances. Kathleen recommended Nancy Evans to Britten as the alternative Lucretia, an idea he took up.

The atmosphere at Glyndebourne was friendly. Kathleen already knew Joan Cross, Nancy Evans and Peter Pears and immediately took to Otakar Kraus, Owen Brannigan and, Pears's 'alternative' tenor, Aksel Schiøtz. She even had a friend in the orchestra, for the flautist was John Francis, with whom she had shared the punt for her memorable

---

[1] Information based on interview with Lady Barbirolli and extracted from two biographies, *Barbirolli, Conductor Laureate* by Michael Kennedy, MacGibbon and Kee; and *John Barbirolli* by Charles Reid, Hamish Hamilton.

performance at Burton-on-Trent. But this did not lessen her difficulties when she was given her stage movements.

She later confessed, in a BBC radio broadcast: 'Could I even *walk* across a stage without falling over my rather large feet? . . . I couldn't believe how difficult it was just to do the simplest arm movements without feeling like a broken windmill. I used to practise them everywhere, on the lawn, in my room, for hours in front of a mirror.'[1]

The second act was particularly trying, notably when Lucretia confesses to Collatinus that Tarquinius has 'torn the fabric of our love'. After an hysterical outburst, she kills herself. Hysteria was not part of Kathleen's make-up, and she found it embarrassing to act such a highly charged scene. In desperation she went to Joan Cross, and asked what she should do. 'She came to me with her arms outstretched,' recalls Miss Cross. 'She didn't know what to do with them, or her feet. My advice was simple. "Why don't you leave them alone? Your voice expresses all you need." After that she stood still on stage, and that was enough. If you confine acting to movement on stage then she was not brilliant, but if you define it as the ability to convey great depths of emotion, then she was a fine actress.'

Kathleen and Nancy Evans rehearsed at different times, so that they would not borrow from each other's performances, and they had separate coaching sessions with Hans Oppenheim, the associate conductor. 'Some expected there to be rivalry between Kath and me,' Nancy remembers. 'The truth was different. The only bit of rivalry was in our studies with Hans Oppenheim. Kath worked hard and was a quick learner, so I had to work like mad to keep pace, as there was no way I was going to let her get ahead of me. That way, we kept neck and neck. But after our individual coaching, we'd go off somewhere together to study.'

Singers cannot be rehearsed all day, so Kathleen had a lot of spare time in which she could enjoy the gardens, use the tennis court and take snaps with the new camera she had bought. Joan Cross remembers her posing her subjects, setting up the camera, then rushing in front of the lens to be in position herself when the delayed action shutter clicked.

[1] Taken from the 1948 BBC broadcast by Kathleen Ferrier, *My First Opera*.

In the evenings, there would sometimes be more music. The cast would gather round one of the cottage pianos for impromptu sing-songs, for which Kathleen was usually the accompanist. Rudolph Bing discouraged this, feeling the singers should save their voices for rehearsals, but they paid him little attention. Nancy Evans recalls that Margaret Ritchie, the soprano playing Lucia, organised surreptitious madrigal parties in her bedroom, and these became popular. Encouraged by her success, she pinned a notice on the board advising all who were interested in singing madrigals to meet in the evening by the lily pond, where the setting would be perfect. This charming idea never bore fruit. When Bing saw the notice he exploded with rage and all madrigal parties, both in and out of doors, were banned.

Kathleen was sad about the ban as the madrigals had provided a welcome respite from rehearsals. Despite the encouragement of the cast she was finding the acting a strain. She was also unhappy about her costume. The part demanded she wear a wig specially constructed of papier-mâché to give it a sculptured, marbled effect. This uncomfortable headpiece reached down to the middle of her back, restricting movement and inducing headaches. It also prevented her from raising her eyebrows, something she unconsciously did when reaching for high notes.

There was one particular high note in the role which she could not sing. It was in the already problematical hysteria scene, where Britten had scored a top A. This was a full tone beyond her range; at that time she was not particularly happy about singing even a G in public. When she told Britten, he readily altered the note down to an F sharp, which she could comfortably manage.

Although she felt she had come to terms with the first act, the hysteria scene was causing her sleepless nights, and she was far from confident at the dress rehearsal. Her morale was further sapped when she missed an entrance, having taken too long over a costume change. The wig proved calamitous, and jammed between her shoulderblades every time she tried to move her head, forcing her to free herself by a series of inelegant jerks. 'Oh, for a peaceful *Messiah*', she wrote to Winifred.

On the morning of Friday, 12 July, the date of the first performance, everyone was strung up. Even a minor difficulty provoked displays of temperament, as when the props department dressed the stage with artificial flowers which proved disappointingly drab. As Glyndebourne was full of roses, Mrs Christie instructed her gardener to replace the artificial flowers with real ones. This raised an outcry from some of the more superstitious singers who insisted it was unlucky to use real flowers on stage and refused to go on unless they were removed. An uncomfortable situation arose as Mrs Christie, châtelaine of Glyndebourne and a lady of no mean temperament herself, claimed to be unacquainted with this superstition, and refused to remove them.

Kathleen saved the day by thanking Mrs Christie for her thoughtfulness and assuring her she would be delighted to use the roses in her scene (she was later rewarded for this by pricking her fingers on their thorns during the performance).

Unaware of the frayed nerves behind the scenes, the audience started to arrive. The weather was splendid, and the gardens quickly filled with elegantly dressed people, many of whom had travelled miles for this gala re-opening. The atmosphere became festive as cocktails were liberally purchased, despite their expense – Blue Nile, 4/6d; Attaboy, 5/6d; and Between the Sheets a staggering 8s.

Just before the curtain rose, a bouquet arrived for Kathleen from Nancy, with the message, 'Lots of love and a big success, from the other one.' The audience took their seats and, forgetting their tempers, the cast wished each other well.

Lord Harewood, and his mother, Princess Mary, were in John Christie's box. Christie was concerned that some of the language in the opera might shock the Princess, and whispered, 'That is how soldiers talk.' In his autobiography, *The Tongs and the Bones*, Harewood summed up his impression of Kathleen's performance with the words: 'The glorious voice of Kathleen Ferrier invested Lucretia with her own form of sober glamour.'

Most of the critics agreed, *The Times* adding in summation; '. . . in Miss Kathleen Ferrier, the opera has a protagonist who was able, without strain, to present tragedy with a splendid voice and great dignity of bearing.'

The opera itself did not receive the same universal acclaim. Comment varied from the *Daily Mail*'s 'His [Britten's] mastery of subtle orchestral colour and dramatic effect is nothing short of genius', to the *Daily Express*'s 'The orchestral accompaniment ... often distracts and sometimes overwhelms.' The critic for the *Evening Standard* was more outspoken: 'I do not know who is to blame but, without warning, we are confronted with the last act of *Madame Butterfly* ... it only needed Tarquinius to return with a Roman wife and the parallel would have been complete and, quite frankly, I prefer Puccini's music ... there were moments when one longed for the excellent little orchestra to go out and have a drink.'

Kathleen sang eight more performances of Lucretia that July, and during that time the role developed strength although, as Britten said, 'It was a little time before the second act became comfortable.'[1]

Towards the end of the run, Britten was standing in the wings, and was startled to hear Kathleen sing the top A he had lowered. After the performance she confessed this had been a surprise to her, as it was the first high A she had sung in public, but she had been so carried away by the part that she had forgotten her fears and had sung the note before she had been aware of it. She sang it in all future performances and Britten reinstated it in the score.[2]

The Rape of Lucretia followed its Glyndebourne run by a two-month tour of Manchester, Liverpool, Edinburgh, Glasgow, Oxford, London and Holland. Holland would be Kathleen's first trip abroad, and she could hardly wait to get on the boat.

Unfortunately, she left Britain with depressing memories of Lucretia as the British tour had been neither a critical nor financial success. Bing dubbed it a 'box office disaster'. The theatres in which they played were nearly empty and, in Manchester, one audience member was so incensed by this lack of support that he wrote to the *Manchester Guardian*:

Sir,

I went to hear Mr Benjamin Britten's new opera *The Rape of Lucretia* on Saturday night and received the surprise of my life. First, the Opera House was far from full, though this is by any standards the most exciting musical and theatrical production which Manchester has seen for ten years, or twenty for all I know. I am told it has been the same each night.

[1] Taken from the BBC broadcast *The Singer and the Person*, later issued as a gramophone record BBC Antrim REGL 368.
[2] *Kathleen Ferrier, A Memoir.*

Secondly, the opera itself is in every way more beautiful than the critics, and I have read most of them, have led us to imagine. To be sure the libretto has obvious weaknesses but it also contains passages of genuine poetry which have, so far, gone almost unmentioned. To be sure the music is difficult but it contains songs of the most haunting beauty of which, again, for some reason, few critics have bothered to tell us. To my way of thinking, and to judge from the applause at the end I was not alone, this was one of the finest artistic experiences offered to us in recent years.

Well, the composer and performers need not worry for the tide will inevitably turn. . . . Those who should worry are the critics who damned with, and sometimes without, faint praise a new British opera of astonishing maturity and the citizens of Manchester who were not there to applaud it. In ten years time I shall take a malicious pleasure in saying to everyone I meet, 'Do you remember that lovely performance of Kathleen Ferrier's in *The Rape of Lucretia* in 1946?' How few, how pitifully few, will be able to say 'yes'. The rest will blush, I hope, and turn away and mumble something about the holidays.

The cast of Lucretia left for Holland on 30 September 1946. Advertised throughout the country by huge posters, the opera attacted a great deal of interest and the advance bookings were considerable.

Kathleen was met at the Hook by Dutch impresario Peter Diamand, who escorted her on the train to Amsterdam, where the first performance was to be given. In Amsterdam she joined Britten and Pears, who had gone ahead, and they took her to lunch. The food was a delight after the austerity of post-war rations, and she gourmandised on steak, chips, peas, gâteau and red wine.

A somewhat high-spirited tea followed, where Britten muddled up his guilders and Pears mimed to the waitress what they wanted. 'My eyes are popping out with excitement,' Kathleen wrote to Winifred.

In contrast to British audiences, the Dutch warmly welcomed *The Rape of Lucretia*, and there was special interest in Kathleen. Peter Diamand noted this and, astutely, secured a promise from her that she would return to Holland for a solo recital.[1]

The Amsterdam performance of 5 October was broadcast and an amateur enthusiast made a home recording on acetate. Nothing was known of this until 1980, when Educ Media Associates of America

[1] Interview with Peter Diamand.

learnt of the recording and acquired it, proposing to issue the opera in record form. The Britten Estate withheld permission for this on the grounds that Britten had revised the score in 1947. Several enthusiasts, Harewood and John Amis among them, disagreed with this decision. Eventually, permission was granted for Kathleen's scenes to be issued, and in 1981 those appeared as an LP.[1] It is the only known recording of Kathleen singing Britten, with the exception of a few folk songs he arranged.

The quality of the recording is poor and if release permission had rested with Kathleen it is certain, as with the Columbia test pressings, she would have withheld it. She might, on this occasion, have been wrong. Although the record does scant justice to her voice, this early performance of *The Rape of Lucretia* is of such historic interest that, however weakened, it is worth preserving.

After her Dutch tour Kathleen took a short holiday in Denmark, then returned to Britain and a schedule packed with bookings. She had thirty-one engagements in the following two months.

She realised that she urgently needed to extend her repertoire – this was brought forcibly home after a performance in Ireland when she had sung every song she knew, and had left an audience still clamouring for encores. She contacted Hans Oppenheim and arranged to study lieder with him. In addition she was studying Rubbra's settings of Psalms 6, 23 and 150, the premiere of which she was to give in the January of 1947.

After putting her under contract, Decca had wasted no time in enticing her into their studios, and she had already made several recordings. Her first session had been on 6 February 1946, when she had sung 'Have Mercy, Lord, On Me' from *St Matthew Passion*, but she had been dissatisfied with the result, and it was never released.

Her next recording, made on 27 February 1946, went on to become a perennial best seller. The Decca 'What Is Life?' is a vastly different matter from the Columbia demo-disc of 1944. Not only has she the benefit of Sargent and the London Symphony Orchestra but her voice is lighter and more agile. She sings surely and takes the top notes at the finale with ringing confidence.

[1] Educ Media IGI 369.

'What Is Life?' enjoyed wide sales and actually topped the best-selling charts for some months. Its sincerity cut right across musical barriers and many who claimed to have little interest in classical music included it among their favourite recordings.

When reviewing the record, *The Times* commented that her perform-ance was 'free from the characteristic vices of contralto singers. . . . These records encourage a brighter view of English singing than the one now despairingly held.' Why the reviewer should have held such a despairing view of English singing at the time is difficult to imagine. The scene was particularly bright, with many splendid voices about.

Not all the reviews were glowing. Tucked away in the *New Statesman and Nation* was the comment: 'Her low notes have the goiterous quality that seems endemic among English contraltos.' Although the remark must have stung, it also seems to have amused Kathleen, for she frequently quoted it. And why not, for by now she had a press book full of good reviews.

Her next recording was Pergolesi's *Stabat Mater* in which she sang with the Boyd Neel String Orchestra, conducted by Roy Henderson. The *Stabat Mater* is considered Pergolesi's masterpiece. Completed in 1736, it is a sequence of pieces reflecting the prevailing Italianate taste of the day. Again she was congratulated for recording rarely-heard music but, this time, the credit must go to Roy Henderson. Decca had invited him to record the Pergolesi – naturally, his choice of contralto had been Kathleen.

The Boyd Neel Orchestra accompanied her again, when she recorded 'Woe Unto Them' and 'O Rest in the Lord' from *Elijah*. She knew the arias well, having heard them since childhood, and sung them on numerous occasions. The *Musical Times* pronounced her singing 'stainless'.

Kathleen was on home ground with the Mendelssohn arias, but with the Rubbra psalm settings she was treading new territory. They received their premiere at St Bartholomew's Church, Smithfield, on 24 January 1947, in a programme that also included the *Four Serious Songs*. Critic Roy Johnson considered the psalm settings 'virtually un-singable', but added, 'Such was the lustre, the exaltation of Kathleen Ferrier's singing, their difficulties almost disappeared; though it needed the suavity of Brahms's *Serious Songs* to display her voice for what it is – the loveliest contralto in Britain.'

Shortly after this performance, Glyndebourne announced that Kathleen would be singing in *Orfeo ed Euridice* in its 1947 season. The choice of opera showed not so much a revival of interest in Gluck, as the wish to provide a showcase for Kathleen.

She arrived at Glyndebourne for rehearsals on 12 May feeling fairly optimistic about *Orfeo ed Euridice*. She was word perfect and delighted to be back among the gorgeous surroundings. The opera was to be sung in Italian, so she had taken lessons in Italian pronunciation. Sadly, however, as soon as she started working with conductor Fritz Stiedry she realised this engagement would not be as congenial as her previous one.

Stiedry made it clear that he had expected to work with a competent actress, and had no patience with Kathleen's lack of stage technique. If she did not get her movements right first time, he was scathing, dismissing her as nothing more than an oratorio singer. On several occasions his wounding jibes reduced her to tears. She was particularly humiliated since she knew there was some substance in his remarks, and realised how fortunate she had been in *The Rape of Lucretia* to have had Britten's gentle encouragement, and the help of Joan Cross, Peter Pears and Otakar Kraus.

She had a friend in Ann Ayars, the American soprano playing Euridice. She helped her all she could, and encouraged her to see the humorous side. She also cut her hair into a becoming, curly bob, which looked well as the youthful Orfeo.[1]

The other principal part, Amor, was sung by Greek soprano Zoe Vlachopoulos, of whom Kathleen made a great fuss. She thought Zoe might feel excluded as she spoke no English, save the sentence, 'Don't be vague, ask for Haigh', which some stage hands had taught her.[2]

There were constant alterations to the score, and Kathleen's effort to learn the Italian words seemed to have been largely in vain. She spent

---

[1] The role was created by the distinguished castrato Gaetano Guadagni but is now usually sung by a contralto, although tenor Alexander Young and baritone Dietrich Fischer-Dieskau have both also interpreted the part with success.

[2] *The Life of Kathleen Ferrier*.

entire evenings relearning her part only to find, in the morning, that the words had been changed yet again.

As Orfeo, she was required to carry a lyre and, to get her used to this, the stage manager had made her one from plywood. 'It's going to make a lovely weapon when the conductor tries me too far,' she wrote to Winifred. 'One of these days he won't know what's hit him! He still shrugs his shoulders in despair, calls me an oratorio singer and shouts himself hoarse. He was vaccinated yesterday, so heaven help me in a day or two when his temperature goes up! I wish I didn't cry so easily. *I* can shout too.'

She concluded her letter, 'I've been doing fourteen hours a day, but last night I went to the local with the stage manager and had a dirty big pint. Did me a lot of good.'

There were also problems in the wardrobe department, although she was not required to wear anything as uncomfortable as Lucretia's wig. Due to the war, certain items of clothing were scarce, and there was difficulty in acquiring a pair of tights for Orfeo. This scarcity was remedied by her friend, Hans Schneider who had designed the clothes for *The Rape of Lucretia*.[1] Schneider recalls he had come to visit her at Glyndebourne, and a few days after this she received through the post a parcel containing a pair of his long, woollen underpants, dyed green, which suited the costume requirement to perfection. She wore them throughout the run, and had fun in the wings each night, doing outrageous things with the fly buttons to the amusement of other cast members.

The opening night, 19 June 1947, was as glittering an affair as had been that of *The Rape of Lucretia*. To mark the occasion there was an addition to the cocktail list, as the barman proudly introduced 'The Kathleen Ferrier', a delicious blend of lime juice, brandy and crème de menthe.

Kathleen took sixteen curtain calls, and next day the critics lavished praise on her, the normally staid *Observer* enthusing: 'Timorous epithets will not suffice, Kathleen Ferrier's is a noble voice.'

---

[1] In response to the clothing shortage, Schneider had made many of the costumes from butter muslin; a lesson in economy for some of our more extravagant designers of today.

As with *The Rape of Lucretia*, however, the production itself was not without its critics – a consistent complaint being that the tempo of 'Che Faro' was too fast. If the recording of highlights is anything to go by (made in London on 22 June 1947)[1] then, compared to the lush Sargent version, it does indeed seem hurried. Yet, Alan Blyth points out, '. . . Stiedry took it at a faster tempo, deliberately stripping it of [some of this] sentiment, but the pace is possibly nearer the one Gluck intended.'

Despite the accolades, Kathleen was dissatisfied with her performance, feeling her acting had let her down. Harry Vincent came to the second performance and called at her dressing room before curtain-up. She asked him to examine her performance and tell her anything he felt could be improved. 'That will be more help,' she said, 'than trying to gloss over it and cheer me up.'[2] Vincent did as he was asked.

Her first booking, following the Glyndebourne season, was at the Decca studios. She took part in a complete *St Matthew Passion* which was conducted by Jacques.[3] The recording was done directly on to wax discs, which meant that if a mistake occurred then the whole side had to be re-recorded. This made everyone tense: a tragedy took place towards the end of one particular session, when after a perfectly executed take, the harpsichordist dropped the pencil with which he was making notes, and the whole piece had to be redone.[4]

The cast would relax with a few drinks after each taxing day, and Kenneth Wilkinson, one of Decca's senior engineers, remembers one such occasion. Kathleen stood to propose a toast. A respectful silence ensued, into which she solemnly intoned:

> Here's a toast to the girl on the hill,
> She won't, but her sister will,
> Here's to her sister.

[1] Decca Historical Recording 417 182–1.
[2] *The Life of Kathleen Ferrier*.
[3] Decca AK 2001–21 (78 rpm catalogue No. At time of print not available on LP).
[4] Anecdote supplied by Winifred Ferrier.

TEN

For many years, festivals have been a feature of musical life in Britain. The famous Three Choirs Festival dates from 1724; the Festival of Birmingham began in 1768 and lasted until 1912; and the Crystal Palace Handel Festivals began in 1857 and continued annually until 1926.

After the war, Rudolf Bing and Audrey Mildmay conceived the idea of an annual summer musical festival, to be held in Edinburgh, which could house performances of the Glyndebourne Company and other events of international calibre. The first Edinburgh Festival was held in 1947 and the prestigious German conductor, Bruno Walter, had been invited to conduct the Vienna Philharmonic Orchestra for some of the inaugural performances.[1] The combination of this famous orchestra and Bruno Walter would, as Bing said, 'put them on the map'.

For this Festival debut, Walter had elected to conduct Mahler's *Das Lied von der Erde*. The suitability of such a work had thrown the organisers into conflict. Mahler was virtually unknown in Britain, and what had been heard was largely considered too rich in texture for British palates. And the inclusion of a German language work, so soon after the war, might be seen as being in dubious taste. Conversely, it was argued that to perform so controversial a symphony would be forward-thinking, and that its very un-Britishness would stamp the Festival as truly international. More to the point, Bruno Walter had made up his mind, so little could be done.

Mahler had never lived to hear *Das Lied von der Erde* performed, and it fell to Bruno Walter, who had been his pupil, to give the first performance. This took place in 1911, the year of the composer's death. There was something of the crusader in Bruno Walter's dedication to the music of Mahler, and in particular his strength of feeling for *Das Lied von der Erde*.

[1] During the war Bruno Walter had worked in America, mostly at the Metropolitan Opera House, where he was engaged from 1941–6.

The work is scored for contralto, tenor and orchestra, and is divided into six movements, or songs, three for each of the soloists. The work is climaxed by the last song, 'Abschied', which is an impassioned farewell to the earth and its beauty. One of the longest songs ever written, 'Abschied' can last well over twenty minutes, depending on the performance, and it is Mahler at his most ecstatic.

Music of so individual a character demands singers of singular quality. Walter had already chosen Peter Pears as his tenor but had not yet chosen the contralto.

Both Rudolf Bing and Peter Diamand had recommended Kathleen, but at first Walter was not interested in hearing her, preferring to make his choice from singers with whom he had already worked. But, as time passed, and no suitable other contralto seemed available, he finally agreed to audition Kathleen.

She was thirty-four at the time, and made a tremendous impact on the seventy-one-year-old Walter. He later wrote of their meeting: 'She came in, not shy and not too bold, but in modest self-confidence, dressed in a kind of Salzburg costume, a dirndl, looking young and lovely, pure and earnest, simple and noble, and the room seemed to become brighter for the charm of her presence. She had the charm of a child and the dignity of a lady.'[1]

He asked her to sing some songs by Schubert and Brahms. Then, pointing to the score of *Das Lied von der Erde*, he asked her to try some of the phrases. Although it had doubtless been pointed out to her that Walter was looking for a contralto to sing *Das Lied*, she had no practical knowledge of the work, and sang the phrases from sight.

'She overcame their great difficulties with the ease of a born musician,' Walter wrote, 'and I recognised with delight here was potentially one of the greatest singers of our time.' More than that, it was 'a voice of rare beauty, a natural production of tone, a genuine warmth of expression, an innate understanding of the musical phrase – a personality.'

Bruno Walter's search for a contralto was over. 'It's love at first sight,' Bing telephoned Diamand, and that remark, made in jest, contained something of the truth. From then on, Walter championed two causes, Mahler and Ferrier, and his relationship with Kathleen was 'a musical association which resulted in some of the happiest experiences of my life as a conductor'.

[1] *Sunday Times*, 9 May 1954.

As far as Walter was concerned, Kathleen had the perfect voice for Mahler. It would be wrong, however, to assume that he was impervious to her physical charms. Their relationship was platonic but, in the presence of his daughter, he confided to Diamand, 'What I could do with that girl if I was twenty years younger.' Catching a quizzical look from his daughter, he added, 'I mean musically, of course.' 'Father,' she said slowly, 'that pause was just a little too long to be credible.'[1]

When Bruno Walter announced he would gladly come to Frognal Mansions for piano rehearsals Kathleen was flattered, but this quickly turned to alarm at the thought of so distinguished, and elderly, a gentleman having to struggle up the many steps to her front door. She also felt humiliated at the thought of asking him to play on her Cramer piano which, by now, was showing distinct signs of wear, and she was concerned that her German pronunciation would not pass muster.

Walter dismissed all these fears. He chugged up the stairs without mishap, had played upon worse instruments than the Cramer and complimented her, not only on her German, but on her grasp of Mahler's work. He later wrote: 'Her uncomplicated mind had the intuitive understanding of the full variety of human emotions, and she could express them in her art with persuasive intensity.'[2]

When Walter started coaching her in 'Abschied', Kathleen found that she had to keep breaking off, as with Brahms's *Four Serious Songs*, because the emotion of the music overwhelmed her. 'The tears streamed down her cheeks,' Walter wrote. 'With all her willpower and vigour she could not help it, and only by and by did she learn to control her feelings, but nothing could be further from her than sentimentality – in those tears spoke strength of feeling, not weakness, and a deep comprehension for another great heart.'

Kathleen was embarrassed by her tears, but Walter patted her understandingly on the shoulder. 'They all do it,' he told her comfortingly. He had coached other singers in *Das Lied von der Erde* and was aware of its effect.

Her father was introduced to Bruno Walter, and the great conductor complimented him on Kathleen's success. 'Yes,' he replied. 'Kath's not doing badly.'

[1] Related to the author during an interview with Peter Diamand.
[2] *Sunday Times*, 9 May 1954.

Kathleen was to make three appearances at the Festival. The first, in the manner of a preparation, was a chamber concert, conducted by Jacques, where she would sing 'Prepare Thyself Zion', from Bach's *Christmas Oratorio*, then there were to be two performances of *Das Lied von der Erde*, the first of which would be broadcast.

She was inspired by the Vienna Philharmonic at rehearsals, finding its reputation not exaggerated. This presented an additional problem. The orchestral playing heightened the intensity of 'Abschied', and she was terrified she might break down while singing.

And that is what happened at the first performance. She was in splendid voice throughout, but during the final bars, where the '*ewig*' (eternally) is repeated, unbidden tears choked her and she could barely utter the words.

She ran to the green room afterwards in a state of panic, convinced she had betrayed Walter's trust in her. 'What a fool I've made of myself,' she sobbed to Neville Cardus, who happened to be there. 'What will Dr Walter think of me?' Cardus replied he was sure Walter would say, 'If we had all been artists as great as you we should all have wept – myself, orchestra, audience, everybody.'[1]

Walter had been as moved as Kathleen but he was too overcome to speak for a while, and simply stood in front of her, nodding his head, and patting her shoulder.

The critics were divided in their reception. *The Times* considered the work in danger of surfeiting the hearer with excess emotion; Ralph Hill of the *Daily Mail* noted, surprisingly, 'There are parts which appear to me childish and commonplace', while in contrast the *Edinburgh Evening News* verdict was 'simply superb'. But it was *Punch* that summed up the feelings of so many on that historic evening:

Das Lied von der Erde is the golden sunset of the romantic period and the most complete expression in the whole of music of human's grief at his own evanescence. In it Mahler unfolds his vision of the universe and of all beauty and colours luminous with agony. And in the 'Abschied' a knell tolls as if for the whole of creation. Days afterwards I still seemed to hear that haunting, heartbreaking Farewell and Kathleen Ferrier's glorious voice singing *Ewig, ewig, ewig* . . . across time and space.

[1] *Kathleen Ferrier, A Memoir.*

The Edinburgh Festival had attracted visitors from all over the world and, as a result, Kathleen found herself deluged with offers to sing in Italy, France, Scandinavia and America. The American invitation involved a tour with no less than three appearances in New York, one at Carnegie Hall where she would sing *Das Lied von der Erde* under Bruno Walter. She accepted, and was due to sail on the *Mauretania* on New Year's Day 1948.

It took Ibbs and Tillett a considerable amount of effort to reorganise her bookings to accommodate the American trip, as she was already fully subscribed for 1948, and this caused ructions on the concert circuit.

There were also changes at home. Winifred had accepted a post as headmistress of a school in Chiswick and, finding the journey from Hampstead too much, had taken a flat nearer the job, in Shepherd's Bush. William was approaching eighty, and neither of his daughters liked the idea of leaving him alone while Kathleen was on tour, so it was decided that Kathleen should look for someone to act as a secretary, who could also keep an eye on William.

Roy Henderson recommended a girl called Paddy Jewett, a pupil of his who was studying to be a soprano. She was delighted with the proposal and moved into Frognal Mansions at once. William was equally pleased, and took great pleasure in going on walks with the lovely Paddy holding on to his arm.

On 1 October 1947, Kathleen began another tour of *The Rape of Lucretia*, starting at Newcastle. This time there were some cast changes and Emilie Hooke and Richard Lewis replaced Joan Cross and Peter Pears, and the conductor was Stanford Robinson. This tour included two London appearances on 14 and 17 October, and these were at no less a venue than the Royal Opera House, Covent Garden. 'From Carlisle to Covent Garden in five years! Lucky Kaff!' she wrote to Winifred. Her success left her breathless at times.

She was at the Leeds Festival following *The Rape of Lucretia*, where she was to sing with Elsie Suddaby. Miss Suddaby could not make the rehearsal and it seemed as though the orchestra in the soprano items would be unrehearsed. Rather than allow this, Kathleen gamely sang the soprano arias, skipping the high Bs and Cs, to the amusement of the orchestra players.[1]

[1] *Yorkshire Evening Post.*

That November she made three appearances at the Royal Albert Hall. The last of these, which was broadcast, was a performance of Beethoven's *Choral Symphony* with the London Symphony Orchestra conducted by Bruno Walter. Her fellow soloists were Isobel Baillie, Heddle Nash and William Parsons.

Some years after Kathleen's death this broadcast was issued as a record in America. It makes disappointing listening, in that the quality of the reproduction is poor. Kathleen's voice, although recognisable in her few solo passages, is generally lost in the morass of distortion and surface noise.

Dame Isobel fares better, as the soprano voice carries more easily over the background interference. She appears to be in good form but in fact had been in anything but an agreeable frame of mind.

Bruno Walter and Kathleen had recently triumphed at Edinburgh, and Walter was determined that everything should be right for Kathleen in the Beethoven. Dame Isobel, left much to her own devices, was unaccustomed to being so cavalierly treated. To add to her feelings of injury she did not particularly like the work she was performing. 'I have participated in countless performances of the *Choral Symphony*, a work for which I have to admit, sacrilegious though it might appear, I do not have a particular fondness.'[1] All of which makes it greatly to her credit that she gives such a fine performance. Even so, the record does little justice to any of the performers, and would never have been issued had Kathleen and, indeed, Dame Isobel had their way.[2]

While Bruno Walter was in Britain, he introduced Kathleen to Mahler's song cycle *Kindertotenlieder*. Influenced by Wagner's *Wesendoncklieder*, Mahler wrote the cycle in 1904, and it consists of settings to music of poems by Rückert, which deal with the grief of a mother over the death of her children. Initially, Kathleen found the subject matter morbid (as had Mahler's wife), but as soon as Walter started to coach her in the songs she found them compelling. She first performed them in a BBC broadcast on 25 November 1947.

She followed this by a broadcast, on November 29, of Mahler's *Third*

[1] *Never Sing Louder than Lovely.*
[2] In 1982, Dame Isobel wrote, 'I recently discovered, with some consternation, that the performance . . . is now in general circulation.'

Symphony. A private recording of this is believed to exist and may, possibly, appear on compact disc or tape some day.

She was back at the Decca studios on the 18 and 19 December, recording Brahms's *Alto Rhapsody*, with the London Philharmonic Orchestra and Choir under Clemens Krauss. Kathleen was fortunate to have Krauss as her partner. As the Wagnerian soprano Gertrud Grob-Prandl wrote, 'He possessed the unique combination of being imaginative and yet giving the singer a sense of total security. He knew voices and brought the best out in them.'[1]

The first performance of the *Rhapsody* had been given in 1870 by one of the outstanding singers of her day, Pauline Viardot-García. Obviously she was up to Brahms's demands as he was said to be so pleased by her performance that thereafter he slept with a copy of the score under his pillow.

In 1951, Kathleen told W. S. Meadmore in an interview with *The Gramophone*, that making records was 'the most difficult thing under the sun. Whatever the record, whenever I hear it in my own home, I always wish I could have done it once more. Perhaps the best record I have made is the Brahms *Alto Rhapsody*.'

She made this statement before her Mahler recordings and may well have felt differently with those to choose from.

Her last performance for 1947 was on 29 December, which allowed her to spend New Year's Eve with Winifred and William, while putting the finishing touches to her packing, before sailing the following day for New York.

[1] *The Last Prima Donnas*, Lanfranco Rasponi, Gollancz.

ELEVEN

Kathleen's friends turned out in force at Waterloo Station to wish her luck. Among them was Emmie Tillett (John Tillett's wife), Roy Henderson and Joan Cross. John Tillett was to travel with her as her manager, Emmie would take care of the agency while he was away.

There was a stevedores' strike at Southampton, from where the *Mauretania* was due to sail, and they had to wait an hour and a quarter before their luggage was loaded on board. But when she was eventually installed in her first-class cabin she found a mountain of good-luck telegrams and flowers awaiting her.

Although the weather was stormy, that trip was one of unmitigated joy to Kathleen. She wrote home:

Well, aren't I a lucky lass (fingers crossed). Fourth day at sea and I've eaten every meal, and am still intact despite 'heavy swell' – Klever Kaff.

I start the day off with a tray brought in by a stewardess. A colossal grapefruit, toast and a week's butter ration, marmalade and tea. She also brings the ship's newspaper, and events of the day – I get up slowly and have a shower then meet Mr Tillett on the sun deck and believe it or not, we had quite a few hours of sunshine yesterday. Then we pace round and round till we've done a couple of miles – then down to the promenade deck to our chairs, where a steward wraps us up in blankets and brings us chicken soup and a biscuit! Whattalife!

A rest for a bit, then a cocktail, and some Smith's crisps in a lovely bar then lunch – oh boy! Won't make you jealous, loves, but I'll bring some menus home.

Then back to our deck chairs with a book and sure enough a snooze and lo and behold it's tea time, and there's our nice steward with a tray of tea and a choice of Persil white bread and butter – delicious cakes and chocolate biscuits. Then there's a gram recital and a flick – we've seen *I wonder Who's Kissing Her Now* and *While I Live*. I have missed *Sabu* today because I've seen it. Then twice round the deck and dress for dinner – last night we were invited to the Chief Purser's for cocktails – tonight to the Captain's, so we're getting around.

A special dinner has been ordered for us tonight on the orders of the Purser, so we're having caviar, sole, fillet steak, new potatoes, salad, special ice with gorgeous little iced biscuits and coffee!! Oh, dear, I keep thinking about you struggling along to make the joint spin out, but I'll send some parcels when I arrive then you both have a good tuck in.

Mr Tillett's a bit liverish today, but if he will have two eggs for breakfast he's asking for it, isn't he? He's grand really, and hasn't been ill either – there are very few who haven't, but thanks to Dr Morton's pills which I have taken in small doses, I've been fine.

Last night there was horse racing on deck – wooden ones that move up as the dice is thrown. I borrowed 5/– from Mr T and won 17/6d with backing No. 4!!

Yesterday, when the sun shone, we were North of the Azores – now as we get nearer Newfoundland, the skies are stormy and there are white horses, but I hear a lot of snow has cleared in New York.

Ernest Ansermet (who conducted *Lucretia*) is on this boat with his wife – we picked them up at Cherbourg – small world, isn't it? I nearly forgot to tell you we share our table with an Australian lady and James Mason's mother-in-law – Mrs Ostrer!! Fame, begorra! Viscountess Rothermere is on board too!

Despite all this excitement, she studied each day, and managed to learn the German words to 'Erlkönig' while on board. For all her coaching with Hans Oppenheim, she was still painfully aware of her limited German repertoire.

On arrival at New York, journalists boarded the boat to photograph her, and question her about her New York performances. There was great interest in her Carnegie Hall debut with Bruno Walter. This was his first appearance of the season and, not previously noted for magnanimous statements, he had told the press that Kathleen was 'the greatest singer since Calvé'. Alma Mahler herself, the composer's daughter, had announced her intention of attending the concert.

Not all the reporters had done their homework. One, seeing the bustle about Kathleen, mistook her for a movie star. 'He wanted to know who this gorgeous beauty was!' she wrote to Paddy and William. 'I could have bit him, but only grinned and they were very nice and didn't hustle me, as I'd been warned.' Reporters never upset Kathleen, she appreciated the value of a good press and willingly kept them up to date with her news.

In the midst of the press conference, Ann Ayars arrived to welcome her to New York. They had not met since they had sung together in *Orfeo ed Euridice* at Glyndebourne. Finally, Kathleen disembarked and took a taxi with Mr Tillett to the Hotel Weylin, where they had reservations. Her room was on the first floor, overlooking Madison Avenue, and was filled with flowers, among which was a potted scarlet azalea from theatre star Ruth Draper, who was having a great success in New York at the time. This was a compliment indeed, for during the 1940s this great American artist topped the bill wherever she performed, be it in Britain or America. She was one of the last of a disappearing breed of entertainers, the 'diseuse', an artist who specialises in monologues. She peopled the stage with imaginary characters, some comic, some poignant. Ruth Draper left a note with the plant saying that a box at the theatre was at Kathleen's disposal any time she cared to visit. Pianist Benno Moiseiwitsch was also staying at the Weylin, and called to pay his respects.

The weather was cold, and a bitter unyielding wind blew through the streets, but this did not stop Kathleen and Mr Tillett from walking down Broadway that night, marvelling at the neon lights and the bustle. Kathleen bought a postcard of the Rockefeller Center, which she sent to Winifred: 'Here I am, thrilled to bits every minute of the day. New York is just unbelievable. The shops are like fairyland and the buildings superb. WISH you could be here to enjoy it.'

Unfortunately, Mr Tillett was not as quick on his feet as Kathleen, so she could not stride along at her usual brisk pace, and arrived back at the hotel frozen to the bone. She gratefully threw herself into bed, exhausted but happy, only to be woken a few hours later by the loud blaring of motor car horns and shouting in the streets. Her room overlooked two nightclubs that seemed to be throwing out their customers. Suddenly the view of Madison Avenue was not so attractive.

The hotel, however, provided her with a different room the next day, which she found more satisfactory. Euridice (her nickname for Ann Ayars) arrived to take her to have tea with a friend, and after that she treated herself to a hair style at the smart Elizabeth Arden Salon. Her other purchases that day included some woollen underwear and fur boots to try to offset the weather, a face flannel (difficult to buy in England under the clothing coupon scheme), some Lux toilet soap (a rarity in England), some sweets (on ration at home) and some bananas (virtually unobtainable in England).[1]

[1] Information from various letters to Winifred and William Ferrier.

All three New York concerts had been sold out well in advance, which so encouraged her American agents, Columbia Concerts, that they offered her another contract for the following year, irrespective of the fact that she had not yet sung in America.

After discussion with Mr Tillett she signed, although she was less than enchanted with Columbia Concerts' terms. She was to be responsible for her travel and hotel expenses, as was the case with her current tour and the cost of living in America was, as she wrote to Winifred, 'exorbitantly expensive, I shall have to go canny with my purchases or I shan't be able to pay my hotel bill. We're going to be very hard-up for money, as hotel, food and everything else is very dear, so I'm not shopping much till I see how I stand.'

There was a clause in the contracts which stipulated that if for any reason she was unable to sing, then she would not be paid for that performance, but would still be liable for her expenses. She cynically noted, 'As there seems to be more paying out than receiving, I'm not thrilled – but I expect it will work out all right.' Her financial problems were aggravated by British regulations which restricted her from taking more than a small amount of cash out of Britain. Consequently, she had no funds upon which to fall back in times of difficulty.

Mr Tillett did not provide as much guidance as might have been hoped for during these negotiations. He seemed to be confused by America and was finding currency, traffic and living conditions frustrating. His health was uncertain, and the sudden intake of rich food, after a wartime diet, did not help matters.

Neither was Kathleen in the best of health. She had a streaming cold, which she blamed on the icy weather and the contrast of the centrally heated hotel rooms. Four days before her scheduled first performance she found she had no voice. Cancelling all social engagements she stayed in bed, but she did not get the peace she sought as the telephone rang, seemingly, every quarter of an hour with friends, or friends of friends, who wanted to meet her. She did not have the heart to tell the operator to stop the calls. Ruth Draper came to see her, took one look, and telephoned for her own doctor.

Kathleen was immensely relieved when, after a couple of days, the fever broke and her nose started to run. This eased her vocal apparatus and meant the worst was over. On the morning of the concert she felt much better and, although her voice had certainly been in better condition, she knew she could go through with the concert.

Her room was full of flowers which had been sent by well-wishers. From all of these she selected a small corsage of orchids from Euridice and pinned this to her dress – the one that Winifred had made from the curtain brocade. Thus attired she made her way to Carnegie Hall for her American debut.

The tenor for *Das Lied von der Erde* was Set Svanholm, a favourite with Metropolitan Opera audiences. He was charming to her and she liked him at once. Bruno Walter wished her well but she could not help feeling nervous as she heard the New York Philharmonic tune up. She hastily looked at her words again, for despite Henderson's embargo on taking words on to the platform, she had written out the more difficult phrases on a piece of paper.

Eventually, the cue was given and she walked on to the platform, followed by Svanholm and Bruno Walter. Just a splatter of applause greeted her appearance, which disappointed her as, by now, she was accustomed to receiving the warmest of welcomes. 'I was stunned,' she wrote to Winifred. 'I thought I must have dropped my pants.' There was no time for further anxiety, however, as the strident opening bars struck up.

Kathleen felt she had sung well, and the audience was enthusiastic, which made a pleasant contrast to the insipid start, and as she left the platform a member of the orchestra called out, 'Bravo, beautiful!' Bruno Walter was pleased also, and Anna Mahler full of congratulations, so she made her way to the after-performance party in good spirits. Within a short time of her arrival she was asked to sing and cheerfully obliged. Unlike many professionals, Kathleen could always be relied upon to sing at parties.

She got a rude awakening next morning. According to the critics, the concert had not been the triumph the audience had led her to believe. Both the New York *Sun* and *Times* were dismissive, the *Sun* claiming, '. . . her voice has neither the breadth nor depth to convey all of what Mahler meant', and the *Times* '. . . she could not . . . give full significance to her text and music'. On the credit side, the *Telegram* considered 'phrasing and diction both showed a sure grip of style,' and the *Herald-Tribune* enthused, 'Miss Ferrier's phrasing was exemplary and her claim to complete artistry rests not alone on the unsullied beauty of tonal texture with which she invested her lines but on the unfailing perceptiveness and inwardness which pervaded her conception of this music.'

The bad reviews depressed her, but there was little time to mope, for her second performance of *Das Lied von der Erde* was the following afternoon, and this was to be broadcast coast to coast. She believed she had sung well in her first performance but was better pleased with her second, although Mr Tillett did nothing to boost her morale; he overheard an audience member remark that her voice was small and – with astounding insensitivity – repeated this to her. 'If they knew the score,' she wrote to Winifred, 'they would realise that I have to start pp and stay there, more or less, until the orchestra gets noisy.'

After the broadcast, there was such a demand for tickets for her final New York appearance, that Columbia Concerts asked her to fit in an extra concert.

I'm not going to [she wrote to Winifred], until I've done some lieder with Bruno Walter! YES! – He's going to give me some lessons when I get back from Chicago – *what* an opportunity! He is truly thrilled with me and my German interpretation, and is already seeing to my dates for next year, so I don't mind so much now. I suppose it's good for one not to hit the headlines all the time, but I did want to on this occasion. Well, love, it hasn't ended in a blaze of glory, but it's all experience. Loads of Love, Not So Klever Kaff.

She was mightily cheered by a letter from Leopold Stokowski, who had heard her broadcast and wrote to her agents:

The mezzo-soprano who sang in Mahler's *Das Lied von der Erde* yesterday was simply superb. Her voice was so full and beautiful, the intonation always perfect, the phrasing so elastic, the interpretation so eloquent. Altogether it was a superb performance and I wish to thank you for the pleasure I had in listening to it and to congratulate you on having chosen such a perfect artist for this masterpiece.

Before leaving New York for her next appearance, which was to be in Ottawa, Illinois, she went to a party with Bruno Walter. Madame Mahler's daughter, Anna, was there and someone asked if she were

Kathleen's mother. 'She took it in good part,' Kathleen wrote. 'She's only forty-three – she might have been furious.' Kathleen was thirty-five.

Kathleen and Mr Tillett travelled to Illinois on one of the new luxury diesel trains, and were joined for the journey by Arpad Sandor, her accompanist for the tour. She was delighted to have his company, as Mr Tillett was proving a ponderous companion. She wrote to Winifred:

> I have to coddle Mr T a bit. He's feeling his age, I think, and it takes him hours to decide whether he ought to wear a jersey, or if he's enough dimes for a stamp, or whether his underwear will go down on the laundry list as combinations or shorts – and as for choosing a meal – well, our father's positively lively in comparison. I try to curb my impatience as I know I do everything quickly, if slapdashly – but I could punch him sometimes!

Sandor made himself agreeable on the train, and pointed out to the waiter in the dining car that Kathleen was English and needed building up, due to wartime rations; this ensured that she received large portions. But for all the splendid food, the journey was still uncomfortable as the train was inadequately heated. 'I slept in everything I had,' she wrote to Winifred, 'including my new woolly breeks, but I didn't sleep much, the beds are sprung so. I bounced up and down all night like a rubber ball.'

She felt less than her best the next morning, and her spirits plummeted even lower when she saw Ottawa: in contrast to New York it seemed a drab, cheerless place. They had been promised that someone would meet them at the station but no one arrived. They waited, shivering under the grey early morning sky for a long time and then, finally gave up and took a taxi to their hotel. It was an unpretentious building, and did not inspire confidence. All three were hungry, having eaten nothing since dinner the night before, but there was no dining room. Utterly depressed, they prepared to go up to their rooms.

Then circumstances improved. The man who was to have met them arrived and apologised, shame-facedly, for having met the wrong train. He had stood on the platform for a good half-hour, equally depressed, believing Kathleen had failed to turn up. Now when Kathleen bemoaned her lack of breakfast she was immediately taken a few doors down the street to a drug store that served an excellent cooked breakfast. With this inside her, she was further heartened when she noticed a hairdressers and was assured she would be able to have her hair done before her recital that evening.

Back at the hotel her room turned out to be warm and quiet and she went to bed and slept until the afternoon. Then she went across to the hairdressers and had her hair done. Unfortunately this further glimpse of the town unsettled her: it seemed very provincial and she feared that her programme might prove too highbrow.

She had selected Gluck's 'Che Faró'; Handel's 'Ombra Mai Fu'; Schubert's 'An die Musik', 'Gretchen am Spinnrade' and 'Erlkönig'; Vaughan Williams's 'Silent Noon'; Stanford's 'The Fairy Lough' and Brahms's *Four Serious Songs*. She was particularly worried about the Brahms cycle, but it was too late to change items now.

The recital took place at the assembly hall of Ottawa High School, which seated about nine hundred. This cheered her. Even though in New York she had sung to audiences of 3,500, for recitals she much preferred the intimacy of smaller halls. One of her consistent complaints throughout her various American tours was that agents booked her into halls that were too large. Understandably, they wanted to gross as big a box office as possible, but Kathleen felt her programme suffered as a result.

Her concern about the suitability of her programme proved groundless. From the moment she opened her mouth to sing there was a respectful silence, followed by enthusiastic applause at the end of each song. Her audience may not have been as chic as in New York, but they demanded just as many encores.

The next day she made the two-hour journey to Chicago where she was to give two recitals. This time she was so staggered by the splendour of her hotel (The Blackstone) that she was afraid she would not be able to pay the bill. Shortly after checking in, she was descended upon by reporters and photographers, who stayed for two hours. She obligingly supplied numerous poses – singing, playing the piano, even combing her hair.

The windy city was living up to its reputation. That night the temperature dropped to seven degrees below zero and the snow was driven horizontally past her window. She hoped the storm would abate the next day as she was about to give her first recital at Park Ridge, about twenty miles out of town. This was in the nature of a preparatory event, as her main Chicago recital was a few days later, on 23 January, in the Ballroom of the Blackstone Hotel.

She had dinner in her room, then an early night, and wrote to Winifred:

> Bed at last, and what a bed – this is the loveliest room I've ever had, with beautiful lampshades, and a lavatory it seems almost indelicate to use – it's in the form of a wicker chair and lift the seat and there you are. I apologise every time I use it – I expect it to blush. . . . The manager of the hotel has just sent the bellboy up with a silver bowl with an apple, orange, pear, banana, and a bunch of grapes, not to mention a fig leaf. I'LL NEVER PAY ME BILL!!!!!

In contrast to the blizzard of the night, the next morning was crisp and sunny and Kathleen went for a long walk. 'This is the loveliest city yet,' she wrote to Winifred. 'Walked along the shores of Lake Michigan yesterday – all frozen – and stretching as far as the eye could see. Loving every minute of it now.'

A flatteringly large limousine arrived to take her to the recital, and the chauffeur explained he would wait and return to the Blackstone afterwards. Kathleen felt very grand, snuggled into her fur coat, as the car swished out of the hotel drive. She asked Mr Tillet who was paying for this handsome vehicle. 'You are,' was the blunt retort, which brought her down to earth.

The recital in Park Ridge provided another shock. It was the local cinema, the acoustics were poor and the plush, which seemed to be everywhere, deadened the sound. When she walked on stage she was blinded by a spotlight which stayed on throughout her performance.

It was unknown for critics to travel out of town to cover a newcomer's recital and in the circumstances, Kathleen felt that it was as well. In fact, she expected no press coverage from either of her Chicago appearances, having been disappointed to learn on arrival that her promoters had made a serious error of judgment. They had booked her main appearance for the 23 January, and this coincided with the only appearance in Chicago of the great German soprano Lotte Lehmann. Lehmann had an enormous following and audiences, and critics, would surely choose to attend her recital rather than that of a newcomer such as Kathleen. But Kathleen had not reckoned on the vigilance of one of the most renowned of American critics, Claudia Cassidy. Although Miss Cassidy had no intention of missing Lehmann, she had been sufficiently curious about Kathleen to make the earlier trip to Park Ridge to hear her. So, on the morning of Kathleen's Blackstone Hotel appearance, she was astonished – and delighted – to read the following review in the *Daily Tribune*.

> Miss Ferrier is a notable newcomer with the germ of greatness. . . . Her essential quality is a kind of bedrock simplicity, a native serenity stemming from strength, and her great gift is a singularly beautiful contralto, almost as natural as Flagstad's soprano in placement and unmistakably her own in its firm, dark texture and supple yet satisfyingly solid tone. Her range just now seems a bit skimpy at the top, but she is too wise to do any forcing. Let it come – with that wonderful middle voice and that velvet-slipping-downstairs of her descending scale, she can wait.
>
> With Arpad Sandor competently at the piano, Miss Ferrier sang a full-scale program in the big style. Handel, including the noble *Largo*. Gluck, to give us rewarding glimpses of her Glyndebourne *Orfeo*. Schubert – well, Schubert is elusive. 'Gretchem am Spinnrade' was valid music drama, beautifully done, but 'Erlkönig', which can be all things to all singers, tried too hard and overshot the mark. The English group was quite lovely – Vaughan Williams's 'Silent Noon', Stanford's silvery song called 'The Fairy Lough', Britten's way with the 'Sally Gardens' and Hughes's 'I have a Bonnet', and the delectable tale of 'The Spanish Lady'. But most extraordinary of all were Brahms's *Four Serious Songs* which she sang with courage, not in mourning. She did not make them problem songs, so no one was baffled by them. They were sombre but not sodden and I have rarely found them so moving. 'O Death How Bitter' which is magnificent in itself, was superbly sung.

After Chicago Kathleen returned to New York for a few days' holiday and, more importantly, some coaching in lieder from Bruno Walter. She enjoyed those days in New York enormously, because it seemed as though the city was filled with celebrities all wanting to meet her. She dined with Ruth Draper, Artur Schnabel and Elisabeth Schumann.

The only sour note came when she made the trip to the tax office on the seventy-sixth floor of the Empire State Building, to pay income tax on her American earnings. By the time this was done, her accompanist paid, and the hotel bills settled, she left New York with only very little more money than she had arrived.

LEFT Kathleen, aged one, with her mother, sister Winifred and brother George
ABOVE Aged ten, with her uncle, Albert Murray

At the microphone for EMI, 1946

Kathleen playfully poking out her tongue at Gerald Moore during rehearsal

Kathleen at the piano
she had won, 1946

The first Edinburgh Festival, 1947. Kathleen with Peter Pears, who was singing the tenor part in Mahler's *Das Lied von der Erde*

Lieder recital with Bruno Walter at the Usher Hall, Edinburgh, 3 September 1951

As Orfeo at
Glyndebourne, 1947

With Winifred
outside Notre Dame
Paris, March 1951

With Bernie in University
College Hospital, 1951

With Peter Pears and
Benjamin Britten
(*from left to right*), using
a telephone directory
as a score for a photo
call, 1952. Kathleen
was wearing a veil so
that her face would not
reveal how ill she was

Kathleen and Rosie

TWELVE

It was as though she had never been away. Kathleen was at the Albert Hall the evening after her return to London for a performance of *The Dream of Gerontius* under Sargent. Princess Elizabeth, Princess Margaret and the Duke of Edinburgh attended the performance and, during the interval, she was presented to them. The royal party offered her a glass of champagne and although Kathleen never drank during a performance, for just that once she broke the habit of a lifetime and accepted it. This abstinence was not based on moral scruples so much as practical commonsense, as alcohol, and gassy champagne in particular, could cause digestive problems.

Barbirolli had been coaching her in *Gerontius* and, now that she was back in London, they resumed their work together. He considered she had improved tremendously and went on to conduct her in many performances. After her death, he wrote: 'The generation of music lovers privileged to hear Kathleen Ferrier in *The Dream of Gerontius* have a memory of physical and spiritual loveliness that will surely have enriched their lives forever.'[1]

Barbirolli also invited her to sing *Kindertotenlieder* in the forthcoming Hallé season, a work he had not conducted since 1931, when Elena Gerhardt had sung it.

Meanwhile, the Dutch agent Peter Diamand, was trying to arrange further work for Kathleen in Holland, and had even made the journey to London to negotiate with Emmie Tillett, who was gradually taking over Kathleen's bookings from her ailing husband.

Mrs Tillett was not keen on Diamand's proposal. She told him Kathleen was 'too English' for continental audiences, who would not appreciate her. Diamand would not accept this, reminding her of Kathleen's Dutch success in *The Rape of Lucretia*. Diamand promised to cover all expenses, and although this considerably mollified Mrs Tillett

[1] *Sheffield Telegraph*, 19 November 1953.

she was still concerned that the concert might injure Kathleen's career. When Diamond persevered she tried another approach.

'Let's be clear about this,' Diamond remembers her telling him. 'You're just in love with this girl. Rather than lose money over a concert, why not simply buy her a present. It costs less; and it's less hurtful if she doesn't have a success, which could leave a scar.'

Finally, he struck a bargain with Emmie. 'If the concert's a success, let me handle all her continental bookings. If it isn't, I won't trouble you again.'

'Go ahead,' she replied. 'But I've warned you.'

Diamond did go ahead, and Kathleen left for Holland on 8 April 1948 for a short tour. Her first two appearances were in Amsterdam. Advance bookings were poor and it seemed that Diamond's faith had been misplaced; without the attraction of a new opera to back her she appeared to be of little interest to the Dutch. Her first recital in Amsterdam was one of the most depressing of her career, with a mere 150 in the audience.

For all this lack of public support, the critics knew her name, not just from *The Rape of Lucretia* but also from her numerous BBC broadcasts which they had been able to pick up. Diamond recalls the events of the following day:

> An incredible thing happened. There was a review of the concert on the front page of one of the main newspapers, something I've never seen before. Within minutes of my reading this I had a telephone call from the box office. They had already sold out for her second concert and such was the demand for tickets that the management offered to fit in another recital if I could secure a date from Kathleen.

At first she was hesitant, wondering if it was wise to reappear quite so soon in the same city, but when Diamond told her it would benefit him financially – as well as her – she agreed and was booked for a third Amsterdam recital, which was to take place in two weeks' time.

Her next recital was at the Hague, which was followed by a broadcast of *Kindertotenlieder* in Hilversum. On 16 April she appeared in Rotterdam, returning to Hilversum for a further broadcast. On the 22nd she was back in Amsterdam for the extra recital, which was in the small hall of the Concertgebouw. Every performance was to a full house and the critics were enthusiastic.

Diamand's organisational ability impressed her; he arranged all hotels and transportation and was always at hand to smooth the way. She enjoyed his company and found the many hours of train travel a joy. 'Blue skies, sparkling water and millions of flowers,' she wrote to Winifred. 'Thoroughly enjoying my book.' This was *Huckleberry Finn*, which she liked to read as she travelled.

Her pianist, Isja Rossican, was competent and good fun. 'He speaks no English, we converse in pidgin German and original deaf and dumb and get on very well,' she told Winifred. 'I am being ruined here.' Part of the ruination came from Otakar Kraus, who was also in Holland and always made a great fuss of her.

She arrived back in London on 24 April, in good spirits, ready to give the radio premiere of Sir Lennox Berkeley's *Four Poems of St Teresa of Avila*, a new British work. For some time she had been working on the texts, which are based on translations from the Spanish writings of St Teresa. Berkeley had composed the orchestral settings especially for Kathleen, often seeking her opinion on them while the work was in progress. 'She put herself at the service of the music,' he said, 'seeking to enter into its spirit rather than use it as a means of displaying her voice.'

She was hoping to introduce these songs to America on her next tour, but reluctantly abandoned the project when she learned that in order to make the tour viable her promoters were insisting she sing in large halls. It was not simply that the subject matter was too intimate for a large hall, but that the tessitura of the songs was also too low to render them audible in a big space.

Kathleen never recorded the songs, but Berkeley made his own private recording from the broadcast. In 1978 this was included in the BBC radio tribute to Kathleen, *The Singer and the Person*, and the recording was made available to the public the following year.[1]

In the March of 1948 Kathleen learnt that HMV were issuing a complete recording of *The Rape of Lucretia*, with Nancy Evans as Lucretia. This was a bitter disappointment. She liked Nancy, and

[1] BBC Antrim REGL 368.

genuinely wished her well, but had cherished hopes of recording Lucretia herself. Now, since *The Rape of Lucretia* did not have the sales potential of a popular Puccini or Verdi opera, these hopes were dashed. Kathleen knew there was no room in the catalogue for two versions.

On 26 April she returned to the BBC for a lieder broadcast that included Brahms's 'Gestillte Sehnsucht' and 'Geistliches Wiegenlied'. She had just recorded these songs for Decca in December 1947, but was unhappy with the results, and had refused permission for them to be released. She had recorded them again, in June 1948, and again rejected them. It was not until February 1949, that she eventually recorded versions she found satisfactory.

The day following her broadcast she flew to Holland for a performance of *Das Lied von der Erde* under Willem van Otterloo. She was nervous of flying and never conquered this. 'My stomach dropped a yard when we took off!' she wrote on a postcard to Winifred from Amsterdam. 'Had lunch served and mags, and sat back and enjoyed and pretended not to feel white about the gills!! Was in Amsterdam by noon, isn't it amazing. *Das Lied* went very well, considering not *too* wonderful an orchestra. Everyone seemed pleased. More bouquets, beginning to expect 'em!'

The sad news greeted her, on her return to London, that Mr Tillett had died. Although he had proved trying in America, Kathleen never forgot that it was he who had given her a hearing, and had loyally represented her in her early days. Thus she was saddened – and also concerned that Emmie, with whom she had become staunch friends, would be lonely.

Kathleen was acquainted with loneliness. She had a wide circle of friends, but there were few in whom she could confide. Winifred was her only confidante. Roy Henderson was close to her, as were Britten and Pears, but she chose not to reveal her innermost feelings to them; she had a reserve that prevented her from wearing her heart on her sleeve. Joan Cross noticed this during *The Rape of Lucretia*, calling her a private person.

Sometimes she could not help feeling a twinge of envy when she observed her friends who were happily married. On one occasion she told Ena Mitchell she was lucky to have such a good husband. Another time, when she was on a train, she shared a compartment with a lady who was crying. When Kathleen asked if she could do anything to help, her companion confided that her husband was in hospital to have a leg amputated. Kathleen's reply was that he still had two arms with which he could hug her.

Kathleen enjoyed the company of men and had several men friends. Lately one had become particularly close. Rick Davies was a young antique dealer from Liverpool. He was good-looking, with a lively personality, and she enjoyed his company more than that of any other man she knew, with the exception of Barbirolli, who was thirteen years her senior, and in any case happily married.

Returning to Holland on 1 July, for her third visit that year, Kathleen sang *Das Lied von der Erde* under George Szell. As there were nearly six weeks before her next appearance she and Rick went for a holiday to Roaspenna, in Northern Ireland. Ireland was a popular place in which to holiday as food was plentiful and unrationed.

Feeling fit after her holiday, Kathleen returned to London and set about redecorating her flat. By now it was beginning to look quite elegant. She learnt about antiques and began replacing her utilitarian furniture with pieces of Buhl and Chippendale. In her sitting room was a portrait of herself by Maurice Codner.

The weeks drifted past pleasantly enough, and she returned to the concert hall on 17 August with a Proms appearance at the Albert Hall, where she sang the *Alto Rhapsody*. The following day she left for the second Edinburgh Festival where she was to give a recital with Gerald Moore, and a performance of Bach's *B Minor Mass* under Sargent, by now Sir Malcolm Sargent.

As before, she stayed with the Maitlands. Full of plans for her forthcoming American tour, she excitedly described how it would last sixteen weeks, during which time she would be touring from the east coast to the west and also giving performances in Canada.

From Edinburgh she travelled by train to Worcester for performances of *St Matthew Passion*, *The Dream of Gerontius* and Debussy's *La Demoiselle Elue*, which she had not sung since the Stockport performance of 1944.

That September she braved another aeroplane and flew to Denmark for a tour, arranged by the Danish agent Einer Gylling, whom she dubbed 'Einer Kleiner'. She gave two concerts in Copenhagen with the

Royal Danish Orchestra under its conductor Egisto Tango, and then sang her way across the country, through Naested, Holback and Odense.

October was packed with appearances, the highlight of which was a broadcast of *Kindertotenlieder* under Barbirolli. She then sang the cycle at Bradford, Manchester and Sheffield. 'Think of me as a throat,' she laughingly told a friend, but quickly added, 'I wouldn't change it for the world.'

Kathleen's pain returned to her chest from time to time and with it her old dread of cancer. To reassure herself she was well she underwent a thorough examination at St Mary's Hospital, Paddington, and was pronounced fit.

She returned to the Albert Hall on 12 January 1949, for a broadcast performance of the orchestrated version of the *Four Serious Songs*; Sargent was conducting the London Symphony Orchestra. This was later issued as a record,[1] and in emotional intensity eclipses the studio recording Kathleen later made for Decca, in which the songs were sung in their original form, with John Newmark at the piano. Kathleen invariably gave something extra when she was in front of an audience.

The broadcast was heard by Kathleen's former headmistress, Miss Gardner, who sent her a letter of congratulation. Kathleen replied:

> I think of Blackburn and my school days with deep pleasure, and my great regret is that I had to leave so early. In my particular work, how grateful I should have been for fluent French, German and Italian. The bit of Latin I did has stood me in good stead, but I have spent many painful hours trying to memorise German and Italian. . . .
>
> I'm so glad you enjoyed the Brahms *Serious Songs*, they are one of my favourite cycles, but it was strange to sing them with orchestra. . . . I think they are such wonderful and moving words to sing and I always love doing them.

Her last engagements before leaving for America were tours of Holland and Ireland, plus an Albert Hall performance of Dvořák's *Stabat Mater* under Raphael Kubelik, followed by four days in the Decca studios recording folk songs.

[1] Decca 414 095–1.

THIRTEEN

This time she travelled to America alone, leaving Southampton on 18 February 1949 in the *Queen Mary*. Kathleen had taken up painting as a relaxing hobby and, before leaving the flat for the voyage, she was struck by how romantic her luggage looked as it stood in the hall. Two plush teddy bears someone had given her for luck were perched on top of the cases. She painted the scene, entitling it 'Ready for Off' and signed it *KK Opus One*.

The voyage was rough, delaying the ship's arrival in New York by thirty-six hours, but as Kathleen had a week of rehearsals before her first performance, this did not worry her. Quite the reverse, she was delighted to have another day and a half of Cunard hospitality.

Her first appearance was in New York at the Town Hall, in a concert version of *Orfeo ed Euridice*, with Ann Ayars as Euridice, and the orchestra conducted by Tom Scherman. This time the New York critics were unanimous in their praise, but for all the acclaim Kathleen was unimpressed with the production, describing it privately as 'scratchy and amateurish'.

She was beginning to understand the truth of the lesson that Joan Cross had given her some years previously in Wales, that any artist must insist on the best possible working conditions. On tour, conditions were frequently poor, and sometimes it took a great deal of persistence to get them improved. This time Kathleen did not have the luxury of travelling with a manager, even one as frail as Mr Tillett, so she had to deal with problems herself.

Her situation was not eased by Arpad Sandor, her recital accompanist. He had played excellently for her on her previous American tour, but now, to her alarm, she noticed that inaccuracies were creeping into his work. Possibly his state of mind was to blame for he was not the cheerful, stable companion of last year, but was suffering from a deep depression.

His psychological condition, however, had not affected his business acumen. On her arrival he told her firmly that his fees had risen by a hefty twenty-five dollars a performance, plus four dollars per night subsistence. Kathleen was already reeling from one financial shock – Columbia Concerts had informed her that she was several hundreds of dollars in debt due to the amount they had debited from her account to cover advertising costs. On top of everything, the cost of living in New York had risen. She wrote to William:

> I can't cope with prices here. The simplest toast and coffee is at least 5s and a steak!! I had just a steak before my Orfeo concert and the bill was $4.45 – drug stores for me in future.
>
> So, I'm going to be a bit careful with my money, but I'll send you some tins as soon as I've got a bit of spare cash.
>
> I'm talking prices tonight, but do you know how much my room at the Weylin was, with no food! $9 a night! It's staggeringly expensive. I'm going to have a bath and leave a tide-mark just to get me money's worth.

While in New York, Kathleen took the opportunity of consulting singing teacher Clytie Mundy, who had been recommended to her by Peter Pears. Kathleen was always wary of those few middle notes in her voice, near her break, and never ceased working on them. She found Madame Mundy's method of great help and was reassured that, whatever else might lie in store for her, at least her voice would not let her down.

She also attended a performance of *Götterdämerung* at the Metropolitan Opera House. Kathleen was no devotee of Wagner, but she wanted to see a production at the world-famous theatre.

The first leg of the tour was Granville, Ohio, which was a two-day train journey from New York. Accommodation had been reserved for her, curiously, at a stud farm, so as the weather was mild she was able to sit outside in the weak sunshine and watch the horses being exercised. Whatever Columbia Concerts might have spent on advertising, the effects did not seem to have filtered through to Granville. 'The concert was about a quarter filled,' she wrote to William, 'and some of them knitting!! I could have spat at them.'

Additionally, Sandor's playing had become so erratic that she put through an urgent telephone call to Mr Mertens of Columbia Concerts, entreating him to try to book Gerald Moore or Phyllis Spurr for the rest of the tour. Had he been successful she would have gladly paid off Sandor but, not surprisingly, neither player was available at such short notice.

Her next appearance was in Montreal, Canada. She arrived there at midnight, in the middle of a blizzard. But the taxi drivers did not seem to find this inconvenient, and she was whisked off briskly to her hotel, where she slept solidly for the next twelve hours.

Her concert was at three pm. 'I arose slowly,' she wrote to Winifred, 'had a bath and left a tide-mark, and donned a face and white satin. Surprisingly, I felt fine. The hall was packed – it was one of the most important concerts – and from the first they purred – so different from Ohio. It was well worth the long journey and they've booked me again for next year.' To Roy Henderson she wrote, 'This concert just saved me from getting the next boat home, because it was packed with ardent music lovers, and they just went mad.'

Sandor's playing continued to deteriorate. 'He plays Schubert-arranged Sandor!' she fumed to Henderson. 'Leaves out notes and puts notes in. He's temperamental and in a brown study most of the time.' There was no alternative other than to confront Sandor. He confided to her that his wife was ill and that the worry was unsettling him. She felt she could not be too hard on him after that.

The financial arrangements with Columbia Concerts still exasperated her. The fees for her appearances were sent directly to Columbia. She could request a subsidy when necessary, but her travelling expenses were so heavy that her cash was constantly running out, and she had to go begging humiliatingly often.

From Montreal she made her way to Indianapolis. The train broke down four times on the long journey, and she arrived four hours late, in the dead of night, with no one to meet her. The next destination was Pittsburg, where she sang at the Foster Memorial Hall. 'I've now got six concerts off me chest,' she wrote to William. 'They have all gone well. Pittsburg was a huge success, thank goodness.'

On the train to Newark she gave vent to her frustrations about Sandor in a letter to Winifred:

He played so softly in the Ash Grove, the other night, I could hardly hear him and had to say LOUDER out of the corner of my mouth, in between verses, but of course he couldn't hear me! He's the only thing that makes me nervous for my recitals here – I never know what he'll do next. At Pittsburg we did 'Heidenröslein' as an encore, unrehearsed, and he put in trills where there weren't any – I stood with my mouth open – the audience would think it was a peculiar interpretation. Twice he's put in major chords when it's only an octave, in the 'Erlkönig'. I asked him to play it, and 'Röslein' again at a rehearsal the other day he played them both just as written!! I think he'll go gaga one day very soon.

Nothing however could be done. Columbia's Mr Mertens had tried every accompanist of repute that he knew, and they were all unavailable. Kathleen was particularly worried about her return New York engagement, on 28 March.

She was briefly diverted when someone introduced her to the joys of nylon underwear, something that was unknown in Britain. It needed no ironing and revolutionised her nomadic life. She wrote to Winifred:

Yesterday I bought myself a girdle for me spare tyre. It's a beauty and comes to right above my waistline. Instead of oozing at me waist I just ooze at top and bottom – it's beautiful. I also got a petticoat and three pairs of pants in nylon, all needing no ironing, and it works too, cos I washed a pair of the pants to make sure!'

As the day approached she called at the offices of Columbia Concerts to discuss details with Mr Mertens and was understandably indignant when one of the employees proceeded to advise her on stage make-up. 'She also told me what to wear on my nails, my ears, my arms and neck in the way of jewellery, and I was in trouble for not having taken my make-up down to try it out and also my frock. I felt about fourteen, until I started to laugh and told her I'd done a few recitals before. What a silly witch.'

The witch seemed even sillier on the afternoon of the recital when she interrupted Kathleen's pre-concert nap by telephoning her not to forget her eyeshadow.

The recital was completely sold out, with over a hundred people actually sitting on the stage. Both Bruno Walter and Elisabeth Schumann had sent good luck telegrams and were in the audience.

The first half of her programme consisted of Bach, Handel and Schubert, and she was called back for three curtain calls.

In the second half she sang *Four Serious Songs*, some lieder and several British folk songs. She wrote to Henderson:

I put my all into it, and the audience just shouted and stamped. It was lovely, Prof dear, and I think you'd have been happy if you'd been there. Bruno Walter rang me up next morning . . . he said some of the loveliest things I could ever have dreamed of hearing, and he said two or three times he was very proud of me. I said, 'What about the Brahms?' because he said I shouldn't do them. He says he thinks that, musically, they can never live up to the words and only a Bach or Beethoven could have done so, and he's still of the opinion, I think, that they are unsuitable. His only 2 criticisms were that the 'Junge Nonne' [sic] could be a little wilder and that I must watch the top notes in 'Du bist die Ruh'. I think I spread them a bit in my effort to make a stunning crescendo!! because he approved them mightily when we rehearsed. But I'm watching them!

I wore my new red dark satin and no jewellery whatsoever except my ring – the witch hasn't spoken to me since!!

People were standing . . . it hasn't happened before for years, I was told. I cheered up at this news because, at least, for all my pains, I would now be in pocket, which is also, except for Maggie Teyte and Lehmann, unheard of! (At least, there'll be hell to pay if I wasn't.) And, true enough, I've made over 500 dollars – well over £100.

Well, the papers the next day were mixed. They all criticised something. One said I could have been better gowned! One said I was breathy – another said I wasn't intense enough – another very intense – another it was a pity that, like Marian Anderson, I couldn't sing the bottom F sharp in 'Todd das Mädchen' [sic]. Of course, it's D, and a third lower if he had the sense to know, which makes quite a difference! But in a grudging way they said I was worth watching. . . .

Well, well, I can't cope with the New York critics – it seems to be the biggest political racket ever, and what Bruno Walter said to me just blots out their silly ravings and I honestly haven't lost a wink of sleep. I think the audiences are often the judges in the long run, and they were wonderful.

To Winifred she added, 'Quite honestly, I'm past caring. They were the most lovely audience and they're the ones who've paid for their seats!'

To her delight, Bruno Walter had agreed personally to accompany her at her forthcoming Edinburgh Festival appearance, and also at an additional London recital. Maestros of the calibre of Walter rarely act as accompanists, so it was the highest compliment he could pay her.

While in New York, she and Walter worked on their Edinburgh repertoire. 'He altered my programme quite a bit,' she wrote to Henderson. 'Now I have six new Brahms to learn and two Schubert, but he's such a love I don't mind except that I wish I had the chance to try them out before Edinburgh. Phew!'

Returning from one of these sessions to her hotel one evening, she had an unexpected visit from Sandor's wife, who told her that far from being ill herself, it was her husband who was sick. He had been suffering from a mental illness for almost a year, and was actually undergoing psychiatric treatment. 'Kinda cheering when we're going off together for six months,' she wrote to Henderson. 'I thought there was something most peculiar. Well, now at least, I know what it is!'

Hearing of his wife's visit, Sandor rang her the next morning in a fit of hysteria, ending the conversation in tears and begging to be released from his contract. That evening, at dinner, he composedly apologised, and announced that he was determined to continue with the tour. 'Oh, for dear Phyllis,' Kathleen sighed in a letter to Winifred.

In an effort to get their relationship on to a better footing, she re-rehearsed her entire recital programme with Sandor. 'Please don't rush, play lightly and in correct time – don't go quicker in between verses – don't put trills in "Heidenröslein" where it's only a turn – play all the notes in the Brahms – play what's written – let me hear the diddle diddles in the right hand of the "Junge Nonne", etc, etc.' She wrote to Henderson of her procedure, and added, 'It was much better, but oh! dear!'

More stimulating was her last session with Bruno Walter, when they spent another 'wonderful' four hours on their Edinburgh programme.

She left New York to resume her tour in a sanguine frame of mind, determined to make the best of a bad job with Sandor. Her first venue was Ottawa, Canada, where she arrived at noon, grey with tiredness, having travelled overnight, via Montreal. She was staying at the lovely Château Laurier, but there was a hitch: 'I was furious,' she wrote to Winifred, 'because when we arrived they said there wouldn't be a room ready until late afternoon and I enjoyed myself for five minutes telling them what I thought of them, and they had one ready for 1.30! Very nice too, I've wiped my face on every towel and opened four pieces of soap!'

She went to bed as soon as she had unpacked and had had a bath, and slept until it was time to get ready for her recital. The hall was huge, seating three thousand, but it was very nearly full, which cheered her, despite the extra effort needed to make the songs carry.

On 1 April she was in Chicago and described her free day to Winifred:

I've had a wonderful day snooping around with my camera. I've taken a picture of a Red Indian for our father, but it's only a statue, I'm afraid! Tonight I went walking again, and passing a flick went in and saw Loretta Young in *Mother Is A Freshman*. There was a stage show too, and I sat next to the blackest Negro you ever saw, who roared with laughter at everything. I enjoyed him more than the show. Loretta Young is quite beautiful – it was very amusing and lovely colour so see it if you get a chance. Then I came out and went into a favourite drug store and had a sandwich about two inches thick and a lovely ice-cream with pineapple juice and cream, so I'm fat and full.

I'm looking really fit and feeling fine because the air is wonderful and I've been doing a lot of walking. Hope you two loves are all right, too.

The showdown with Sandor came in Chicago when, after another outburst, he finally realised he was too ill to carry on and asked to be released from his contract immediately. Mr Mertens had still not managed to come up with a substitute accompanist, but Kathleen had a Canadian pianist called John Newmark recommended to her. She was impressed when she learned that he had worked with Aksel Schiøtz, who spoke highly of him. 'If he has a sense of humour, I can bear anything,' she wrote to Winifred, passing her information to Mr Mertens with an urgent plea to try to book him.

This was not easy, as Newmark was in the middle of a tour on Prince Edward Island, accompanying bass-baritone George London, and could hardly leave him in the lurch. But by now, Kathleen was a big name in Canada and America, and George London knew it would be a marvellous opportunity for Newmark to work with her, so he generously released him from his contract.[1]

Newmark immediately caught a plane to Chicago and arrived at about lunch time. Kathleen was at a business lunch, discussing her 1950 Chicago appearances, for Emmie had already organised an American schedule for the following year. Kathleen left a letter of welcome for Newmark:

> Dear Mr Newmark, Bismark Hotel, Chicago
> 14 April 1949
>
> I am so very sorry not to be able to meet and welcome you. . . . I have heard such lovely things about you from Mrs Russell-Smith, and I am looking forward with great pleasure to working with you, and I hope with all sincerity that this may be the happiest of tours for you.

She wrote to Winifred: 'Thank God he looks bright and hasn't got a drugged look about the eyes. We rehearse tomorrow, but I've a feeling he's going to be all right.' As the tour progressed she wrote again: 'He does play beautifully, and does all the dirty work like enquiring for trains and planes, and seeing the piano and stage are all right, etc., and he bosses me completely, which is quite a new feeling for me! He has terrific concentration and energy and absorbs everything he sees and hears and never forgets it again.'

She passed on the good news to Emmie and, in reply, Emmie informed her that she had had to decline several Dutch bookings due to pressure of engagements. Kathleen, who was already booked for the Holland Festival shortly after her return from America, accepted this without question.

Not so Peter Diamand, who now handled her Dutch bookings and who sent Kathleen a terse letter suggesting that if she was really so busy, then perhaps Emmie was overworking her. She responded in like spirit, bluntly pointing out that Emmie was turning down the Dutch bookings at her personal request. As usual, Winifred was her confidante, and she poured out her annoyance in a letter to her.

[1] Taken from a broadcast Newmark made on his relationship with Kathleen for CBC Radio, Canada, translated from the original French.

I have sung more in Holland than anywhere – and every song I know – so I have personally told Emmie autumn 1950 at the earliest, as I can't keep it up. Then he [Peter Diamand] wrote to me to learn two Bach cantatas – brutes – and Flothuis[1] wrote wanting me to do his cantata and I'm to do Ben's Symphony[2] which I haven't seen yet and on top of this *Orfeo*.[3]. And he's the one who talks about not working me too hard. . . .

He also, after I arranged the sending of the *Orfeo* orchestral material to Holland, said I must help him find the scores for the chorus as he couldn't get them back from Novellos [the music publishers] – I'd just had a bad overnight journey so I said I was in the bleeding Rockies – they'd never heard of *Orfeo* there. I'm humbugged to death on this trip – yesterday Mr Mertens wrote saying there will be papers to sign for taxation when I'm leaving and 'I do not see how you can leave by boat or train without permitting yourself at least one day in New York'. He's the silly bugger that booked me in Wisconsin on the 26th when the boat leaves on the 28th – and despite all my curves, I can't stop the *Queen Eliz.* sailing until I've paid me income tax – Really! I wanted you to know about Peter though, because he was only stating one side of the case – and I won't have a word said against Emmie – not unless I say it.

Kathleen's indignation in the letter is perfectly justified, but the untypically violent spirit must have been brought about by the frustrations of fatigue and travel, for she had by now been in America for nearly three months. She soon made it up with Diamand and he carried on representing her for many more Dutch appearances. But Columbia Concerts' chronically slack organisation continued to goad her, as did the amount of red-tape with which she was obliged to contend. 'If I just had to sing, and no visas, taxes and dates to think about, I shouldn't know what to do with myself – but I'd probably sing better!'

In between Chicago engagements she made appearances in La Crosse, Wisconsin, where some of her audience had travelled over two hundred miles to hear her. In La Crosse she made friends with Mrs Benita Cress, one of the concert organisers.

Aware of the food rationing in Britain, Mrs Cress entertained Kathleen royally – it seemed that wherever she went Kathleen was

[1] Dutch composer who wrote especially for Kathleen.
[2] Britten's *Spring Symphony*, which she was to premiere.
[3] All Dutch engagements.

being entertained royally. 'Listen, buddy – how do I lose weight?' she enquired of Winifred. 'I'm 12 stone 1 lb!! I got the shock of my life. That's been creeping on for twelve months, so I must do something about it!' If frustration can cause weight loss, then she should have shed several pounds when she returned to Chicago. She sent the following account to Winifred:

I've just had the time of my life – I've been telling the Chicago manager what I think of him and the whole managerial set-up here – and what's more I didn't cry!

Mind you, it won't make any difference, but at least I've got it off my chest!! I've been really miserable until now with my money disappearing down a drain of advertising and managers' pockets!

I said I wanted to know where, if the concerts were non-profit-making, the money went. I have an average of 3,000 in the audience – which means at least 3,000 dollars and they pay me 800, out of which I pay an accompanist 105 – twenty per cent managers – rail travel for two (which is a colossal amount here) hotel, taxis, porters and tips – and income tax! I told him I was the highest paid artist in England, and was wanted in every country on the Continent – that I hated the halls here – they were too big for recitals, and if I was going to suffer and not enjoy my work, I wanted well paying for it – not go home penniless (Klever Kaff, don't you think). Otherwise I would cut down my visits here to the minimum and sing in England where they'd been waiting to get me for three years! I also said I came to this country as an established artist and didn't want to be treated like a beginner, and I told him how one of the girls at the office in New York had told me what nail-varnish to wear – what hairstyle – how much eye shadow – the colour of lipstick, and I said I didn't want to outshine Hollywood and remove all signs of character.

I said a lot more – for a whole hour and a half – and I feel wonderful. I did say that if American artists came to England we didn't tell them how to dress – nor did we send them to Gt Horwood to sing for two hours and then be out of pocket. I think I've made him think. He agreed with most of what I said! He's a nice man, and a businessman and I had a good dinner out of him too.

I'm learning to talk straight here – but am becoming hard-boiled in the process. We're firm friends now! But isn't it hard work!

At Carlton College, Minnesota, she sang to an audience mostly comprised of voice students and, afterwards, was amazed at the technicalities of their questions: 'They all clamoured round, asking me how I did this and that – I felt about 90 – and most of the things I didn't know I'd done.'

There was always the odd adventure en route. Her hotel in Battle Creek, Michigan, was also housing a grocers' convention and she was kept awake late at night as the grocers gaily tossed cans of produce down the stairs. In Kentucky, Newmark's page-turner was so overwhelmed by her singing that he sobbed noisily throughout her performance. And in Havana, Cuba, she had her first Baccardi daiquiri, which she thought so delicious she had three more. She was observed in the Prado, shortly afterwards, holding on to Newmark's arm and singing Irish songs.[1]

Her concert in Havana was at the Sociedad Pro Arté Musica, where she sang to an audience of two and a half thousand. If the effect she produced on them was even half as profound as the effect she produced on a local music critic, then she must have caused quite a stir! The following review, translated here from the Spanish, appeared in an Havana newspaper of 7 May 1949:[2] Newmark was so impressed he carried it around for years:

When we write today about the art of Kathleen Ferrier our pen hesitates as if the rich treasure of Spanish words were not able to describe it. And really, it is not sufficient. Because Kathleen Ferrier uses her voice like one of the most perfect instruments one can imagine in a supreme beautiful synthesis of technique and naturalness, giving the sound such beauty that, would one describe it it would also be necessary to do so with musical sounds. What can be expressed about her in words can be done in one: a miracle! Kathleen Ferrier is more than a mere singer, she is a real miracle, a happy blend of admirable musicality and vocal quality, of angel-like purity and delicious timbre, of technique and schooling, of finesse and nuances, of overwhelming tone production and sureness: elegance, wonderful restraint, exquisite diction, flawless phrasing, unique gift for voice projection, effortless, like breathing and talking, noble and dignified expression without any exaggeration or false pathos, a control whose proud nobility yet contains great human sweetness; with it a quite unique personal charm

[1] Information from John Newmark.
[2] Author and publication unknown.

in appearance and with all this (much too little to do her justice) the greatest gift to move her listeners that we have ever found in a singer. In one word: one has to come back to it: she is a miracle with a capital M! What else we could say about Kathleen Ferrier can only be found in the words of the Ave Maria! We cannot remember to have ever assisted a concert that left us in such a turmoil of emotions, neither a symphony nor a choir, neither chamber music nor instrumental works. When we say 'concert' the expression is wrong because what Kathleen Ferrier and her accompanist John Newmark offered yesterday was actually not a concert, but a sacred offering in the temple of music, a lyrical donation, a blessing of the souls. We come back from this sacred hour as if stunned, drunk with beauty and the impact of the hard reality hits us like a whip. We wish this superhuman experience would never be forgotten and the memory of it would last on the soul as long as a tattoo on the body. For hours afterwards we were still unable to do anything or to express ourselves in words, like somebody completely taken away from the terrestrial sphere. What magic! Do we have now to talk about the works Kathleen Ferrier sang? Why? It was the same perfection, the same ecstasy in Bach as in Handel, in Schubert as in Brahms, in Parry and Stanford as in Peter Warlock or Benjamin Britten. Only the style of the music and the pathos of each period changed. May it, thus, to give details of the programme be sufficient to say that she sang an aria from the *Christmas Oratorio* by Bach and three from operas by Handel. Also seven songs by Schubert ('Du bist die Ruh' was the sensation of the evening, something really extraordinary). Also the *Four Serious Songs* by Brahms with biblical texts and finally songs by Parry, Stanford and Warlock, a wonderful aria from Britten's *Rape of Lucrecia* and Scottish folk songs. At the end the whole audience stood for a long time in raving enthusiasm. A voice called for 'Carmen! Carmen!' May God forgive him!

The British Ambassador was in the audience and, afterwards, invited Kathleen and Newmark to dine with him. Her host was fascinated when, after the meal, Kathleen accepted, and smoked, an Havana cigar. Kathleen had smoked cigarettes moderately for years, but tried to cut down when her singing schedule was heavy, restricting herself to just one cigarette after a performance. Passing Cloud was her favourite brand.

While driving back to her hotel in the Ambassador's car she told the driver to stop and wait while she and Newmark had a liqueur and ice-cream at a café. A peanut vendor passed by and she sang his vending song with him. But her mellow mood was fragile. When someone asked her when she would be returning to America she snapped 'probably never!', angrily remembering her high overheads and the bureaucratic demands made on her.[1]

After the Havana concert Kathleen and Newmark separated for a week or so as her next concert, in Miami, was to be with an orchestra. She flew there four days ahead of schedule in order to take a holiday in the sun. Before leaving Cuba she received a parcel of letters. Columbia Concerts had instructions to forward her mail to her, wherever she was, as she loved to get letters from home, eagerly devouring the news, whether it be about the horrors of the leaky cistern at Frognal Mansions or accounts of Winifred and William's outings. 'That's lovely,' she replied to a letter from Winifred, who had told her that Paddy had taken William to Kew Gardens. 'But tell them always to have a car – I've a big credit account – when Pop's going along, never hesitate.'

In truth, she would have preferred a Kew Gardens trip with William to her holiday in Miami, as she was feeling homesick. It was the height of the Miami season and when she arrived, after a bumpy flight, she discovered that the hotel had not received her reservation. The receptionist told her there was no accommodation available, and it was only after a heated discussion with the manager that a room was found.

But at least the weather was magnificent, so she bought herself a swimming costume and took a bus to the beach. 'I'm pink in some amazing places,' she wrote to Winifred that night, 'but feel self-conscious with my lilywhite legs here – everybody else *dark* mahogony! They paid me cash in Cuba so I've been having fun, bought two sun dresses, two pure silks, none of the frocks cost more than £4.10s each! I had only one thin one with me and I can't wear more than one layer here.'

The four days passed pleasantly enough, even though she was on her own, and she reported for her orchestral rehearsal in high spirits. She was to sing Elgar's *Sea Pictures*, and she wrote to Newmark:

You were expected to come with me to play the encores, but I'm sure the audience will have had enough by the time I've splashed my way through, I

[1] Taken from a broadcast made by Newmark for CBC Radio, Montreal.

have a horrible feeling I shall go under 4 times and only come up 3. Whattalife!

I am a bright, puce lobster colour, and must have a temperature of at least 205, but have been in the water twice and it's just heavenly. This hotel is about twenty miles away from the University [where she was to appear] and I have a twenty-five-minute bus ride even to get to Miami beach!

My great sorrow is that the masterpiece I took of you at the yacht club (in Havana) has intermingled itself with the Hotel Nacional swimming pool, so I am two snaps missing, but the others are rather good – especially one I took of a sunset that I never expected to turn out. Klever Kaff!

Look after yourself – I look forward already to Louisville, and hearing your superb accompaniments again. God bless.

After the recital she flew to New York for talks with Mr Mertens and described the scene to Winifred:

I played hell with Columbia this morning! I'm just beginning to enjoy playing hell! I had lunch with Mr Mertens and dinner with him, and the big white chief, and I never stopped! I didn't cry either (Klever Kaff) and I think I've made them think. I pointed out that they hadn't put my fee up for next year – got it put up on the instant! My, but isn't it hard work! Only fifty dollars a concert, but better than nowt. Actually, I wouldn't have missed this tour for anything, especially Miami and Cuba, but I don't like being *put on*!

To give me courage I bought a new hat, bag, shoes, stockings, and summer nylon pantie girdle and could have coped with the whole blinking board of directors. I have only sagged a little now, having discovered that the tab of my dress had been sticking out at the back of my neck all the time. I *thought* people were looking at me, but I thought it was admiration!! That'll larn me!

On 22 May, she flew to Louisville, where she was to be joined by John Newmark. The flight, as described to her father and Paddy, proved to be as stormy as her lunch with Mr Mertens had been:

Well, I never expected to reach Louisville. We started off from New York in a downpour of rain – splashed through a lake of water to get to our places and came through a tornado in West Virginia. It rained, it lightened [sic], it leapt up and down, it nearly turned ruddy somersaults, and we were three hours late, and t'was a good job we'd had no lunch or I should have lost it! There were thirty-seven people killed in the tornado and much damage, but the old airplane came down eventually, safely if lopsidedly in the wind! Talk about being glad to be on terra cotta!!

This morning I couldn't raise my head! – it was draughty in the plane and getting wet was very uncomfortable. I've got a concert tonight and tomorrow and I've been to an osteopath, but I don't think she's a bit of good. I still can't do my hair or scratch my back!!

On 26 May she returned to Wisconsin for the final concerts of the tour. Benita Cress made her a present of a large decorative ring to be worn over a glove, as a memento. 'I've got my sticky labels marked,' Kathleen wrote to Winifred. 'In four days I'll be sticking them on and look out Hampstead, here comes Kaff!'

When she arrived at New York there was just time for a bath at the Weylin before making for the port. An American news company was waiting for her on board, and asked if she would film for television. 'I must have looked a mess,' she wrote to Benita, 'because the bags under my eyes were bulging like the rest of my luggage.'[1]

At sea the next day, she had lunch with Benno Moiseiwitsch and Heifitz, who were also on board. 'So I had a wonderful voyage and some unexpected debauchery,' she wrote to Benita. 'It did me good.'

During the sixteen weeks tour she had earned $17,500 gross. American income tax amounted to $3,500 and her fares were a further $1,000. To avoid starting the following year's American tour in debt she left $1,500 with Columbia Concerts to cover advertising costs. Thus, by the time she had deducted accompanists' fees, agents' commission and subsistence costs, she estimated she had made a net profit of $1,500 (£375). 'Better than a kick in my nylon pants,' she wrote to Winifred. 'But, still, I haven't arf worked hard!'

[1] The first page of this letter is reproduced in the photograph section.

IV

Orpheus

FOURTEEN

The flat was fresh and sparkling, as Paddy had given it a special spring clean to welcome Kathleen back home.

As her birthday, 22 April, had occurred while she was in America, there was now the pleasure of opening her cards and presents. Among these, unfortunately, was a distressing letter from Decca.

Bruno Walter had expressed a wish to Kathleen that they should make a recording together of Mahler's *Kindertotenlieder*. They both knew, however, that this might prove a problem since they were contracted to different recording companies. Nevertheless, Kathleen had optimistically written to Decca, asking permission to be released from her contract in order to make this one recording with Walter on his American Columbia label. The letter from Decca contained a refusal. And a Columbia release for Walter wasn't possible either. Her reply to Decca shows the depth of her frustration:

> I can't tell you how disappointed I am that you have decided not to release me for this recording with Bruno Walter. I rang Mr Lieberson [Walter's representative] this morning and agreed with him when he said it was too uneven an exchange of artists – Bruno Walter for me! He said he was willing to exchange any pianist, singer or any other executant in this case as Bruno Walter had asked for me personally. If you don't release me to do this, they will have an American singer – of whom there are many.
>
> Can't you see that with all this competition what an honour it is for you, as well as for me, to be singled out to have to borrow an artist?
>
> When I came to Decca at first it was with the promise of a recording of *Messiah* – which never materialised. This same recording is one of the biggest hits in America, and one of the largest money-makers. I never expect to make money with a recording of *Kindertotenlieder* – but the honour of appearing on a label with Bruno Walter would put me in the top flight of artists both here and in Europe and would compensate completely over my disappointment over *Messiah*.
>
> Please reconsider your decision, Professor Walter is an old man and such a chance would probably never come my way again.

Inevitably Kathleen saw the situation from the artist's point of view. Decca, however, had spent much time and money building up her recording career and by now she was one of their few classical artists who made a profit. It was reasonable for them not to want such a valuable asset to be handed over, even temporarily, to another company.

Kathleen's disappointment may have been compounded by the fact that shortly before leaving for America, she had recorded several British folk songs for Decca. These included 'Ma Bonny Lad', 'Drink to Me Only', 'Have You Seen But a Whyte Lillie Grow?', 'Down by the Salley Gardens' and many more established Ferrier favourites.[1] Rather than delay release proceedings until her return, Kathleen had jointly empowered her accompanist Phyllis Spurr and Winifred to listen to the songs at the Decca studios and, if they thought them satisfactory, grant release permission.

They found the songs beautifully sung, and had no hesitation in signing the release documents. When Kathleen heard the records upon her return to London, however, she was disappointed, and rounded on Winifred, 'I thought you were my severest critic.' Kathleen would have liked them withdrawn but happily, by that time it was too late. The records have sold in their thousands and, listening to them today, nearly forty years after they were recorded, it is difficult to imagine what improvements could have been made. As *Time* magazine put it, 'They are all sung with incomparable beauty.'

But there was little time for regrets. On 10 June, Kathleen left for the Holland Festival. She was to spend five weeks in Holland and, in addition to several recitals, she would sing Bach's *Magnificat* and Cantata 169, premiere Britten's *Spring Symphony* and give seven performances of *Orfeo ed Euridice* under Pierre Monteux.

She caught a severe cold during rehearsals, for which she blamed the unseasonably cold weather, but her main problem, as always, was to give a convincing theatrical performance in the opera. She wrote to Benita Cress:

I'm working quite hard, but need every minute of it, as I think I'm *lousy* on

[1] Decca ACL 309.

stage. Can cope with expressing sorrow, happiness and fright on me old dial, but, oh! my large extremities! I fall upstairs, downstairs, even over my own feet – there is a nice pet of a producer who's very patient and long suffering. And, it'll perhaps be all right on the night – I hope so!

Fortunately, my first night is next Friday (phew). I shall have tummy ache that night with fright. I've taken my iron pills, Vick in every exposed spot! and a hot rum tonight, so my old vocal cords should be just ashamed of themselves if they're not functioning soon.

I'm doing a Garbo act here in that I just go to rehearsals, come back, eat, wash me smalls and go to bed.

Invited to the opening night of *Orfeo ed Euridice*, Winifred reluctantly explained that this was impossible as she had to work. Kathleen would not accept that, and wrote back:

Now look 'ere, our Winnie! Peter Diamand's going to be disappointed, cross and put out if you don't come to Amsterdam for *Orfeo*, specially as he is arranging a Saturday and Sunday performance for your benefit.

Now here's an idea! and be honest and tell me if you don't like it – catch morning plane Friday, lunch in Amsterdam – stay three nights – fly back Monday morning. You could be in school by two pm. The journey and hotel expenses would be my birthday present to you with my love. Howzat? Go on, be a devil!

After that, Winifred decided she would be a devil. Rick Davies came to the opening night, too, and by now Kathleen was seriously considering whether or not she should become engaged to him.

The opera was a great success. Queen Juliana and Prince Bernhard were the guests of honour and Kathleen was presented with ten bouquets. She was then taken to an official banquet which went on long into the night.

On 5 July 1949, she wrote to Newmark in Canada:

American Hotel, Amsterdam

Johnny dear!
You must be sweltering in the heat just now, whilst here, I am wearing a woolly frock!

Wish you were here, love! This is a lovely festival. *Orfeo* has gone well –

four performances already, and all sold out. Everybody ruining me, and I'm surrounded by Dutch flowers and overwhelming kindness. I am just going for a final rehearsal for the Bach tomorrow, also a Purcell *Te Deum* which I hadn't been told about – but which is very short and straight-forward.

The Bach Cantata 169 is gorgeous and oh! the *Magnificat*! I'm in my element with this sort of music. I still haven't really started the Britten *Spring Symphony* but have been so tired and so hard worked I could only tackle one job at a time – and I had many cuts to learn in *Orfeo*, but after tomorrow I really must get down to it.

I have also seen many things, the Dutch Opera in *Manon* – very good. Vienna Opera in *Entführung*, *Rosenkavalier* and *Don Giovanni*. The Mozart was wonderful, Krips conducting beautifully and I suppose *Rosenkavalier* was good too, but I was hearing it for the first time. I was slightly embarrassed in the first act, it hurt my ears in the second and I'm afraid I was bored and had corns on me situpon by the third. But then, I'm no Wagner fan and I suppose it's the same school. But, oh! the Mozart!! the music is overwhelming, isn't it? Must dash now – will finish this when the Bach concert is over.

Wednesday – no, Thursday morning 2.20 am!

Just home after supper, and in bed after trying to dispose of ten bouquets in a small single room! TEN! Honest! It *is* time I went home – I'm ruined here! All went smoothly, Johnny love, even the Purcell – learnt in five days! But this [the Concertgebouw] is such a wonderful hall in which to sing – it makes anything sound beautiful. The 169 Cantata is gorgeous but another six performances in public and I shall be less tense!

And now for Ben and his beastly augmented 9ths!!

Britten's *Spring Symphony* is a large-scale work for voices and orchestra and Britten had written the contralto part with Kathleen in mind. Her fellow soloists were Peter Pears and soprano Jo Vincent. The Concertgebouw Orchestra was conducted by Eduard van Beinum.

The premiere took place, at the Concertgebouw, on 9 July 1949, and was a triumph, only marred by Britten's annoyance at the large amount of publicity accorded Field Marshal Montgomery, who had been among the audience. Not noted for his support of musical works, the Field Marshal had been pressed to attend by the British

Ambassador, as a public relations exercise, and scooped most of the press coverage.

When Kathleen returned to London on 17 July she was, for the first time in her life, thoroughly exhausted. This was understandable, as the taxing Holland Festival had followed hard on the heels of her strenuous sixteen weeks in America. But it seemed to Winifred that some of her sparkle had gone, replaced by an uncharacteristic listlessness. She was relieved, therefore, that she and Kathleen were soon to leave for a week's holiday in Switzerland where she hoped Kathleen would quickly recuperate.

The weather in Switzerland was warm, and they had a magnificent view of the Jungfrau from their hotel rooms. They had booked into separate rooms in order that Kathleen should have a complete rest. But her listlessness seemed to linger throughout the entire week. She spent the mornings in the hotel, sunbathing, or painting. She would sleep every afternoon, then get up for tea. Sometimes, as the sun set over the mountains, Winifred could hear her singing some wistful phrases from 'Abschied' to herself.

She was worried about her forthcoming appearances in the Salzburg Festival, where she was to give two performances of *Das Lied von der Erde* under Bruno Walter. She would be the first British singer at the Festival, and was conscious of the responsibility, terrified she would let Walter down. Her German pronunciation was also worrying her, as she would obviously be singing to a predominantly German-speaking audience, and one with a greater knowledge of Mahler than any she had previously encountered.

Winifred went with her to Salzburg, and a downpour of rain greeted them as they stepped off the train. The sight of her hotel did nothing to elevate Kathleen's spirits. The city was full of American servicemen, whose officers had taken all the finest accommodation, so Kathleen and Winifred had been obliged to make do with what was left, which was decidedly second-rate.

As there was nothing much to do that evening, after she had eaten Kathleen went for a walk, and lost the glove ring that Benita Cress had given her. She retraced her steps in vain, and the police, to whom she reported the loss, offered slim chances of the ring being handed in. She went to bed thoroughly miserable.

The weather improved next morning and, in brilliant sunshine, she made her way to rehearsals with Bruno Walter and the Vienna Philharmonic Orchestra. Most of the players knew her from Edinburgh, and stood and applauded as she walked on to the rostrum. She was in good voice, and received another ovation after the rehearsal, but she was so dreading the performance next day that she convinced herself that people were merely being nice because they were sorry for her.

She was to sing at the Festspielhaus, and her first performance was at eleven am, an ungrateful hour for singing, as the voice has not yet had time to settle. Then, as she walked on to the stage, she recognised in the audience, the eminent and intimidating faces of Karajan, Krips and Furtwängler. Nevertheless:

> Her performance was one of those experiences which occur seldom in a lifetime, the perfect realisation of a work of art.
>
> *Sunday Times*

Her second performance was as successful as the first. With these behind her, she recovered her zest for life, and permitted herself a two-day holiday in Salzburg before returning to London. She spent most of the time with Walter, who took her to her second performance of *Der Rosenkavalier*, but she liked the opera no better. Still, she enjoyed the restaurants: 'I'm getting a corporation,' she wrote to Benita. 'I'm getting so fat people are thinking of pouring me into my tights.'

Her next major engagement was at the Edinburgh Festival where she gave performances on six consecutive evenings. Four of these were with Bruno Walter, where she sang two performances of *Kindertotenlieder* and gave two recitals in which he accompanied her. Their second recital was broadcast. In 1975 this broadcast was made available to the public in the form of a two-record set.[1] Alan Blyth reviewed it for *The Gramophone*.

> I would say these records are the first to do full justice to Ferrier's Schubert and Schumann. 'Junge Nonne' has that much more urgency at the start,

[1] Decca 6BB 197–8.

serenity at the close than on her previously available performance. There is a wonderful rapt *Innigkeit* to the third verse of the *Rosamunde* romance. 'Tod und das Mädchen' has a subtle change of timbre between the impersonation of the girl and of Death, whose comforting, sombre message is presented with a grave, unearthly beauty that tells us what an Erda we might have had if the singer's life had not been cut so cruelly short. 'Du liebst mich nicht' was always one of her successes in recitals, so it is particularly pleasurable to have it preserved after all, especially in such an intense, immediate reading: you feel the sentiments were deeply understood. 'Suleika' is a comparative failure; as Capell stated, it does not transpose down comfortably. 'Du bist die Ruh' suffers a little in the same way, but the singer's wonderful swell of tone at the close silences such criticism. Walter's very personal and positive support obviously pushes Ferrier to give of her very best. What a remarkable partnership it was.

The Schumann cycle (*Frauenliebe und Leben*) is much freer, more spontaneous than the former interpretation, all the songs being more intensely 'felt'. Any kind of sophistication is anathema to Schumann and von Chamisso's concept. Ferrier moves through the woman's growing maturity to her final grief with unfailing sureness of expression, and with nuances attended to. The smile in 'Er der Herrlichste', the belief and certainty of 'Du Ring an meinem Finger', the little jab on '*fallt*' in the last song are all moments to cherish. Odious comparisons with other singers are here definitely out of place; Ferrier's is, in a sense, *hors concours*. Walter's accompaniment is likely to surprise the purist. It is to say the least free and individual, also great in its very idiosyncracies.

Others felt more strongly about the idiosyncrasies of Walter's playing. In his book *Farewell Recital*, Gerald Moore comments:

His playing on this particular evening was deplorable and showed how necessary it is for the accompanist to have prepared himself by assiduous practising and to have maintained the discipline (much more difficult for a pianist than anybody) of self-listening. For example his playing of 'An die Musik', a hymn of thankfulness for the art of music, was painful. A violoncello-like bass affectionately reflects the vocal line; above it are repeated chords in the treble to be treated tenderly and smoothly and to be played, naturally, with the lightest touch to allow the bass tune to predominate: but these parenthetical chords were dabbed down by Walter as if he were beating eggs. Throughout the concert his habit – elementary and amateur – of playing one hand after the other in all his chording (did

Kathleen know with which hand she should synchronize?) had old ladies in ecstasy, they sighed that 'It reminded them of old Vienna'. I become annoyed at the recollection of it, but when I expressed myself at the time to Audrey Christie she suggested that I was jealous, though I hope it was said to tease.

As Moore says, there were those who enjoyed Walter's style, and any criticism must be balanced against the inspiration he gave to Kathleen.

The Edinburgh recital takes up three sides of the four-sided set, and the final side consists of a BBC recital broadcast on 12 January 1953 – less than eight months before Kathleen died. In this recital, in which she is accompanied by Ernest Lush, she sings the Rubbra psalm settings, and songs by Howard Ferguson and William Wordsworth.

So much of Kathleen's fame rests on her interpretations of Mahler, Gluck, Handel, Bach and the lieder composers, that it is easy to overlook that she sang much modern music.

At the BBC recital Kathleen performed Ferguson's cycle *Discovery*. The songs are settings of poems by Denton Welch from his post-humously published anthology *A Last Sheaf*, and when Kathleen decided to sing them, she invited Ferguson to Frognal Mansions to run through them with her. 'Though she had not sung them before in public,' Ferguson remembers, 'she knew the songs perfectly and (as you can imagine) did them with the greatest warmth and under-standing. I don't remember having to make any suggestions at all. I've no idea how Kathleen got to know about the cycle, but she certainly did not appear to have the least difficulty with it.'

The three Wordsworth songs are 'Red Skies', 'The Wind' and 'Clouds'. She liked the songs and told the composer she would like to sing more of his work, notably *The Four Sacred Sonnets of John Donne*.

'Her performances of "Red Skies" and "Clouds" are perfect,' Wordsworth states. 'Perhaps "The Wind" is more a man's song. *The Four Sacred Sonnets of John Donne* are also, perhaps, men's songs – but I would have loved to hear her do them.'

In the manuscript for 'The Clouds' a misprint occurred, where an F was printed as a G (page 5, second line, bar 2). Kathleen naturally sang the F sharp as written and when she discovered the mistake wrote to Wordsworth, 'I hope my F sharp didn't offend your ears too much, and that my interpretation did not cause you too much agony.' 'It sounds quite good as sung,' Wordsworth comments.

Following their Edinburgh performances, Kathleen and Walter made two London appearances. The first, a recital at the Westminster Central Hall, and the second a Mahler concert, with the VPO, at the Royal Albert Hall. On 4 October 1949, they realised their ambition to record *Kindertotenlieder* together. Decca had finally relented, and granted Kathleen dispensation to record with Walter; the company had been spurred in this decision both by pressure from Kathleen and by the hope of securing Bruno Walter for a future Decca recording.

When reviewing the records,[1] Andrew Porter likened their relationship to that of Elena Gerhardt and Arthur Nikisch, commenting: 'Future Dr Burneys, noting a sudden revival of interest in Mahler in our time, will surely remark how largely it was due to the collaboration of Miss Ferrier and Bruno Walter.'

[1] Originally issued as 78 rpms Col. DB 8939. Now available on LP, HMV HLM 7002.

FIFTEEN

The morning after recording *Kindertotenlieder* Kathleen flew to Copenhagen to start a three-week tour of Scandinavia, commencing that very evening with a live radio broadcast of Brahms's *Alto Rhapsody*. The flight was late arriving and she was frightened she might miss the broadcast, but as soon as the plane landed she was whisked through customs ('Just had a very rude search through customs, whooopeee!' she later wrote on a postcard to Winifred), and hurried to a waiting car which sped her to the studios where the orchestra and choir were waiting. There was no time for a proper rehearsal but the broadcast went without a hitch: 'Was nearly a corpse when I arrived,' she wrote that night to Benita Cress, 'but have perked up since.'

Her schedule included two recitals in Copenhagen, and these had been sold out weeks in advance. She agreed to fit in an extra recital and this, also, sold out within hours of being announced.

At a performance in Oslo, the organisers planned what they hoped would be a charming surprise for Kathleen; they recorded her concert and then played it back to her. This intended treat backfired as, as was usually the case, Kathleen was disappointed with her performance and said so. The recording was stored and forgotten until 1957 when it was rediscovered, and Decca released it as a record.[1] 'Radiant, like the leaves on a copper beach tree,' stated the reviewer for *The Gramophone*.

On 8 October 1949, she wrote to Newmark from the Hotel Stockholm:

> I wish you were here to play these all-lieder recitals I'm doing in Copenhagen, Stockholm and Oslo. They are going very well and I had a full hall last night here, for a first concert in Sweden, which was a nice surprise – thank goodness for records – they *do* help!
>
> I'm having argie-bargies with Andre Mertens [of Columbia Concerts, USA] and so far I haven't been sacked but who knows? Now he says I ought

[1] LXT 5324.

to go January 1951 instead of autumn [1951] – however, I've stuck out, as I must have a rest and learn a repertoire.

It's been wonderful working with Bruno Walter. The two recitals in Edinburgh and London were a wow, and he seemed very pleased. He altered very little in your Brahms[1] – only '*Botschaft*' slower – but apart from that he couldn't find anything to say! Klever Johnny. They're lovely songs – I adore singing them.

Am very thrilled that Decca let me record for Columbia – what a lucky twerp I am! Only hope that they are all right. We heard the playbacks and he was thrilled to bits, so I hope the finished article *is* all right.

Hope all is well with you – God bless – Love Kathleen

Her flight from Stockholm to Copenhagen was in an elderly and draughty Czechoslovakian plane, and she woke next morning with her right arm swollen and painful, and a severely stiff neck. She sent for a masseur who eased the pain and assured her that rheumatism was the cause of the trouble. Despite the masseur's treatment the pain returned during the day, and she gave her recital that evening in considerable discomfort. Her movements were so restricted that she was unable to bow to acknowledge the applause: 'So they had to be content with superior nods of the cranium,' she wrote to Winifred.

That 'rheumatism' was to prove increasingly troublesome in the future. Back home she wrote to Benita Cress:

The Scandinavian trip was fine – I was spoiled wherever I went, but I did have to work hard – eleven concerts in three weeks in three different countries – but it was very rewarding and my managers are thrilled to bits and have done me proud so we're *all* happy. Now I'm off at a rush again – recording tomorrow, then Albert Hall *Messiah* (1,000 in the choir!); Paris; Scotland and all over the place until I leave on 21 December.[2] Then I can have a rest on the boat and I'm looking forward to it already.

Have just been staggered by the death of Ginette Neveu, in a plane crash to the USA – she was one of the finest fiddlers in the world, and just thirty! Just can't think why that should have had to happen – also brother killed at the same time – isn't it a waste!

[1] While in America, Newmark had coached her in lieder.
[2] The start of her third American tour.

Just before leaving for the boat-train for Paris, Kathleen had an unexpected visit from Ena Mitchell's son.[1] He rushed in, full of excitement, to tell Kathleen that he had just gained a position with a symphony orchestra and that, after six pm when the rates were cheaper, he would telephone his mother with the good news. 'What?' said Kathleen. 'Would you deprive your mother of six hours' happiness?' Pointing towards her telephone she told him to call Ena right away.

Her Paris recital was at the Salle Gaveau, and she had decided upon a programme of lieder. There was concern over her choice of exclusively German material as many of the French held bitter memories of German occupation. But as Kathleen knew no French music with the exception of *La Demoiselle Elue*, and felt her English songs inappropriate, there was not a great deal else that she could sing. She performed six Schubert and six Brahms songs and *Frauenliebe und Leben* and her advisers' fears were not realised: 'This English singer conquered Paris with the opening bars of her Schubert lieder,' wrote the reviewer of *Paroles Françaises*. She sent a postcard to Winifred, dated 9 November 1949: 'Fancy KK in gay Paree! The bits I've seen are lovely but have been busy rehearsing. Concert tonight – pianist tries hard but is not Gerald or Bruno! But he kisses me hand so life has its bright side.'

She left Paris on schedule, on 21 December, for her tour of America. After all the straight-talking with Columbia Concerts, followed by some curt letters from Emmie, she was optimistic that, this time, her itinerary would be better organised. John Newmark was booked as her pianist, and Columbia Concerts gave her the welcome news that only $1,000 of her $1,500 deposit had been spent on advertising, therefore a cash surplus of $500 awaited her in America. This would usefully tide her over until she received funds from her concerts.

Unfortunately her optimism was dispelled as soon as she arrived in New York. Columbia Concerts informed her that, as a Canadian citizen, Newmark had been refused a further work permit for the United States.

Kathleen was not accepting that, and telephoned Newmark at once.

[1] Ifor James, now a well-known horn player, and a conductor of brass bands.

He was as distraught as she, and already taking legal advice. From New York, Kathleen telephoned every government official she could think of who might be useful, and used all her influence. Eventually, she and Newmark between them, managed to get the decision reversed. An exultant Newmark telephoned Kathleen that he was already on his way.

Now good news came from Columbia Concerts, that a further $1,000 had been credited to her account. This amount consisted of fees which, due to an oversight, had not been paid her during her previous trip. The agency seemed to be going out of its way to be helpful, and there was now a respect in its approach which had been missing before. 'It seems I can do no wrong,' she delightedly wrote to Winifred.

Her first recital was on 4 January 1950, in Nashville, Tennessee. As the train journey took twenty-four hours she had to leave New York early on the morning of the 2 January. Ruth Draper was giving a party for her on the evening of the 1st, so, in honour of the occasion, Kathleen had her hair permanently waved, 'like Claudette Colbert's bang'. This permanent wave proved a good investment throughout her tour, as there was not always time for her to get her hair done before a recital.

After her hairdressing appointment and lunch, she took a singing lesson with Clytie Mundy. While in New York she had several studio photographic portraits taken. These photographs later caused her much amusement, as they were retouched until all facial lines were removed, and with them most of her character. In one photograph her face appeared to be a different shape as the photographer had altered her jawline by painting out a wedge on each side. 'My glamour-puss photos', she called them.

Despite her early start for Nashville the next morning, she stayed late at Ruth Draper's party and, with Newmark at the piano, sang most of her repertoire to the delighted guests.

The audience at Nashville was no less appreciative and, she considered, well worth the long journey. Then followed an appearance in Pennsylvania and a return to New York where, on 8 January 1950, she appeared at the Town Hall. 'You couldn't blame the crowd for giving her one of the biggest hands of recent Town Hall history,' commented the *World Telegram*.

Dame Myra Hess was also in New York, giving a recital at Carnegie

Hall, and they dined together, but as their concerts clashed they were unable to attend each others' performances.

Kathleen had another lesson with Clytie Mundy, then left for recitals in Nebraska, Kansas, Wisconsin, Illinois, Missouri, New Mexico and California. She travelled continuously for twenty days, and much of this time was spent hurtling along the railroad, eating and often sleeping on trains, passing scenery which varied from ice-fields to sun-baked sand dunes.

Kathleen was a great film fan and went to the cinema whenever she had the chance. In Chicago she was able to compare her bang with Claudette Colbert's, as the star was appearing in *Since You Went Away*, which also featured Shirley Temple and Nazimova. Critic Bosley Crowther had damned the film as 'a rather large dose of choking sentiment' but Kathleen, who had moved hundreds to tears with Mahler and Brahms, cried throughout. Newmark, who was with her, thought she had a cold until he realised she was sobbing.

At a party in Missouri she reduced a young man to stuttering infatuation. Having learned that he had offered to drive her to the station the next morning she marched over to thank him at once, in front of the other guests, which he found overwhelming.

On 20 January, she reached La Crosse, Wisconsin, where she was to sing Pergolesi's *Stabat Mater* and Brahms's *Alto Rhapsody* with the local choir. She was staying overnight with Benita Cress, and had written to her: 'Can you bear it? I'm a good washer-upper and bed-maker and can toss a pancake. Don't praise me too highly, I'll never live up to it.'

Benita, naturally, was thrilled to have the diva actually staying at her house: 'Her eyes just popped with excitement all weekend,' Kathleen wrote Winifred.

She was treated so kindly, and the reception for her singing was so warm that as a thank-you gesture she gave another recital free of charge: 'They were all thrilled and pleased with me, and pleased with themselves for tackling such nice works,' she told Winifred, 'so all was very well. I had a bouquet of red and yellow roses from a millionaire (dollars – no good), and one of lovely pink ones from the choir, so I was a real prima-donna.'

Benita gave her a dressing gown as a parting present. It was on the big side, but she altered the buttons on the train and 'quite took

Johnny's breath away when he came upon me suddenly, wearing same'.

Her next destination was a return visit to Chicago, and she wrote to Winifred: 'We're happy as larks. Johnny's playing gets better, which I didn't think was possible, and we get on very well. Our journey was grand, though I was awakened at 5.50 getting into Chicago, and could have willingly strangled the porter.'

In New Mexico, which was under snow, the altitude was 7,000 feet. High altitude can adversely affect singers, causing them to lose high notes, but Kathleen had no trouble apart from an initial shortage of breath.

From New Mexico she journeyed to Los Angeles, California, where she was to stay at the luxurious Beverly Hills home of Bruno Walter. Bruno Walter was not there – he and his family were currently staying at his other home in New York – but he generously lent her the house, complete with servants, swimming pool and Cadillacs. As she was making only one appearance in Los Angeles, and had two weeks at her disposal before her next engagement, she was able to take a holiday and enjoy the Walter home.

While there, she received a letter from Paddy, telling her that she and William were redecorating the flat at Frognal Mansions. Kathleen replied:

I enclose a cheque for £10, just so's you won't be short, and don't skimp *anything* on either paint, distemper, food or drink. I'm delighted with anything ya do, so don't worry about any expense – think what it would cost it we got Mr Enigma Variations[1] – so just get the best of everything, when you're putting all that work into it, and I'll send you a cheque anytime. Gee whizz, I'm looking forward to seeing it all, not to mention you two poppets.

She endeared herself to Walter's two servants, Fanny and Adolph, by singing them songs in their native German, inviting them to sit in the music room with her, with their shoes kicked off. The huge cars were fun and, with Adolph at the wheel, she and Newmark went sightseeing in the convertible, visiting the Hollywood Bowl, the orange groves and the film stars' homes. Edward G. Robinson, star of many gangster

[1] Mr Elgar, the local decorator.

movies, and a connoisseur of the arts, proudly showed her his collection of French paintings. She left suitably impressed.

Her recital was on 2 February, but another artist, the Polish conductor Artur Rodzinski, was appearing in Los Angeles the same night, and scooped all the press coverage: 'There wasn't a single criticism, I could spit,' she wrote to Winifred. 'But the audience loved it, so what the hell!!'

Ann Ayars's parents, who lived in California, had attended her recital and, the following day, took her on a picnic to Laguna Beach. Almost before the car had stopped Kathleen was out, running ahead. She tore off her shoes and stockings, leaving them on the beach and, bunching up her skirt, waded into the ocean.

Back at Walter's house she found a letter from Mr Mertens, who continued to urge her to sign a contract for a return visit to America starting January 1951. She was adamant that she would not return until the autumn of 1951.

By the same post her regular letter from Emmie awaited her. Emmie had various offers to discuss, the most exciting of which for Kathleen was a forthcoming production of *Orfeo ed Euridice*, conducted by Bruno Walter.

'Oooooooooh, boy,' she replied on Walter's typewriter, '*Orfeo* with Dr Bruno??????? YES PLEASE. Would forgo all my holiday for that.' With reference to a forthcoming Holland trip she responded:

> What shall I do about an accompanist? I wish I could take John Newmark, he's absolutely superb, but he'll be out of pocket to come to Europe, even if I paid his fare. Acht, well, we'll see. I can do *The Apostles* for Hanley – it's the 'Music Makers' that gets me doon. Lovely to do *Gerontius* for the Royal Choral Society on May 24, Whoopee. All this work, aren't I a lucky old twerp?

Emmie had also passed on a request from Barbirolli for Kathleen to sing the little known Chausson *Poème de l'Amour et de la Mer*. Barbirolli had already mentioned this to Kathleen but she had been evasive in her reply. She would do almost anything to please Barbirolli, but thought the tessitura of the Chausson too high for her and, as she spoke no French, was worried about her pronunciation.

She discussed the Chausson with Newmark and he urged her to accept, promising to help with her French, which he spoke perfectly. She cabled Emmie: 'Accept Chausson. Tell Sir John to play loudly to cover my Lancashire accent.'

Newmark did coach her, and he also wrote to a French-speaking friend in Montreal, asking him to record the Boucher poems, upon which Chausson had based his work, so that Kathleen could replay them when she was back in London.

Fond as Barbirolli was of the Chausson, there had been an ulterior motive in his choice. He believed, as did Nancy Evans, that Kathleen had not yet exploited her full vocal potential, and judged that the exacting technical demands of the work would do her good. 'I felt there were ranges of nuance and colour yet unexplored. Frankly, I became a little terrified she might degenerate into that queer and almost bovine monstrosity so beloved of our grandfathers . . . the "oratorio contralto" '.[1]

Alan Blyth agrees with Barbirolli's judgment:

I would say that from the time I first heard her sing in the mid-1940s her tone and style altered very little, except for a welcome extension upwards of her register under the careful tutelage of Barbirolli and Walter. Obviously chary in early days of anything much above a G, she gradually grew more confident and competent at the top. Undoubtedly she had those higher notes, but her contralto training had probably led her to believe that they were not required of her. When Walter, and Mahler, came along, the situation changed and she was able to encompass mezzo territory.

Kathleen's first booking after her holiday in Beverly Hills was a recital at Sacramento, followed by three performances of *Orfeo ed Euridice* in San Francisco. Pierre Monteux was conducting the San Francisco Symphony Orchestra. This was the first time the opera had been produced in San Francisco, and performances had long been sold out.

At the rehearsal, Kathleen noticed a huge Negro woman sitting in the stalls. Kathleen started to sing, the woman clapped her hands and very audibly exclaimed, 'My God, what a voice – and what a face!' Afterwards Kathleen asked Monteux who she was and was introduced

[1] *Kathleen Ferrier, A Memoir.*

to Marian Anderson, the possessor of one of the most thrilling contralto voices in the world. Not only had Miss Anderson a range of nearly three octaves, but her singing was distinguished by a fine intelligence. Kathleen knew her voice well, having listened many times to her broadcast recordings of lieder and arias from *Samson and Delilah*, and she later described their meeting as 'the biggest thrill of the tour'.

Despite an international career as a concert and recording artist, Miss Anderson had yet to make her debut at the Metropolitan Opera House. In fact this did not occur until 1955, when she was aged fifty-two and her voice had lost some of its bloom. It was generally accepted that Miss Anderson's ethnic origin had been the barrier to her progress.

'San Francisco was a wow!' Kathleen wrote to Benita. 'Everybody thrilled and want me back next year – whoopee!' After the first night Pierre Monteux presented her with a kiss on each cheek and a gift of a black fox stole.

From San Francisco she made her way, via recitals in Oregon, Washington and Wisconsin, to Wheaton, Illinois. There was a miners' strike in Wheaton, and the hall in which she was to sing had no coal to fuel its central heating. The temperature hovered around the zero mark, and the audience sat in overcoats. There was no way Kathleen could sustain a performance in her evening dress, even with the bonus of the Monteux stole, so she had to appear in her overcoat.[1]

Working north, she sang her way up to Montreal. 'The most beautiful contralto voice of our epoch,' stated *Le Canada*.

A stack of letters awaited her in Montreal, among which was an offer to appear in a feature film. Producers Michael Powell and Emeric Pressburger were making, in England, a screen version of Offenbach's *Tales of Hoffmann*. This would be in colour and Beecham had agreed to conduct.

'Me in a film? Pon me soul!' she wrote to Emmie. 'I don't know the part or if it's suitable, and could the cameraman remove my curves? But I couldn't give a definite answer just now till I know more about it. It would be interesting if it were rewarding – musically and financially.'

In the end commitments would not permit her to accept the offer, but it is unlikely she was too disappointed, as the idea of acting in front of a

[1] *Daily Express*, 20 March 1950.

camera filled her with terror. Also, she did not relish the idea of working with Beecham who could be, to say the least, impolite to singers on occasion. Although she recognised the kudos of working with him, she had no desire to become a target for any possible abuse. When she had auditioned for him at Glyndebourne her circumstances had been different. At this stage in her career she could afford to be choosy.

Anyway it was probably just as well Kathleen had not taken the role, as when *Tales of Hoffmann* was released critic Gavin Lambert dismissed it as 'the most spectacular failure yet achieved by Powell and Pressburger'. Nowadays, it is a curiosity which, from time to time, pops up on television.

Kathleen continued, in her letter to Emmie:

Zurich. I wonder if they would be interested in Lennox Berkeley's *Four Poems of St Teresa*, I am awfully short of orchestral things. Am just learning Chausson's 'Poème', but would rather not do a first performance there, but if you are stuck then I could manage it. What about Brahms's *Serious Songs*, they are orchestrated, but I suppose I would have to do them in German and that's an awful sweat.

She dashed off a note to Benita Cress: 'All goes well, though it's a ruddy blush now, but our concerts are a pleasure and we even floored a Columbia representative – he rushed straight back to write nice things – Clever him.'

From St John, New Brunswick, she wrote to Winifred:

Howdy, Toots,

Have never stopped since San Francisco. Just got here from Montreal and have a concert in four hours. Came straight to bed for my siesta after the train and haven't seen nuttin'. Montreal was wonderful notices, just raving KK! I'm so pleased because they're all such poppets there . . . Have you ever had the whiskers in your nose freeze? Well, I have, all those last few days in Montreal. It's been 10 degrees below freezing – give me California!

Her next appearances were in New York and New Jersey, where she was to give a recital with Bruno Walter and two concert performances of *Orfeo ed Euridice*, conducted by Tom Scherman. When she checked into the Weylin on 14 March she found dozens of letters awaiting her attention, which Columbia Concerts had not troubled to forward. She protested vigorously. More depressing was the news from Bruno Walter that their hoped-for production of *Orfeo ed Euridice* together had had to be cancelled, as he would not be free to do it. That particular dream was never to come true.

Columnist Newell Rogers had been following Kathleen's performances in America and wrote an account for the British *Daily Express*:

> One of Hampstead Heath's most musical dollar exports is queen of the moment in New York concert halls. Twice in two nights I have heard contralto Kathleen Ferrier sing to sell-out audiences. In a powder blue sequin-spangled gown she crossed the river Styx as Orfeo, in a concert version of Gluck's opera to rescue Euridice from Hades. With her Hollywood host, famed conductor Bruno Walter, for pianist, she sang Brahms and Schubert. . . .

Rogers was not the only person writing about Kathleen. The beautiful American film star Judy Holliday had also seen her Orfeo and had been so taken with it that she wrote the following limerick, which she gave to Kathleen when they met, some time after the performance:

> There was a young lady called Ferrier,
> Whose voice is just like her exterrier,
> She sings so delicious
> That all I do wish is
> That no one will ever bury her.

The pains had returned to her neck and shoulder in Pennsylvania and, once again, she was unable to bow to the audience in response to the applause. Her health improved, however, for her concert in Chicago on 23 March 1950. This booking was almost as important to her as had been her New York recital. She sang *Kindertotenlieder* with Fritz Reiner and the Chicago Symphony Orchestra. Much interest had been centred on this concert: not only was it Reiner's farewell to Chicago before joining the Metropolitan Opera House, but it was also the first time that *Kindertotenlieder* had been performed in the city.

Kathleen's records of *Kindertotenlieder* had recently been released in America: she had not heard them since the playback and, 'I'm rather pleased with them myself, for once,' she wrote to Winifred, 'but will probably change my mind when I hear them again.' However, the critics of the Chicago recital did not take to the music at all. 'Joyless offerings', was the summary of the *Sun-Times*, and the *American-Herald* considered it 'somewhat austere'. Claudia Cassidy, always Kathleen's champion, suggested that if the work had to be heard at all, then it was as well to wait for Kathleen to sing it.

Her final recital was at the Massey Hall, Toronto, and this was the jewel in her crown, with the audience awarding her a standing ovation and demanding encore after encore.

Back in New York, she had two days free before leaving for Southampton. She sorted out the many letters again awaiting her unforwarded at the Weylin despite her previous protests, and wrote to Emmie, enclosing some glowing press cuttings:

> I would like, if you agree, to have an insertion in *The Times* and *Telegraph*, with a few quotations, just to let people know I've been working hard and not disappeared for three months, wanted you to see I've been behaving myself. It's been a lovely tour and I haven't signed owt. Klever Kaff. Won't be long before I arrive in me new hat and the white flour under me arm. Oh, boy! My French grows apace, I can say Darling, *je vous aime beaucoup, – passé partout, cul de sac – voulez-vous coucher avec –* oh no, that's the rude one!! Heigh ho! *Quelle vie –* ain't I a lucky old buddha.

She was met at Southampton by Paddy and John Turner. 'I could show them around the *Lizzie* before sliding, innocent-eyed, through customs,' she wrote to Benita.

Some weeks later Kathleen was asked to be guest of honour at a lunch at the Savoy Hotel. This was her debut as an after-lunch speaker and she made what she described as 'a shocking red-faced speech'. She paid tribute to America, particularly the audiences, the plumbing, her sojourn in Beverley Hills and some of the halls in which she had sung, especially the San Francisco Opera House. Her only complaint (which was mild) was about the amount of tax she would have to pay. She also told her audience, 'I can honestly say I haven't a single bad memory.'

SIXTEEN

That April was particularly balmy, with bright spring blossoms everywhere. Paddy and William had distempered the walls of her flat and washed the paintwork, making the whole place sparkle, and there was a new carpet, and new curtains in her bedroom. Kathleen felt very happy to be home again.

One of her first performances was in the *St Matthew Passion*, at Glyndebourne. Among the orchestral players was her friend, Alison Milne. She recalls that as this was her first visit to Glyndebourne, Kathleen showed her round the house. In the music room they noticed that the lid of the piano was propped open by a volume of Burke's *Peerage*, 'What else would you expect?' asked Kathleen.

She did not have long to enjoy England. Within a very few days, she was off to Amsterdam for performances of *Kindertotenlieder* under Eduard van Beinum, then returned to London on 18 May for a further performance of this work at the Albert Hall, where van Beinum was again the conductor. They then travelled to Scotland together for a performance in Edinburgh. According to the reviewer for *The Scotsman* Kathleen's interpretation 'lacked drama' on this occasion. Claudia Cassidy was also covering the concert and more or less agreed with *The Scotsman*, but added, 'Listening, I thought of the Frenchman who recently told me, "Ferrier, yes a good singer, but a statue, cold." The Irish could tell him there are fires that burn the house and fires that warm the heart.'

The fire that Kathleen would have most appreciated at the time was one which would have warmed her body, for despite the spring weather, she was feeling the cold intensely. She thought this was possibly because she had been spoiled by the American central heating.

When she got back from Scotland she wrote to Benita: 'I'm just negotiating with Decca to bring Johnny over to make some recordings with me, and they are all for it – so if he is happy with their terms, we should be working in July. Won't it be gorgeous?'

A few days later, on 28 April 1950, she was able to tell Newmark:

Well! I had lunch today with Victor Olof – the musical adviser of Decca. He is all for you coming to make the *Frauenliebe* with me here, and doesn't think there will be difficulty about labour permit, but is finding that out in the morning. I shall hear more news tomorrow when he rings me, but, so far, he suggests paying your fare from Paris and your hotel from the night before you record to the night we finish, and so much a record – I don't know yet how much, but I said it must be their top fee for accompanists. He wondered if an American contract would be better for you, then there would not be English tax, and there is another difficulty of taking money – more than five pounds out of this country[1] – but we shall see what happens, but it is as good as in the bag!! O BOY! He wants to do much more than *Frauenliebe* – lots of lieder, so keep your fingers crossed, darling! My only slight cloud is breaking the news to Phyllis Spurr, because she's a nice poppet, but these things have to be done, and we can record other things together. . . . Joseph Krips, conductor, has asked to play it for me on records, but I want *you* to do it, and am going to stick out – Klever Kaff!

Hampstead is looking simply superb with all the blossom and spring flowers doing their best to outshine each other – it has never looked so green and fresh, and I wish you could see it just now, but praps it is just as well you're not here, as our flat has dry rot and fungi growing on the bricks, and the builder can't understand why I haven't floated out in the bath before now! SO, the bath is in the hall, along with the water heater and washbasin, and the lavatory is due to join them any minute!! Our timing for inner cleanliness is something of a feat, and our outer cleanliness is reduced to washing vital parts in the kitchen!! *Quelle vie*! Also the electrician is here putting extra plugs in, the gas man also giving us extra heating, and we are having felt surrounds put down to keep out the draughts, so everything is being done at once – we couldn't be in a worse mess, and we couldn't *care* less, so what the hell! We're going to look quite grand one day, but it may be 1953! Win wrote a limerick for my birthday – here it is: There was a young lady called Kath, who did like to sing in the bath. When the dry rot did creep in, the bath sank so deep in, that Kath had her bath on the path! Will write again as soon as I have news. Much love, Kaff.

This was followed up, three days later, by a further letter to Newmark:

[1] Government restrictions of the time.

I'm a cautious ole budder, but I really begin to have the highest hopes for our recording! Mr Sarton, the business manager, rang me up the following day after I wrote you, and here are his suggestions: Decca will pay your fare from Paris – (you are coming from there, aren't you?): they will pay you three pounds a day living expenses whilst recording and ten pounds for each double sided record – and we can make as many as we can get in – until my cords start steaming in fact. That is the highest they pay for any accompanist – they don't pay by royalties – and I am terribly pleased – I *do* hope you are. I have asked to record in the evening, as my voice has warmed up then, and they will just do anything to get some records on wax. Ain't that nice? I'm pickled tink!! Please let me know at your earliest, definite times when you will be in London, and then I will reserve with them recording times – because much of their time is booked already for sessions, but fortunately not the evenings. Oh boy!

I *think* Miette Dernbach came round to see me after a broadcast the other night, – I know I'm dumb – but there were a lot of people, and it was only after I left her that I realised it was probably she, as she said she knew you. I haven't contacted her yet, because I've been working ever since I came home, and now must get on with the *St Matthew Passion* in German – I have only done it in English before, and I have only one month, so my French is in the background. Except yesterday, I was going through some music and found a volume of Fauré!! Such lovely ones – which may I sing, Johnny? Help please!

Sir Thomas Beecham's secretary has just left me – he was wanting to know if I would record some Delius songs mit him on Columbia, but I don't think Decca will keep on lending me – but it's nice to be asked. He also told me that Ann Ayars is doing Antonia in the film of Hoffman! – it would have been fun to be there with her – but I couldn't do it anyway cos I'm in Wien.

That's all for now – write soon and say you are pleased too about the recordings. Much love. Kaff.

Newmark was as delighted as she, and arrived in London that July, to accompany her in recordings of Schumann's *Frauenliebe und Leben* and Brahms's *Vier Ernste Gesänge*.[1] It was her second studio attempt at *Frauenliebe und Leben*; an earlier version with Phyllis Spurr had been rejected.

[1] *Frauenliebe und Leben* Decca ACL 307; *Vier Ernste Gesänge* Decca ACL 306.

Frauenliebe und Leben and *Vier Ernste Gesänge* were released in LP form, first in America. 'Miss Ferrier is young,' wrote Jerome D. Bohm, critic for the *New York Herald*, 'and her fine voice has never sounded lovelier than it does in her flawlessly phrased, innately musical and deeply affecting accounts of these songs.'

Britain had to wait until 1951 for the record to be released. The reviewer for *The Gramophone* was as enthusiastic as Mr Bohm: 'Miss Ferrier's tone is glorious and she gives a noble, a superb performance of the cycle.'

By now, Kathleen was eager to record *Das Lied von der Erde* with Bruno Walter. He was just as keen, but there were complications. Although Decca had eventually proved so accommodating in releasing Kathleen to Columbia to record *Kindertotenlieder* with Walter, they had no intention of granting her yet another dispensation to record with a rival company. If, however, Bruno Walter could obtain release permission from Columbia, then Decca would be only too delighted to utilise his services in a recording with Kathleen. He had formally requested such permission but the response was not encouraging. He wrote to Kathleen from Beverly Hills:

I am afraid that my efforts to free myself for a recording of *Das Lied von der Erde* with you will not be successful. The Columbia people seem extremely reluctant to commit themselves, and although they have not given a definitely negative answer, my impression is not a very favourable one. I shall see Mr Gilbert at the end of the week and talk it over with him once more. But he told me already on the phone that he sees 'great difficulties' in this matter.

I made a most urgent appeal [to Lieberson] to reciprocate the courtesy of Decca of having permitted you to make the *Kindertotenlieder* with us. I shall certainly continue my efforts, but I did not want to keep you waiting for an answer any longer.

In the midst of these discussions Kathleen had to leave Britain for performances in Vienna, Zurich and Milan. She found Vienna depressing as there were many signs of the Allied occupation: uniformed troops everywhere, and the streets full of beggars and the wounded.

As in Salzburg, the best of the accommodation had been requisitioned by the forces, and the Hotel Astoria, where she was staying, was far from satisfactory. She wrote to Emmie: 'The food is frrrrrraightfully rich – too rich for my old liver, and the pongy lav is a mile down the corridor. Oh, the exercise I've had!'

Fortunately, she met Victor Olof, who was working in Vienna, 'otherwise', she continued to Emmie, 'it would have been "O Sole Mio". Victor came for me after a concert to rescue me from the terrific crowd of autograph hunters – they're worse than in England.'

From Vienna she took the train to Zurich on 25 June where she sang *Kindertotenlieder* with Erich Kleiber. 'Kleiber, whom I was rather dreading,' she wrote to Winifred, 'is a fine conductor and cancelled my final rehearsal this morning as he was so happy. Klever Kaff. I hope he's as pleased at the concert tonight.'

Rick Davies flew to Zurich to join her. After long and hard thought Kathleen had come to the conclusion that she should not marry him: 'I guess I'm meant to be a lone she-wolf,' she continued in her letter to Winifred. 'I don't mind him for a buddy for two days, then I've had enough and want to retire behind an iron curtain and not have to listen and make conversation! Fickle, that's me.' After the Zurich trip she saw less of him and their relationship petered out.

One of the stumbling blocks had been that his enthusiasm for music was less than hers. In her early days Kathleen's singing had been a compensation for a barren home life, but now that she had succeeded it had taken over her entire existence. Dame Isobel Baillie later endorsed this. When asked why, in her opinion, Kathleen had never remarried she replied that she felt Kathleen was 'simply too busy, there was no room for anything else'. Had Kathleen had more spare time she might, possibly, have welcomed marriage although, it seems, her own experience cautioned her for ever. She told Susannah Jacobson that she would 'want a rehearsal' before she ever remarried and expressed similar sentiments to others. But she always enjoyed the company of an attractive man. A contributory reason for her fondness for Cuthbert Bardsley was that he was so personable.

Kathleen was certainly far from 'fickle' in her affections but, according to Bernie Hammond, she did fall in love again. 'There had been a man whom she had loved,' Bernie remembered. 'He wrote and told her he was getting married and sent back to her the letters she had written to him. When she unwrapped the parcel Kath sat on the end of the bed and howled her eyes out. It was ages before she could get it all out of her system. She then burnt the letters and the episode was never mentioned again, and that was the one and only time I saw her cry.'

After Zurich she travelled to Milan where she arrived on 29 June. She was to sing Bach's *B Minor Mass* in La Scala, under Herbert von Karajan. In order to cover her living expenses while in Italy, it had been arranged that Kathleen would be paid certain fees in cash, which should ensure she was financially comfortable. Things did not work out as planned: 'I'm only allowed to spend so much of my fee,' she exploded in a letter to Winifred, 'as part of it must go back to England and I'm only just going to have enough to pay my bloody bill, the barstewards! and will be counting every franc till I leave. Honestlee!!'

A fellow soloist in the *Mass* was Elisabeth Schwarzkopf, who had also sung the work with her in Vienna. According to a letter Walter Legge wrote to Winifred in 1955, the Milan *Mass* was a performance to treasure:

> Karajan has often remarked that Kathleen's 'Agnus Dei' and her duet with Elisabeth in the *B Minor Mass* are among the most treasured recollections of his career. Toscanini ... told Elisabeth, two years afterwards, that Kathleen and Elisabeth's singing in that Scala performance was the greatest experience he had ever had of Bach's singing.

Kathleen wrote to Benita: 'Schwarzkopf is a fine musician and does a terrific amount of work – some things absolutely superb – all these Viennese singers work themselves to a standstill – I just dawdle by comparison.' Schwarzkopf, for her part, later stated in the magazine *Musical Opinion*, that her 'highlight' of 1950 had been hearing Kathleen singing the 'Angus Dei' in that Scala performance.[1]

[1]Some, or all, of that La Scala performance of the *B Minor Mass* has been captured on tape. Engineers from the Columbia Gramophone Company, Ltd, were in La Scala to record Schwarzkopf before the *Mass* commenced. They stayed for the performance and, experimenting with their equipment, taped some (or all) of the *Mass*. EMI has in its possession a tape containing the 'Agnus Dei', sung by Kathleen, and a duet between Kathleen and Schwarzkopf. Elisabeth Schwarzkopf, herself, claims to have heard a complete recording of the *Mass* on radio, but has been unable to locate the source.

Toscanini had been so impressed that he tentatively booked Kathleen for a recital in England. Due to prior commitments, however, it had to be abandoned.[1]

She returned home on 5 July and, among the avalanche of letters awaiting her, was one from Emmie outlining many offers of work. But the pain had returned to her shoulder, and was now extending down her back. This must have been more severe than usual on one morning, for Roy Henderson remembers her arriving in tears.

> I'd never seen her cry like that. When I asked her what was the trouble I finally wormed it out of her that she had a pain in her breast which she was worried about. I asked her if she had a doctor, and she said she had, so I went with her, on the tube, to see him. I waited at Baker Street Station while she ran up the road to his surgery. Well, she came back on top of the world, she shouted at me from quite a way away, 'Look, Prof, he's given me a clean bill of health.' She was thrilled to bits about it.

She was booked for her third Edinburgh Festival appearance at the end of August and for once she insisted to Emmie that she must have a few weeks' rest beforehand, something she had never seemed to need in the past. Indeed, Susannah Jacobson recalls that Kathleen had been physically very strong. During the time she was taking German lessons with Jacobson at his home, once, after a lesson, Kathleen gave them a hand with packing things prior to the Jacobsons' moving house. 'She worked with me for two and a half hours,' says Susannah. 'After that I wanted a rest, as anyone would, but she was fine and went on and did another two hours with Maurice. Anyone else would have been exhausted.'

Among the offers she now turned down was a television appearance – 'no television, *bitte*, too fat!!' – and Hindemith's *Requiem*.

Winifred was about to leave for a holiday, and Kathleen wistfully wrote to her: 'Just thinking about you going off and wishing I was coming too. Have a lovely time and don't go short of anything. Here's a little extra for a good stuff and a gentle booze.'

[1]Toscanini had also arranged to conduct Kathleen in a concert to mark the opening of the Festival of Britain in 1951. This was cancelled due to Kathleen's ill health.

Her Edinburgh appearance was on 28 August and she sang Brahms's *Alto Rhapsody* or 'Brahms's Raspberry' as she usually called it, conducted by Fritz Busch.

The following month she made several broadcasts. She had a premonition about one of these, *Kindertotenlieder*, and wrote to Benita: 'Will be glad when it's over. I don't like broadcasting – always dither and get frogs.'

The premonition was proved accurate, for *The Listener* criticised 'uncharacteristic stiffness and lack of ease'.

The highlight of the month came on 25 September, when she joined Benjamin Britten and Peter Pears for a concert at Westminster Hall to help raise funds for the United Nations. By all accounts this was a delightful evening with Kathleen and Pears singing solos and duets to Britten's accompaniment. In a letter to Newmark, dated 28 September, 1950, Kathleen wrote:

He is a superb pianist. I didn't have enough rehearsal time, and found him a little bit disconcerting, whilst still loving what he did – forgot my words several times as a result, but put in some rude German ones and the Churchills and Atlees who were there would be no wiser, I am sure!!

Edinburgh was exciting – the outstanding things for me were the Hallé with John Barbirolli – de los Angeles voice – Tourel's brain, intelligence, intellect – what you will – Primrose in the Bartok – Curzon in the Brahms – Ariadne, original version, until the opera part started and then I thought she and Bacchus would never stop – but the Zerbinetta was fine – Ilse Hollweg – and disappointing for me the Scala in the Verdi *Requiem* with De Sabata – but I am one of the few who think this, so it must be me! But De Sabata is so acrobatic, and the singers use such varying speeds of vibrato that the a capella bits were terrifying, I couldn't enjoy the performance as a whole – though it was very exciting, but to me never moving and you know it doesn't take much to move ole Kaff!! But it was a wonderful busman's holiday for me, because I had two concerts a day, once my Brahms Raspberry was off my 'chest' – and it was grand to hear so much music for a change.

I saw George London several times and liked him enormously, and loved his voice. He has a nice silly sense of humour and we got on like a house on fire. He seems to be well established over here now. He is back in Wien and going to Bayreuth, and very pleased about that – good for him!

> Look after yourself, dear Johnny, and take pity on a palpitating prima-donna and post her a post card. Much love, Kaff.

In October she wrote to Benita:

> Made a lot of money for the UN. Only hope it works a miracle among the nations, but have me doubts! The cookies were a treat, but they're off for me now 'cos I'm getting too fat – so I'm cutting all starches (when I'm strong enough) and trying to get my bulges a little less rotund. I had some new photies taken the other day and I look like the bull at the other end of the toreador!! Fraightful!! Otherwise all goes well, and we're full of beans. You are lucky still having warm weather – ours is terrible, wet and cold. We've had the worst summer I can remember and now it's cold autumn and we have a gas strike and electricity cuts!! What's wrong with everybody?

Plans were underway for her to appear in the 1951 Edinburgh Festival with both Barbirolli and Bruno Walter. To this end Walter sent her a list of lieder which, he wrote, 'in my opinion, are composed especially for you'. They were all by Brahms and included 'Liebestreu', 'Standchen' and 'Die Mainacht'. He also suggested five Mahler songs, including 'Um Mitternacht' and 'Urlicht'. As the latter is included in Mahler's *Second Symphony*, Walter was careful to explain that it could justifiably be sung out of context.

Walter also requested she come to New York in March 1951, to sing *Das Lied von der Erde* with him. Any request of Walter's was tantamount to a command as far as Kathleen was concerned and she implored Emmie to rearrange her schedule to fit it in.

That November she sang *Frauenliebe und Leben* at Milton Hall, Manchester. 'It could scarcely have been sung more exquisitely,' commented the *Daily Telegraph*. She had been told that she would be singing at Houldesworth Hall, but the venue changed and, due to an administrative error, Kathleen had not been notified. The concert organisers were considerably embarrassed and a letter of apology was despatched, to which she replied: 'Don't be embarrassed about the hall, I will come again and don't be afraid to ask me because I love your audiences – they are a joy and an inspiration.'

Following this, she undertook a three-week tour of Holland. On the 5 December, she wrote to Newmark from the American Hotel in Amsterdam:

Gerald Moore and I are here for three weeks – we both get fatter every day with the superb food. I was on a diet before I arrived here to reduce some too fulsome curves – but what's the good when everything's cooked in butter – I give up, and thereby expand daily! Our musical diet here – Bach cantatas – two recital programmes (8 concerts) – Brahms *Alto Rap.* with Debrowen (3 times) and *Das Lied von der Erde* with Klemperer, so it is a full programme. But everything is arranged so well and I can sleep so late, that I am as fit as a flea and enjoying it all.

Gerald plays beautifully and is a comedian into the bargain, so there is much hilarity too, and I would rather go home poor, through having passed my monies on to him, rather than the income tax people!!! He's very expensive!

I'm furious with Decca – the *Frauenliebe* should have been out two months ago – the chumps. Victor [Olof] has been in Vienna again, so I guess he wasn't there to keep them up to scratch. Do you remember rehearsing Mahler songs at Bruno Walter's, and my dissolving into tears? Do you know, I haven't seen the copy since? You don't have it tucked away anywhere, do you? I can't replace it here – I've tried. Gerald bought the Brahms folk songs for me the other day, in the right keys, so that's a lovely set to have – he wants me to do the Zigeuner lieder – would you?

Shall be sailing to New York on 21 September, and I am looking forward to it already, and to working with you again – what fee do you want, me darling? Have more work that I can really manage, but am enjoying it. Have new fur coat, Johnny – mmm! mmm! Russian ermine – phew! phew! Much too grand ever to wear!! I read the Korean news and it looked so black I went out and blowed all my savings! It all looks enormously serious whenever I have the courage to read the news.

She returned to London in mid-December and within two days was on tour again, in Scotland. But she was home for Christmas, and Winifred joined her and William, as did Emmie Tillett. Emmie brought a friend with her, Bernadine Hammond, a New Zealand nurse who had been looking after Emmie's sick mother. Kathleen's letter to Benita describes the holiday:

Christmas was spent cooking, washing up, fetching coal and dusting. I enjoy it when I haven't anything else to do, but I was in such a mess with correspondence and programmes, having been away a long time, I didn't know which jobs to tackle first. I'm just getting on with my letters but am far behind with my learning. But I cooked a wizard turkey, girl. I haven't forgotten the essentials, but I said my prayers and crossed my heart and it must have worked because it was succulent and tender. Klever Kaff, eh?

SEVENTEEN

New Year's Eve was spent at Emmie Tillet's. Then, on 2 January 1951, Kathleen took off in a snow storm to fly to Amsterdam for four performances of *Orfeo ed Euridice* with the Netherlands Opera, under Charles Bruck. This was to be followed by performances in the Hague, Paris, Zurich, Rome, Florence, Milan and Perugia, plus a return to Paris for a further recital. A taxing schedule but, as she said, 'I wouldn't have it any other way.'

The flight was bumpy, which she did not like at all. She sent a card to Emmie: 'A young man in front lost all his Christmas cheer for the *whole* journey! But I had me Kwells and I tucked in – I was so glad to be up and on an even keel. You're bound to come down once you're up, as the actress said to the bishop!!'

Due to the severe weather the plane arrived late, and she had to go straight from the airport to rehearsals. Concerning the costumes for *Orfeo*, she wrote to Emmie: 'The others look as daft as I feel.' She added in a letter to Benita: 'I wish you could see me in my black, woollen tights, they're all right when I stand up but I bounce like a rubber ball when I try to sit down, they're so tight, and it hasn't helped having what the Dutch call "spit", which is backache, but I hope the audience take my groans for passion.'

Emmie wrote to say Kathleen had been requested for a performance of *The Rape of Lucretia* at Wiesbaden, that July, but Kathleen replied:

Lucretia's Rape. Can you get me out of it, sweetie? The thought of it worries me enormously, my big feet and all that – I don't want to go careering off to Wiesbaden when I'm only just back from Europe – I'm only going to have a few days to relearn the whole bludy thing and I certainly don't want to work any more in July. Can you talk me out of it, do you think? I would be relieved.

Orfeo ed Euridice was performed in Amsterdam on 9, 11, 14 and 16

January 1951. She wrote to Winifred: 'The first night was a wow and nothing awful happened and I quite enjoyed it. If I could act confidently, it's really much easier than a recital but I still feel it's a lot of playacting – where I live, love and die in a song.'

One of the performances was broadcast and recorded on to 78 rpm discs. These were stored and, as had happened in Norway, forgotten. In 1965 an unknown engineer dubbed the records on to tapes and, in the extraordinary manner of Ferrier recordings, they resurfaced in 1977, in the archives of NOS (Dutch Broadcasting Corporation). Great excitement was generated by this discovery and, quick off the mark, EMI set about obtaining permission to issue the tapes as commercial records.

There were, of course, complications, as the original 78s had been owned by another company, KRO, so agreement between KRO and NOS had to be reached. Realising the historic value of the tapes, both companies cooperated to the full. The thorny problem of royalties was resolved by both the Dutch Musician's Union, and Decca, waiving their rights. Winifred, as Kathleen's beneficiary, donated all royalties from record sales to the Kathleen Ferrier Memorial Scholarship Fund, which had been set up after Kathleen's death.

Meanwhile, the tapes had undergone extensive tests, and it was decided to issue the records in the original mono, as there was less likelihood of distorting the timbre of the voices. The records were initially released in Holland in December, 1977 at a special ceremony at which Winifred was the guest of honour. They became available in Britain the following year, and were described in the press as 'the musical event of 1978'.[1]

While performing *Orfeo ed Euridice* in The Hague, Kathleen narrowly escaped a violent death when a heavy iron bar fell from the flies and thudded to the floor, just missing her.

Her Paris recital, on 23 January, was at the Salle Gaveau, and described by critic Christina Thoresby, as 'a triumph of vocal beauty'. While in Paris she had coaching in French from Pierre Bernac. They worked on the Chausson, and Bernac ungallantly roared with laughter when he heard her French pronunciation, 'But,' she wrote to Emmie, 'in the nicest way – now he's getting quite excited. I should love a lesson a day for twelve months, then I should feel I was really getting somewhere!'

[1] EMI RLS 725.

To Newmark she wrote: 'I am in Gay Paree for lessons with – guess who? – Pierre Bernac. Am *so* thrilled and working hard at Chausson I have just about conquered the N in '*chantez*' so am coming on!!'

Gerald Moore had been her accompanist in Paris and from Switzerland, Kathleen wrote to Winifred: 'Gerald played like an angel and was a source of inspiration and confidence, as ever. I could murder the man here in Zurich and he's not really bad – just dumb! and no soul to boot – O Sole Mio.'

Distressing news reached her in Rome. Her father had had a stroke and was expected to live just a few hours.

Kathleen's instinctive reaction was to cancel the remainder of her tour and return home at once, but two things prevented this. First, there were no flights as fog at London airport prevented landings and, secondly, Winifred assured her by telephone that there was no point in returning: William would surely be dead by the time she arrived. Kathleen saw the wisdom of this, but wrote: 'I am at a loss here and feel that I am not pulling my weight. I do hope I am doing the right thing in not coming home and that you don't feel I'm getting out of the responsibility.'

William's death plunged the tour into gloom. 'The audiences are the most uncivilised anywhere,' she wrote to Newmark. 'They arrive three-quarters of an hour late, after starting twenty minutes late, get up and walk in and out, and chatter all the time. I loathe their very guts, darling, but perhaps it's me.'

To Winifred she wrote:

It certainly isn't worth staggering around on my own, trying to cope with strange languages and monies, to sing to such people. . . .

Then the manager came round, with all the people there, and asked me to change my programme for Milan – on the spot – so I let out all my inhibitions and repressions and went prima-donna and waved my arms and said 'Not bloody likely' – or words to that effect – and enjoyed myself. But when I thought about it afterwards, it was really my fault as I had mixed up the programmes – so it was temper – not temperament. . . . The Maitlands have come with me and I think they will be terrified in case the audience shout or spit! . . . the pianist is very good, though he *will* duet with me in a hideous falsetto all the time – but he's a trier and very sensitive, so I can bear anything. I daren't leave anything about here – and I lock my fur coat up all the time – I had all my Swiss francs stolen the day I arrived, about £30, taken out of my bag, and however much you give a porter or a taxi, they shout for more. This is one country I'll never retire to! But I'm getting good at shouting back and saying '*Basta, basta*' – and often adding the 'rd'! . . . The concert is at five pm tomorrow of all awful times.

The beauty of Florence did nothing to cheer her, and the subject matter of *Kindertotenlieder*, which she sang, was hardly helpful. From Florence she travelled to Turin, where she was to broadcast *Kindertotenlieder* with Otto Klemperer. She met Klemperer in Florence, and they travelled together overnight by train in adjacent sleepers. This was mildly hazardous, as the great man was an inveterate smoker, and subject to absent-mindedness. He often forgot where he had put his lighted cigarette and there had been several near accidents, and one very serious one. His bed had caught fire and he had reached for the nearest tumbler, which he thought contained water but which, in fact, was full of brandy. He was severely burnt.

Emmie and Winifred came to Paris for Kathleen's final concert. Struck by how drawn Kathleen looked, Winifred was also disconcerted when her sister threw herself into her arms and hugged her. She was not usually so demonstrative. Winifred put it down to tiredness and the strain of William's death.

While in Paris, Kathleen had several more sessions with Bernac, who later wrote in a letter to Winifred: 'Without knowing French at all, she succeeded in singing it really very well.'

Winifred and Emmie cheered her enormously, but she was, nevertheless, heartily glad to be back in London on 19 February, and busy with rehearsals. Barbirolli was going to conduct her in *Poème de l'Amour et de la Mer* for the first time nine days later.

It was then that Emmie told her there was no possibility of altering her schedule to include the performance of *Das Lied von der Erde* in New York that Bruno Walter had requested. Kathleen had to accept this, but would have preferred singing with Walter to any of her other bookings.

Another offer Emmie had reluctantly to refuse for her was Mahler's song cycle *Lieder eines fahrenden Gesellen*. Kathleen loved the music and, although it is more suited to a mezzo than a contralto,[1] she felt she

---

[1] Although actually written for a baritone.

could master it with practice. But there was simply not the time.

In response to a request to take part in an orchestral concert, Kathleen wrote to Emmie: 'I could do the Bliss, but I have forgotten its proper title, it's something about frying me lover in hot oil.'

The Bliss to which she so flippantly referred, is a cantata of great technical difficulty entitled 'The Enchantress'. It tells the story of a Syracuse woman who, when deserted by her lover, invokes the black arts to get him back. It had been composed for her by Sir Arthur Bliss. She was to premiere 'The Enchantress', on radio, on 2 October 1951, then still seven months ahead. But within those seven months her prospects, which looked so rosy, were to take a tragic turn for the worse.

EIGHTEEN

There was no indication of impending disaster. The greatest worry in Kathleen's life seemed to be that since Paddy was leaving to get married, she urgently needed a new secretary. Originally, Paddy had been taken on to help look after William and act as part-time secretary, and now that Kathleen had become so busy what she really needed anyway was full-time help.

Emmie recommended Bernadine Hammond, the New Zealander who had spent Christmas with them, and who had looked after Emmie's late mother. Emmie was sure that Bernie would be able to handle the secretarial duties and, just as importantly, that Bernie and Kathleen would get on well together. No one suspected that Kathleen would soon be needing a nurse herself.

Kathleen invited Bernie to Frognal Mansions for an interview and almost immediately asked her if she could start the next day. The startled Bernie asked what her duties were to be and was told, 'Just keep an eye on the housekeeping, and help me with my letters and things.' Bernie pointed out that she could not type, but this did not worry Kathleen, so she agreed to start the next day.

As Bernie was leaving, Kathleen called out over the banisters, 'Get a taxi in the morning and let me know how much it is.'

'It seemed like some curious dream,' Bernie reflected. 'I seemed to be watching this happen to someone else. I'd agreed to start and I did not know what my duties were.'[1]

She arrived next morning with her suitcase, and Kathleen came down the steps, purse in hand, to pay the taxi. She then made a cup of tea, and while they drank this, in the kitchen, she told Bernie, 'Just settle in and enjoy yourself, there'll soon be plenty to do.'

In fact Bernie had arrived just in time. Kathleen was shortly to leave for a tour of the north of England with Barbirolli and the Hallé, and did

[1] Information from Bernadine Hammond's unpublished diary.

not want to leave the flat unattended. During the tour she would be giving three concert performances of *Orfeo ed Euridice* and making her debut on 28 February, with *Poème de l'Amour et de la Mer*.

She fretted about this Chausson piece. She had been studying it for a year and she still had reservations about her ability to sing it.[1] The 'Poème' is different from anything she had sung before. Chausson had been influenced by Wagner but had studied under Massenet; thus, although the 'Poème' is rich in texture it is delicate in sentiment, and its intensely romantic nature made her self-conscious. She had learnt the work at Barbirolli's suggestion, however, and trusted his judgment implicitly.

On the morning of 28 February, she wrote to Newmark:

> Well, darling, this is a great day. The first performance with Barbirolli of the Chausson. We rehearsed last night – oh boy! is it lush!? . . . He's pickled tink, and I'm enjoying it – there's such support for the high bits – didn't worry me last night. *Orfeo* at the weekend, that I *am* looking forward to. Barbirolli, with his Italian blood, seems to me just right. But then, I'm a fan, so am probably biased.
>
> Could tell you several after-dinner stories about Klemperer – *Quel homme!* whew!

It seemed that Kathleen's faith in Barbirolli was not misplaced, for the critics were unanimous in their praise. The *Manchester Guardian* claimed that she sang 'the passionate sections of the music with buoyant exuberance and the more delicate parts with fastidious expression', and the *Evening Chronicle* considered her approach 'sympathetic and intelligent'. Despite these assurances, Kathleen was dissatisfied with her performance and had to sing the work several more times in public before she felt comfortable with it.

On 9 March, she and Barbirolli broadcast the work from Manchester. It was not until 1983 that Winifred learnt of the existence of a private recording of this broadcast, owned by a Mr Ian Cosens. Upon request, Mr Cosens sent Winifred a cassette of the recording which she,

---

[1] Winifred believes these reservations were more concerned with interpretation than technique, for by now she knew she could master the high tessitura – she would never have attempted it in public otherwise.

in turn, sent to Decca to assess its potential as a commercial issue. Difficulties were encountered with the sound quality, which is well below modern standards, but eventually all concerned parties agreed that the historical interest of the recording overrode its inferior sound, and Decca issued the record in the April of 1985.[1] Both Winifred, and Barbirolli's legatees, donated their royalties from it to the Kathleen Ferrier Cancer Research Fund.

Alan Blyth, in his review of the record for *The Gramophone*, wrote:

> There is here a remarkable familiarity with the French text, a new-found freedom above the stave (the A flats and As ring out truly), and in the work's final, restrained section, 'Le temps des Lilas', a refined, shimmering tone and tender expression that exactly mirror those qualities in the music.

The three performances of *Orfeo ed Euridice* took place respectively in Manchester, Hanley and Sheffield. Ena Mitchell was Euridice and the Italian soprano, Fulvia Trevisani, sang Amor.

These performances were a remarkable achievement for Barbirolli. He had been suffering from abdominal pain, and had lost two stones in weight. Appendicitis was diagnosed, and his doctor advised an immediate operation. Determined not to let Kathleen down, he secretly persuaded his doctor to keep him going, until after the final performance, and it was not until all the performances had been completed, and they were sharing a celebratory dinner at the Midland Hotel in Manchester, that he confessed to Kathleen what he had done. She later wrote to him: 'I can't ever forget that you put off your "appointment" . . . until *Orfeo* and the Chausson were over. Those ten days working, and being with you, were inexpressively wonderful. . . . It is the loveliest time I ever remember and I keep on reliving it, and purr with pleasure every time I do so.'

Kathleen had been staying with the Barbirollis throughout the tour. During their last day together Barbirolli told her that he felt a concert version of *Orfeo ed Euridice* did not do justice to the opera and that, one day, he would like to conduct it in its proper setting, the Royal Opera House, Covent Garden, with her as Orfeo. Kathleen was not too

[1] Decca 414 095–1.

hopeful, remembering Bruno Walter's unsuccessful plans for the same work.

She left the Barbirollis on 13 March, the day Barbirolli was being operated upon, to sing *Kindertotenlieder* in Liverpool, under Hugo Rignold.

In Kathleen's absence, Bernie had put the flat in order, bought a stock of provisions and neatly arranged messages, letters and press cuttings. Also, encouraged like Kathleen by Emmie Tillett, she had started to paint, and when Kathleen arrived home she found Bernie bent over an easel. She wanted to stop but Kathleen would not hear of it. 'That's ever so good,' she told her, looking at the canvas, she added that it was a joy to see everything so tidy. Bernie did not mention it, but she was horrified by how worn Kathleen looked.

The next morning, seemingly casually, Kathleen called Bernie into her bedroom. 'Have a look at this lump, will you?' she asked. 'I'm sure it's nothing.' She showed her a growth on her breast. Kathleen had first noticed the lump when smoothing down a dress which John Turner had made for her. During her nursing days, Bernie had seen similar growths. 'There wasn't the slightest doubt in my mind as to what it was,' she said. 'I almost froze.'

She persuaded Kathleen to see a doctor but it could not be arranged immediately as she was about to leave for a tour of Holland and Germany. 'Tell the doc, I want a really dashing surgeon,' were her last words to Bernie before departing.

She saw her doctor, Reginald Hilton, on 24 March. After examining her he sent her for X-rays to University College Hospital, where cancer of the breast was diagnosed. A mastectomy was necessary, and arrangements were made to admit her to the hospital on 9 April, for an operation on the 10th. All concert work was cancelled for two months.

The worst fears she had harboured since childhood were now realised and several seemingly curious past reactions began to make sense. It was as if she had been preparing herself for the illness. Admittedly she had moved to London for career reasons, but she had remarked at the time that she believed the hospitals in the capital to be superior. She had wept at Roy Henderson's home before he accompanied her to the doctor for an examination, and her relief had been enormous when told she was fit. And there was her emotional display in

Paris when she met Winifred after William's death; Winifred is convinced this was because Kathleen was suspicious of the nature of the growth on her breast, and had been worrying about it throughout the tour. Finally, she had employed a secretary who was also a trained nurse.

Before consulting Dr Hilton, Kathleen had two previous medical examinations and had been pronounced well. Possibly, if she had had symptoms then, they were too immature to be detected by the technology of the time. But no doctor examining her breast now could have missed a growth as prominent as that which Bernie has described.

Kathleen took the news of the operation stoically, underplaying its significance, but impressing on her friends that she did not want the public to know the reason for it. Sadly there was a social stigma attached to cancer in those days: the disease was something people preferred not to talk about.

'She accepted it without question,' said Bernie. 'There wasn't a trace of poor me, or why did this have to happen. All she said was, "It's worse for you, you've got to stand there and watch." She did not want sympathy, but needed someone to be there.'

Before being admitted to hospital she kept her mind occupied by turning William's old bedroom into a music room. She bought a new carpet, and a little escritoire and, when Dame Myra Hess learned of her plans, she insisted that Kathleen accept the loan of one of her Steinway pianos. It was a great day for Kathleen when the magnificent instrument was installed.

The dear old Cramer had done sterling duty, but it was now showing definite signs of wear. Sir Arthur Bliss had not helped – during rehearsals for 'The Enchantress' he had pummelled the keys so hard that several of them had broken. Eventually, Kathleen sold it.

During those pre-hospitalisation days, Kathleen valiantly tried to stay cheerful, and for the first time in her life she actually managed to take things easy. 'She could relax better than anyone I've known,' says Bernie. 'She stayed in bed in the mornings, read the *Daily Telegraph* from cover to cover, then set about the crossword.' It was a marvellous contrast to her former lifestyle.

Now and then she and Bernie would go for a walk on Hampstead Heath, sometimes meeting Anne Ziegler and Webster Booth, who lived nearby and exercised their dog there. Anne had just had her tonsils removed and was concerned it might affect her voice. Webster meanwhile had been booked to sing in a *Messiah* with Kathleen, but unfortunately it was one of the bookings that had to be cancelled due to Kathleen's illness. This was a great disappointment to them both.

She spent a lot of time listening to music on her radio. 'Must check up on the opposition,' she would say, as she opened *Radio Times*. Occasionally, she would listen to her own records, but not often.

Despite her efforts, the news that she was unwell spread, and visitors constantly called at the flat. Sometimes fans came – and one of these, an Italian count, laden with flowers and chocolates, actually sank to his knees and proposed marriage. 'She split her sides laughing when he'd gone,' said Bernie. An anonymous admirer sometimes left a jar of cream outside the flat door; they never discovered who it was. Cream was hard to come by at that time and whenever the surprise gift arrived, Kathleen would bake a sponge right away.

Just before the operation she confided in Benita Cress:

> Bernie hasn't got out of her nursing as she thought. I have to go into hospital any day now for a rather formidable op. for a lump on me busto. Having her here has lightened the load enormously and I am in the finest radiologists' and surgeons' hands in the country. I have had to cancel a month's tour in Scandinavia, and everything, till the middle of May, but I'm glad of a rest. I feel better now that everything is getting done. I should have gone earlier but I haven't been home for months. The X-ray yesterday was better than they thought so don't worry, love.

On the day of her admission to hospital she was up early. She brought Bernie a cup of tea in bed and after breakfast they went by taxi to the hospital. Kathleen had taken her latest painting with her to hang in her room and, as they were early, they walked down the Tottenham Court Road looking for a suitable frame. When this was bought, Kathleen framed the painting on the spot by hammering in the nails with her shoe.

Bernie spent that night at the hospital and remained with Kathleen until she was wheeled into the operating theatre the following day. She also insisted on staying for several nights afterwards, and was only persuaded to sleep at Frognal Mansions when it was clear that Kathleen was making an excellent recovery. But she would arrive at the hospital at eight thirty each morning and stay until eight at night.

Kathleen took an interest in anything to do with the hospital, and kept Bernie up to date on the love-lives of the nurses, dispensing advice to them when asked. She also kept up with the vicissitudes of the varicose veins of the cleaner, about which she was very sympathetic. 'This is the place to be, love,' she would tell her visitors.

Only after the operation did she confide to Winifred, 'I worried a bit beforehand, in case I should not be brave enough.'

On 18 April, nine days after her mastectomy, she wrote to Benita:

I am writing my first letters for a bit and feeling real cocky – just waiting for the doctor to come – and being glad it isn't this time last week – when I threw up four times all down Bernie's front – poor, sweet Bernie, she's been an absolutely bludy marvel – just don't know what I should have done without her.

I don't know about my itinerary, love, it's at home and I'm not even thinking about singing yet, but I'll let you know in a bit. I shall be in here another week or ten days yet – so I really am enjoying a rest and, Gee, I was ready for it.

I seem to have startled all the staff here with my quick recovery and I'm being spoiled to death and thoroughly enjoying myself.

22 April was her thirty-ninth birthday, and as she was still in hospital she decided to give a little party there. Flowers started to arrive first thing in the morning from Barbirolli, Sargent and others, and Bernie was asked to bring bottles of gin, vermouth and a lemon.

Visiting hours started at two pm, and the first guests to arrive were Ena Mitchell and Gerald and Enid Moore. They were relieved to see how well Kathleen looked and Moore, a skilful raconteur, was soon relating his latest anecdote. Owen Brannigan and William Herbert then arrived, shortly ahead of Emmie Tillett who, thinking alcohol might be forbidden, had hidden a bottle of champagne under her coat. Winifred came, followed by Peter Pears and Benjamin Britten, both of whom had expected to be greeted by a forlorn invalid – but instead, gusts of laughter issued from the room. Finally the ward sister, Rhona Phillips, presented Kathleen with a birthday cake which the kitchen staff had baked for her. After the cake they had oysters and more champagne, which Dame Myra Hess had sent, and the nurses brought in cups of tea. 'This is the loveliest birthday I've ever had,' Kathleen told Winifred.

Before sleeping that night she wrote a letter to the kitchen staff, thanking them for their cake. 'Lucky Kath,' she murmured to Bernie.

Her relief at the success of the operation was short-lived. A few days after her birthday Sister Phillips quietly told her that all was not as well as had been hoped. Secondary symptoms had been located but these could be disposed of by a six-week course of radiation therapy.

When Arthur, the ward attendant, arrived with a trolley to wheel her to the treatment room on the first therapy day, she told him, 'I hope you've got your driving licence.'

Bernie was not permitted into the treatment room, but could view through a glass panel, and speak to Kathleen through an intercom system. 'I'm all right,' Kathleen assured her, as she was being attached to the radiation apparatus. Although Kathleen was determinedly cheerful, she confessed later to Bernie that the treatment was sickening. To her disgust she was not even allowed a bath.

Every day Arthur came to fetch her; usually he was early so they could have a chat. 'I'm getting a dab hand at this,' she told him as she slid from her bed to the trolley.

She was still anxious that as few people as possible should know how ill she was. 'I'm not telling any of my buddies in New York,' she wrote to Benita. 'Such exaggerated rumours get around. You're the only one wot knows.'

After three weeks she had responded so well to treatment that Dr Hilton discharged her from hospital, allowing her to continue the course as an outpatient. Wearing a smart suit, and with her face carefully made up to face the world, she bid an affectionate farewell to the staff. 'Well, that's it,' she told Bernie on the hospital steps. 'Now I can get on.'

As soon as she arrived at Frognal Mansions she tried out her voice at the piano. 'That's a relief,' she said. 'At least they haven't cut out my vocal cords.'

For the next three weeks she went with Bernie each day to the hospital for her treatment. Mostly she was cheerful but, occasionally, she would lapse into silence when, Bernie recalled, 'it would have been an insult to try to cheer her up'. Bernie told Gerald Moore of their routine, and he included it in his chapter in *Kathleen Ferrier, A Memoir*:

. . . morning after morning we went off to the hospital, and Kath would think of something interesting to do on the way home. We would stop at an antique shop and look at some glass; she would handle things with love and say, 'That does give me pleasure.' She loved wood. . . . We would go in search of curtain material (Kath would always know exactly what she wanted), or some new kitchen utensil, or a book she had seen advertised. There was much combined pleasure in the planning of meals, for Kath always maintained that eating was a great art. I remember one dreary day coming home in the taxi and Kath suddenly saying, 'I know, I'll make an apple pie!' Instantly the fog vanished and we were soon eating boiling-hot apple pie.

One of the amazing things about her was her complete acceptance of whatever came her way. . . . This was an enormous help to her. At times when it seemed that she had more than any normal human could be expected to cope with, there would suddenly be that quick smile and there she was counting over what yet remained to her, and feeling sorry for people she considered worse off than herself. She hardly ever complained; on such rare occasions as she did, a saint would have done the same. She was her own greatest, most valiant helper, and never once did she let herself down. . . .

Kath enjoyed life from the moment she woke and purred over her morning cup of tea. . . . During the day she would say so often, 'Lucky, lucky, Kath!' Troubles, and they were not infrequent, were never made much of. If there was anything she could do about it, then she did it smartly, otherwise she waited for it to blow over and turned her mind to something else. She used to say that the value of an illness was that it taught one to draw the dividing line between what mattered and what was of no consequence; she had a wonderful sense of proportion.

She was an ordinary person and an extraordinary one. At first I was puzzled when I saw her on the concert platform, and I used to wonder how this woman, with her divine voice and lovely appearance, could possibly be the same as the one who spent the morning digging in the garden, and had been so excited to find parsley had come up that we had to have an omelette for lunch to do it justice. It suddenly occurred to me that that intrinsic loveliness was present in varying degrees in every single thing that she did. She once said that the Brahms's *Serious Songs* were the best sermon that she knew, and because she herself lived by that creed her singing of them was so deeply moving.

On 22 May 1951 she wrote to Newmark:

All's well, sweetie! I'm still going to the hospital for rays each day, but should have finished with them in ten days. I have only been slightly queasy on a few occasions, when they seem to lay most people completely out – making them violently sick, anaemic and suicidal – so I am feeling cocky and, with the end in sight, I perk up each day. 2,000,000 volts is quite a lot of current going into one's innards, isn't it? The doctors are very pleased with me – I have gained weight this last two weeks and, from wanting to sit and twiddle my thumbs all day, I have the urge to do a bit of work now – which is just as well, as I have lots to learn for Edinburgh.

Voice seems better for the rest, and oh! I *was* ready for one! I'll always approach Italy tentatively in future, wot with one thing and another!

I don't need anything, love – I have lots of tins of meat and butter – the ration is still one chop per person per week! But really we're fine, so don't you worry your ole head, honey-chile!

Much, much love, from a fairly Klever Kaff.

When she felt well enough she entertained her friends at home, and the first to be invited to supper were the Barbirollis. Sir John brought her a gift of home-made marzipan cakes. Kathleen remarked to Bernie that he looked 'like a refugee from the Mafia', as he stood in the doorway in his huge black hat, overcoat and sunglasses. His stipulation, on accepting Kathleen's invitation, had been that he would cook the meal. He was a gourmet cook, and had brought with him some fillets of plaice which he lovingly fried.

During the meal he amused Kathleen by telling her of his days in the army when, because of the difficulties in pronouncing his name, he was known as Bob O'Riley. He also told her how, as a cellist, he had accompanied Anna Pavlova in one of her 'Dying Swan' performances. He was captivated by her fragility and she astounded him after the performance, when she shook his hand with a grip like a vice.

Sometimes Barbirolli and his wife, oboeist Evelyn Rothwell, would bring their instruments and play chamber music, with Kathleen at the piano. As he staggered up the many steps to Frognal Mansions, Barbirolli's small frame would be eclipsed by his cello case.

Dr Hilton was a keen amateur violinist, and he begged Kathleen to introduce him to Barbirolli. As Barbirolli was fascinated by medical topics, Kathleen invited them both to supper. Reggie Hilton arrived with his violin and two Fauré songs which he thought might suit Kathleen. To his delight she sat at the Steinway and sang them, accompanying herself.[1] Emboldened by this, Hilton asked if he could play his violin for Barbirolli. With Kathleen accompanying him, he delivered what Bernie described as 'excrutiatingly awful renditions'. Barbirolli sat throughout with utter composure.

Kathleen used the kitchen table for meals – even though it was actually a mangle with a wooden top, it was the only table she had that was big enough – but she now decided this was no longer sufficiently grand, so she bought a mahogany dining table and six chairs, and converted her tiny spare room into a dining room. Shortly after this, on her way to University College Hospital for treatment, she saw some expensive white carpet in the window of Maples. 'Shall I be a devil?' she asked Bernie. The carpet arrived next day: 'We were able to fit six into that dining room,' remembers Bernie. 'Four were wedged in and only able to move in cases of emergency. I sat in the doorway, so that I could nip into the kitchen. If things got out of hand there, Kath would come and join me.'

The elegance of the flat had been recently enhanced by the acquisition of a silver tea service. Bruno Walter was coming to tea one day and Winifred, who had also been invited, was appalled when she saw Kathleen reach for the big brown teapot she had used for years. 'You should have a silver service,' she told her. Kathleen went out at once and bought one on Hampstead High Street, returning with it in plenty of time for tea.

At the end of her treatment period she had a few friends to lunch at the Casa Prada restaurant in Euston Road, and gave them a bizarre surprise when she took a locket from her neck and revealed inside it the stitches from her operation.

---

[1] Kathleen probably knew the songs quite well, as she was preparing three Fauré songs ('Après un Rêve', 'Lydia' and 'Nell') for her forthcoming tour of America and Canada. It is an enormous pity she never recorded 'Après un Rêve' as it would have suited her to perfection.

By the end of May she was able to take a short holiday with Bernie. As travel abroad was out of the question, she followed Barbirolli's advice and chose the Sussex town of Alfriston where they reserved a double room at the two-hundred-year old George Inn. Reggie Hilton drove them down in his Rolls Royce. Kathleen sat in the front and told Bernie she could play at being Queen Mary in the back. It turned out to be a somewhat protracted journey as the doctor was an amateur ornithologist and stopped his car every time he saw an interesting bird, so that he could follow its flight through his field glasses.

Eventually they arrived at the George Inn, which lived up to their expectations. It had oak beams, steep stairs, and was set in an attractive garden shaded by trees, under which chairs were placed.

The mornings were devoted to their painting, but first they had a large cooked breakfast: 'Might as well, as we're paying for it,' said Kathleen sensibly. Painting brought her peace of mind, and she would sit at her easel for hours, working swiftly with her brushes and palette knife, occasionally tutting when a fly committed suicide on her canvas.

As she was painting Lullington Church with Bernie one morning, a young boy came up to her and reprimanded her for sitting on a grave. She was horrified, having no idea the mound on which she had squatted was a neglected grave, and moved at once. The boy followed, and she asked his name. He told her it was Vincent, and she said hers was Kath. He stayed with her all morning.

At around one o'clock, carefully holding their canvasses in front of them, the two women returned to the hotel for lunch. After this they went up to their room, where the canvasses were pinned to the wall and criticised. Then Kathleen would take a siesta, and Bernie had firm instructions to wake her in time for tea. 'I'd hate to miss out on that sponge,' she told her. After tea, Bernie and Kathleen went for a walk, looking for views to paint the next day. Sometimes they called in for a drink, and a game of shove-ha'penny, at the nearby Plough and Arrow, an inn reputed to be 450 years old.

For a change, one day they took a bus ride to Eastbourne, but the crowds tired Kathleen and she was glad to return to the peace of Alfriston.

She was studying the Brahms songs, which Bruno Walter had recommended for the Edinburgh Festival, and to make Bernie laugh she would put on Reggie Hilton's motoring cap, which he had forgotten, and sing in a gutsy basso profundo.

Before leaving Alfriston, Kathleen visited Gerald Moore who lived nearby. He took her out for a drive and, on the way home, stopped to buy some cigarettes. While he was in the shop Kathleen slipped into the driving seat and moved his car out of sight. She was much amused by his horrified amazement when he finally found her.

Her return to the concert platform was on 19 June 1951, when she was to sing the Bach *B Minor Mass*. She was nervous at the rehearsal as she had not sung in public for three months, the longest break in her career. Alison Milne, who was in the orchestra, remembers that as soon as Kathleen stepped on to the rostrum for rehearsal, the entire orchestra stood and applauded. She was so touched it was a few minutes before she could sing.

Any doubts there may have been about her voice were dispelled. As *The Times* put it, 'her vocal and interpretative powers were unimpaired'. After the performance the green room was crowded with well-wishers, and Kathleen celebrated until the small hours, delighted to be back in harness, and realising how much she had missed it all.

Her next major undertaking was the Holland Festival, where she was to sing four performances of *Orfeo ed Euridice*, and several recitals. Emmie questioned the wisdom of such a strenuous tour, and suggested several cancellations, but Kathleen would not hear of it, insisting in a letter to Emmie that she was as 'fit as a flea and ready for anything'. Her only concession to her illness was that she was taking Bernie with her. It was, in fact, difficult for her to dress without Bernie as, although ten weeks had elapsed since the operation, she could still only raise her arms just high enough to do her hair, and her scars still needed a certain amount of attention.

Peter Diamand met her at Amsterdam airport, as did a film crew. Since Walt Disney was on board the plane also, Kathleen assumed the crew was there for him. She was genuinely surprised when the camera was turned on her. The film was for a Dutch cinema newsreel and, as Kathleen was very busy rehearsing, Bernie was despatched to the cinema to bring back a report. Unfortunately, it was a short clip and someone stood in front of her just as Kathleen was about to appear. So Bernie had to sit through the entire programme again in order to see her. That film still exists and shows a trim, elegant Kathleen making a smiling and assured way across the tarmac.

The first performance of *Orfeo ed Euridice* was on 6 July. 'At the end of the performance,' Bernie recalled, 'the audience stood and cheered until I thought the roof must surely fall in. Flowers were brought on to the stage until it resembled a garden and still the applause continued.' Under the spell of the opera, Bernie called round to the dressing room to help Kathleen change. She found a matter-of-fact Kathleen counting the minutes on her fingers until she could have her supper.

On 12 July Kathleen sang Mahler's *Second Symphony*, with the Concertgebouw Orchestra conducted by Klemperer. This was broadcast, and tapes of it were located in the archives of Dutch Radio after her death and issued in record and cassette form in September 1982.[1] The reviewer for *The Gramophone* commented, 'Kathleen Ferrier's singing of "Urlicht" and the glorious contralto verses in the "Resurrection Hymn" threaten to haunt my waking hours for several days yet.'

For all the success of the performance, Klemperer had been temperamental at rehearsals. At one point he had stalked off the rostrum and threatened to cancel the performance. Kathleen wrote to Emmie: 'Been rehearsing with Klemperer this morning, took Bernie with me for safety and she hasn't yet regained her natural colour. He terrified her!!'

Such behaviour by Klemperer was not unheard of. At another rehearsal he had dismissed everyone from the hall except the orchestra. Outraged when one woman persistently remained, he stormed across the floor to remonstrate with her, only recognising his wife at the very last minute.

Lord Harewood was present at the performance and, afterwards, took Kathleen and Bernie for a meal. He recalls her smarting at Klemperer's irrascibility:

I always found Kathleen had a very lively sense of fun and perhaps also of humour, though she did not respond easily to people who had, she felt, any

[1] Decca K264K22. At the same concert, Kathleen also sang *Kindertotenlieder* which has now also been issued: Decca 417 634–1(LP) and Decca 417 634–4 (cassette).

reservation about her performance. . . . I remember how she hated working with Otto Klemperer and in particular her sharp reaction about him and his attitude towards her when she had taken part in a quite wonderful performance of Mahler's *Second Symphony* in Amsterdam in 1951. I had thought it had been a major event, but she only remembered that he was sarcastic in rehearsal, perhaps because of her connection with Bruno Walter, whom he did not greatly respect. But supper afterwards . . . was nonetheless a convivial and agreeable affair.

The evening does not appear to have been all that convivial. Bernie recalls that there were certain uneasy moments: 'At one point Lord Harewood gave his very definite views on a fellow artist of Kathleen's. She did not agree and said so equally definitely, and that led to a heated discussion. Afterwards she said, "I don't care who he's the Earl of, he wasn't going to get away with that."'

Later, Kathleen and Klemperer were to perform *Das Lied von der Erde* together and there was no trouble on that occasion. He described her performance, quite simply, as 'wonderful'.

In Naarden she sang the *B Minor Mass* under Georges Enesco. As she was leaving the stage door, she found an elderly woman who had been in the audience waiting to see her. The tears streamed down her visitor's face as she congratulated Kathleen on her performance. Kathleen gave her a carnation from her bouquet and told her, 'I know what it's like, love. There have been times when I have almost choked with emotion. Don't you worry.'[1]

The tour tired her more than she had expected, and her back began to ache, but she forestalled Bernie's worries by assuring her it was 'just screwmatics'. But she wrote to Emmie: 'I spend most of my time in bed in between whiles, being thoroughly lazy – it's so tiring here being below sea level, I suppose. *SO* looking forward to coming home.'

On her return to London she was visibly exhausted. Dr Hilton examined her and recommended she resume outpatient treatment at University College Hospital.

The next three mornings were spent lying face downwards on a treatment table, a red pencil mark on her back denoting the area to be treated by radiation. The radiographer was Dr Gwen Hilton, wife of

[1] Taken from Bernie's diary.

Reggie Hilton, who was astonished on the third morning when Kathleen arrived with a suitcase and told her she was leaving for Liverpool after her treatment, to give a performance that evening. She told her he had never known such determination.

Kathleen was not, however, so lively after the performance. Her face was grey with exhaustion. But when, as she was about to leave the theatre, she saw a crowd of autograph-hunters waiting for her and it was suggested that she might slip quietly away by a side door, she would not hear of it. 'I dread the day no one comes for my autograph,' she said. 'Then I'll know I'm finished.' She stayed chatting until the last fan had gone.

She spent the night in Buxton after the performance, and in the morning, 27 July 1951, set off by car for King's Lynn where she was to sing Haydn's *Nelson Mass* under Josef Krips. This was followed by a recital in Birmingham with Gerald Moore. Her back was so painful after the performance that she could not get out of the car without help, and had to be assisted up the hotel steps. 'I'll be all right,' she told Bernie. 'A good night's sleep works wonders.'

So it seemed, for she was much brighter next morning. After her usual hearty breakfast she went to the BBC Birmingham studios and recorded a performance with Britten and Pears. She left by train for London the next day, sleeping all the way to Euston.

It was one of the wettest summers Kathleen could remember. She had a performance at the Dome, Brighton, and thought, as the weather was so appalling, that she would treat herself to a hired car for the journey. Passing Mr Wilson, the flats' caretaker, on her way down Frognal, she happily gave him the royal wave.

On 1 August, she wrote to Newmark:

Dearest Johnny, I'm all right, are you? Only sorry I haven't written sooner, but there have been great issues at stake! I'm *terribly* sorry to tell you my doctor thinks I must cancel my whole trip this autumn. I can't tell you how worried I am on your behalf thinking of all the jobs you must have turned down, and getting this off at the first possible moment in the hope that it may not be too late to get others. (Mrs Tillett asked me to wait two days so that Mr Mertens would hear first. I have money returned from excess income tax in the care of Mertens, and can easily ask him to let you have your Decca money from that – will you let me know?) Holland took it out of me rather – after all it's only just over three months since the operation – and – *entre nous*, darling – I have to have more treatment on my back, which is rather uncomfortable around my sciatic nerve, and the doctor feels that if I needed more whilst I was away it is such an intricate business of X-rays and how to apply them, that it can only be done by a radiotherapist who has the complete details of the case. I am enormously disappointed and sorry, and grieved beyond measure that I let you down. I hope I can make up to you for this very quickly and can only repeat how *terribly* sorry I am.

I hope you are feeling really well and fit again – I have a month off now, before Edinburgh, and shall be glad when that is over, as it is a completely new programme – lots of words to remember!

Dearest Johnny – again I must say how terribly sorry I am to let you down and hope with all my heart that it is not *too* great a loss financially. My love to you and many thoughts. Not so Klever Kaff!

She followed this letter up, on 7 August, by one to Benita Cress:

Here it comes, love! I have to cancel my American trip – not because I'm any worse – I hasten to tell you – but because Holland took it out of me, and the doctor feels that so heavy a tour would be asking for trouble so soon. If I needed treatment it can really only be given here, as it is such an intricate business that only a doctor who knows the case could cope. HELL! HELL! HELL! My tour started off with a recital every day and travelling in between, and it just makes me tired to think of it, but I am grieved to the core to miss my buddies there and especially La Crosse, but I think it is wise, and it will be the first long rest I have had in ten years! I know you will understand and try not to be too disappointed, because by this time next year I hope to be bouncing with health. I think it is better to cancel now than to have to give up in the middle, and worry everybody stiff. Poor Mr Mertens – I *am* leading him a dance.

Shortly after Kathleen wrote this letter, Dame Myra Hess came to supper and suggested she accompany Kathleen in some Brahms songs. They had never made music together, and within a short time it became clear to Kathleen that they never could. Dame Myra was a soloist. She surged into the lead, leaving Kathleen no room for interpretation. Within a couple of minutes Kathleen stopped singing and tactfully informed Dame Myra that her playing was so beautiful she could concentrate on nothing else. Laughingly she took the opportunity to firmly close the Steinway lid. They never attempted to perform songs together again.

Another exalted musician arrived at Frognal Mansions a few days later – Bruno Walter. Kathleen was again nervous for his safety when she saw him shuffling up the many front steps but, as before, he made it without mishap. They rehearsed their programme for Edinburgh.

On 31 August, she and Bernie caught the overnight sleeper to Edinburgh, arriving at six-thirty, when they were met by the Maitlands' chauffeur, who drove them to Heriot Row, where they were staying. Kathleen was to give two recitals with Bruno Walter at the Festival, plus a performance with Barbirolli of the Chausson.

Kathleen took every opportunity to rest. She had intended to go to a ballet one afternoon, but at the last moment excused herself with 'Better not, I've got a concert tomorrow.' Bernie went to every event, morning, afternoon and evening. 'You watch you don't get cultural indigestion,' Kathleen warned her.

Her recitals with Bruno Walter were among the most keenly anticipated events of the Festival and had been booked solid for weeks. On 3 September 1951, she and Walter sat together in the green room before making their entrance, 'God will help you,' he told her to steady her nerves, 'but he wouldn't if you hadn't helped yourself.'

'If any two performers could succeed in investing the Usher Hall with the required intimacy, these would be the artists to choose,' noted *The Scotsman*. 'What superlatives can one find to use about Miss Ferrier that have not already been overdone?'

At the champagne and quail reception afterwards, Bruno Walter delightedly confided to Barbirolli that Kathleen's voice was now much lighter and more agile. Barbirolli refrained from saying how substantial a part, in his opinion, the Chausson had played in this improvement.[1]

She was to reappear in the Usher Hall on 7 September, this time with Barbirolli and the Hallé, to perform the Chausson. But on the morning of the performance her back ached so painfully that she could barely dress, even with Bernie's help. Bernie brought her a cup of tea and some codeine tablets and, after a while, she began to feel better. She rallied throughout the day and, that evening, in her Molyneux gown,

[1] *Kathleen Ferrier, A Memoir.*

managed to look a picture of health and elegance.

Although she did not really feel up to it, there was no way she could miss the party after the performance. It was a civic affair and the Lord Provost was the host. But she left as soon as she was able, and after a comfortable night's sleep she was much improved and ready for the first leg of the homeward journey. There were two overnight stops, at Marple and Ilkley, where she was to give recitals.

Gerald Moore was her accompanist in Marple and reduced her to hysterics in the middle of the night, by knocking at her door and entering her room wearing just a shirt, underpants, shoes and a trilby hat and enquiring in a high falsetto, 'Did anyone call?'[1]

Dr Hilton pronounced her 'a walking miracle' when she confessed to him all she had done. She added that she had engagements the following week in Dorchester and Bournemouth and he protested it was too much. 'Don't worry, love,' she reassured him, 'I'll be sensible.'

In Dorchester, she and Bernie were house guests in a mansion on a country estate. They were given a magnificent room, with a leopard skin on the floor. Kathleen put her hat over its face with a shudder, telling Bernie, 'I don't like dead things.' She found the house distinctly chilly, and was glad to get back to Frognal Mansions.

On 24 September 1951, she wrote to Newmark:

Edinburgh went well, though I always find it a terrific strain as I don't get much rehearsal time with Bruno, and I was doing nearly all new things. But there was a crowded house, and a very appreciative one, and I didn't forget me words!! I did the Chausson the next night with Barbirolli and he was 'pickled tink' with my French abandon! Sang some Fauré the other night, so my repertoire grows – Klever Kaff!

I'm so glad you prefer Walter's interpretation – I hate to work with Klemperer. . . . I find he shouts like a madman – (not at me, not bludy likely) – just to try to impress – though why he should think it impresses I can't think. Perhaps his Mahler comes off sometimes, because he wastes no time nor sentiment – but, ohh!!!! whattaman!! I had to share a train journey and many concerts with him when I was feeling proper poorly, and, oh boy, I was glad to arrive in Rome and have all my Swiss francs pinched!! Brrrrr.

It is sweet of you to repeat you have not lost much by losing my tour, and

[1] Bernie's diaries.

it makes me feel a bit better – but I shall miss your lovely, lovely playing more than I can say – and I *do* hope to make it up to you very soon, and sing better than I ever have as well.

Barbirolli came to cook dinner again. They delighted in each other's company and while she sat with him in the kitchen he put on her gingham apron and, with the perpetual cigarette in his mouth, prepared a complicated spaghetti bolognese, banging on the frying pan with a spoon when it was ready.

The long-awaited premiere of 'The Enchantress' took place on 2 October, in Manchester. Bliss and Kathleen travelled north together and, while there, Bliss took her to an exhibition of modern paintings, teasing her that her ideas were old-fashioned and she ought to adopt a more abstract approach in her work. 'She was in a gay, happy mood,' recalled Sir Arthur. 'The same evening, at a party after the concert, she sang to us, almost in a rapt trance, unaccompanied folk songs.'[1]

Ruth Draper was appearing in England at the time and in a letter to Dorothea Draper, dated 14 November 1951, she wrote: '. . . I went to lovely Kathleen Ferrier's. She has had a serious cancer operation . . . but is recovering well. She told me quite calmly and I felt shattered. She is so brave and so beautiful. . . .'

She was back in Manchester, with Barbirolli, on 16 November, for the opening of the restored Free Trade Hall.

The hall had been damaged during the war, and its re-opening was honoured by the presence of Her Majesty the Queen, now the Queen Mother. The *Elizabethan Suite*, arranged by Barbirolli, was played in Her Majesty's honour, but the climax of the evening came when Kathleen sang 'Land of Hope and Glory'. The *Manchester Guardian* noted: 'Lovers of this tune will fear that, never again, can they hope to hear it in such glory.' Barbirolli himself wrote, 'A noble climax which moved everyone, not least the conductor, to tears.'

She stayed with the Barbirollis for a few days, in their Manchester flat. Sir John took her for drives in the beautiful Cheshire countryside but her greatest joy was when they returned and she could bask in the

[1] *The Life of Kathleen Ferrier.*

warmth of the central heating.[1]

Back home, she had to accept the fact that she was still far from well. She was re-examined at University College Hospital and diagnosed to be in need of further radium therapy. For all her courage, the treatment debilitated her. Already exhausted, she dreaded the thought of travelling to concerts through the coming winter months. Reluctantly, she told Emmie she must have a rest, and all professional engagements were cancelled for the rest of the year.

[1] One of Kathleen's rare extravagances was a magnificent Russian ermine coat; its warmth brought her great comfort. When she wore it she told Bernie she felt 'two-hundred percent'. Ermine is not a hard-wearing fur, and someone told her that if she sat on it, it would wear out. This might have happened over a period of years but Kathleen was taking no chances. Bernie had to hold up the coat while Kathleen settled herself, then carefully drape it around her. Her treatment of it obviously paid off for the coat is still in service, worn regularly by Winifred, as is the fox stole donated by Pierre Monteux.

NINETEEN

Offers poured in while she rested. Among them was an invitation from Herbert von Karajan and the directors of the Bayreuth Festival, to sing Brangäne in Wagner's *Tristan und Isolde*. To reinforce Karajan's invitation, Walter Legge wrote to her:

> I have been further asked by Wieland Wagner and Herbert von Karajan to induce you, to cajole you, to talk you into accepting their invitation. If necessary, to kidnap you, abduct you, bribe you, or even blackmail – as if that were possible – so that you can sing Brangäne with them next summer. . . . Ever since Tristan was projected for 1952, it has been our unanimous wish and hope that you should undertake this part, which both vocally and dramatically is perfectly suited to you. Everything that can be done to make the Festival easy and pleasant for you shall be done. If you need help with the polishing of German inflections before you go there Elisabeth [Schwarzkopf] and I are at your entire disposal, and we should be happy if you would stay with us there if it would make life there easier for you.
>
> You have no doubt read what Ernest Newman has had to say about Wieland Wagner's production of *Parsifal* and *The Ring*. This will be his first *Tristan* and, particularly if you take part in it, one of the great operatic events of our epoch. Your colleagues will be Marthe Mödl [Isolde] and Ramon Vinay [Tristan], Karajan conducting.

It is doubtful that Kathleen would have accepted the Bayreuth invitation, even if her health had permitted. *Orfeo ed Euridice* was the only opera which really interested her as a singer, and she felt that her true strength lay on the concert platform and in oratorio, where she could establish an immediate rapport with her audience without having to project a theatrical character. Yet it must be admitted that her friend Burnet Pavitt recalls her telling him that she would, one day, like to sing Brangäne. Furthermore, Alan Blyth has written that, in his opinion, Kathleen was destined for the part of Brangäne, and adds:

Operatically speaking, she had the ideal voice for Erda and for Madam Sosotris [in *Midsummer Marriage*, not written at the time of her death] and it is sad that she did not live to fulfil this side of her potential. Listening to the live *Orfeo* from Amsterdam, as compared to her earlier efforts in that role, we can judge how far she had travelled in experience of the stage, particularly in pointing her words. We have to be grateful for what we have.

She bought a kitten, Rosie, who nearly died of cat flu a week after her arrival, and it was only thanks to Kathleen that she recovered. She spent hours nursing her, and teaching her games like rolling around the room in a paper bag. For a special treat, Rosie was allowed to sit, in the bag, on Kathleen's knees.

Kathleen would sometimes take Bernie to lunch at Casa Prada after her treatment at University College Hospital, and she was happy to oblige when the manager asked for her autograph. She was even happier when he refused to accept payment for the meal in return. The autograph was later embroidered, framed, and hung in the restaurant.

On Sunday mornings, she, Bernie and Winifred would go to Emmie Tillett's for painting sessions, followed by roast beef for lunch. Then, if Kathleen was tired, she would creep upstairs for a nap. Kathleen painted very rapidly. 'Before we'd even picked up our brushes she would have produced a likeness of the subject,' Bernie recalls. 'Every now and then she would have a look at our efforts, "Winnie, you're coming on," or "Now, Bernie, get your nose off the canvas," were typical comments.'

If Bernie had had her way, she would never have allowed Kathleen out of her sight for more than a few minutes. But Kathleen was insistent that she should cultivate friends of her own, encouraging her to bring them to Frognal Mansions for tea. 'It's a bad thing to put all your eggs in one basket,' she told her.

There were certain musical events Kathleen felt she must attend. One such was a production at Covent Garden of *Turandot*, conducted by Barbirolli and starring the distinguished Austrian soprano Gertrud Grob-Prandl. Kathleen marvelled at Madame Grob-Prandl's[1] vocal technique but was amused at the immense figure she presented on

[1] All female singers, when attaining prima-donna status, are accorded the courtesy title of Madame, regardless of nationality.

stage. She was unable to contain her mirth when, hand in hand with Barbirolli, Madame Grob-Prandl took a curtsey and completely obliterated him from view.

An event she attended willingly was the premiere, also at Covent Garden, of Britten's *Billy Budd*. Peter Pears was singing the role of Captain Vere. Emmie had taken a box and invited Kathleen and Bernie to join her. Bernie did not utter a word about the performance afterwards, but Kathleen knew she was bewildered by the unfamiliar music. In the taxi home, after they had parted from Emmie, Kathleen patted her knee and told her, 'It takes all sorts to make the world, love.' 'It seemed to sum up exactly what I was thinking,' recalled Bernie.

When Kathleen heard that a rumour was circulating in America that she was seriously ill, she wrote to Benita: 'There are malicious rumours going round, so will you keep your pretty pink ears open and, don't let on you know me – okeydoke? And don't believe any of the rumours – I'll let you know the truth first thing – and at the moment I'm just full of beans.'

On 30 December she wrote to Benita again:

We had a grand Christmas. Bernie, Win and I went to Mrs Tillett's on Christmas Day, opened presents and gave some, and painted a pheasant, being in the Christmas spirit. Went over to my doctor's for tea, played Lexicon with them, and their daughter and friends, and the first word I achieved was URINE! Klever Kaff! Couldn't miss putting that down no matter how polite the company. Back to our painting and dinner of turkey and plum pud. Bit of orl right.

Bernie and I had a few friends in the next night, including Gerald Moore and his wife, and Roy Henderson, Norman Allin, a wonderful bass singer, now sixty something and a darling, and we opened some tins of meat and salad and I made some wizard mince pies and sponge cake and we had a right good do. Helped along with a glass of champagne – one of the best Christmasses I remember and the end of this year in sight too!

Sir John Barbirolli came up the other evening and brought his cello – and we went through several sonatas and pieces and had a wonderful time – I adore accompanying and he loves playing, so we were very pleased with ourselves.

I start again at the Albert Hall on 7 January . . . and from then on I am very busy. But I have had a wonderful rest and it has been heavenly to be at home for so long.

The same day, Bernie wrote to Benita: 'Kath is brimming over with health and spirits, and it is grand to see her old vitality back again. As I write this we are both in front of a large fire, having eaten a good meal. Kath is busy cracking an inexhaustible supply of nuts and Rosie has her own chair.'

One of the reasons for Kathleen's good spirits was that she had received welcome news from Bruno Walter. He had at last secured release permission from his American recording company in order to record *Das Lied von der Erde*, for Decca. Decca informed Kathleen that the recording would take place in Vienna in the May of 1952.

On New Year's Eve, Kathleen went to a party at the home of publisher Hamish Hamilton, and returned to Frognal Mansions in the small hours of the new year. Bernie was already in bed, but she heard Kathleen come in, and it was obvious she had a man with her. Then, to Bernie's embarrassment, there was a knock on her door. 'Who is it?' she called out. Kathleen came in and told her, 'I've brought you a tall, dark and handsome man to wish you a happy new year.' In strode Sir Malcolm Sargent, in full evening dress, and kissed her on the cheek.

Kathleen resumed her career on 7 January, with *Four Serious Songs*, conducted by Sargent, at the Albert Hall. On 13 January, she was at the Royal Festival Hall for a performance of the Chausson, under the baton of Gaston Poulet. Unfortunately, the wrong orchestral parts were despatched and the music that arrived was keyed for soprano accompaniment, unusable for Kathleen. No alternative orchestral parts could be located so, after conducting the first purely orchestral half of the programme, Monsieur Poulet was obliged to leave the stage and hand over to Gerald Moore who had agreed, literally at the last minute, to deputise at the piano.

From 14 to 30 January, she undertook a gruelling tour of Grimsby, Scarborough, Newcastle, Carlisle, Manchester, Bristol, Nottingham, Birmingham, Liverpool and Skipton. The winter was bitter, and the government was having great difficulty in organising proper supplies of fuel.

For the first half of the tour she was accompanied by Gerald Moore, who travelled with her, but from Manchester onwards he was replaced by Benjamin Britten and Peter Pears, with whom she was to take part in concerts to raise funds for the English Opera Group.

Britten wrote of these concerts in *Kathleen Ferrier, A Memoir*:

The third close artistic association I had with Kathleen Ferrier was perhaps the loveliest of all, a kind of Indian summer. It was in the early days of 1952, the period after her first serious operation, and when we dared to hope that the miracle had happened, that she might possibly be getting well. It was a series of concerts organised for the funds of the English Opera Group – which, after all, she helped to launch by her wonderful Lucretia performances in 1946 and 1947 – to be given in London and the provinces by her, Peter Pears, and myself. It was a programme which we all could enjoy: early English songs, including some of Morley's canzonets, ravishingly sung, some big Schubert lieder, some folk songs, grave and gay, ending up with the comic duet 'The Deaf Woman's Courtship', which Kathleen sang in a feeble, cracked voice, the perfect reply to Peter's magisterial roar. A masterpiece of humour, which had the audience rocking, but never broke the style of the rest of the concert.

To complete the programme I wrote a Canticle for the three of us, a setting of a part of one of the Chester Miracle plays – *Abraham and Isaac*. It was principally a dialogue for contralto (the boy) and tenor (the father), although on occasions the voices joined together to sing the words of God, and there was a little *Envoi* in canon.

We performed this programme in Nottingham, Birmingham, Manchester, Bristol, and Liverpool, a broadcast, and at the Victoria and Albert Museum in London, the happiest of concerts. Everything seemed to go well, with big friendly audiences. *Abraham and Isaac*, when performed with such sincerity and charm, pleased the public. Only in Nottingham was there a cloud, but we did not realize the size of it. Kathleen seemed to trip and slightly wrench her back walking off the platform and she was in pain for some of the time. It turned out to be a recurrence of her terrible illness, but no one suspected anything – or perhaps she did and said nothing.

As soon as Kathleen got back to her Nottingham hotel, she telephoned Bernie to come to her. Bernie left Frognal Mansions immediately, and arrived at Kathleen's hotel in the early hours of the morning, to find her still awake and shivering. She had spread her fur coat over the bed but still could not get warm. The room itself was freezing as the shilling had run out in the gas fire and she could not bear to get out of bed and look for another one. Bernie soon had the fire re-lit and organised extra blankets, and Kathleen managed to sleep.

As was so often the case, Kathleen quickly rallied and, although her back was still sore in the morning, she was able to walk.

Still in pain, and feeling the cold intensely, she travelled with Bernie to Birmingham for her next concert. At the hotel there, Kathleen asked that a coal fire be lit in her room and then bribed the porter to keep it stoked all evening while she was at the theatre, and to leave her a stock of fuel which would see her through the night. Before leaving the next morning she banked up the fire with what coal remained, so that the staff who came to make up the room would have at least one warm place in which to work. After this Bernie was sent home, under protest, as Kathleen assured her she was 'in fine fettle'.

The press had been somewhat cool in its reaction to *Abraham and Isaac* yet, as Britten says in his memoir, it seemed to please the public. Critic Michael Walsh solved the mystery: 'Don't let it fool you, Ben, it's Katie who gets them.'

On 28 January 1952, she wrote to Newmark from the train that was bringing her back to London after a performance in Skipton:

> I have just started work again – with a heavy programme – nine recitals in two weeks – so have been concentrating on those – thereby neglecting you, which is shameful. Have had some with Ben and Peter P -- Ben wrote a new canticle for the two of us on the biblical story of Abraham and Isaac – the ink was still wet for the first performance! But it's a sweet piece – simple and very moving.
>
> It's heaven to be going home! We have been having a very cold spell of frost and snow, and the coal shortage is rather serious, and I haven't been warm for a week. The hotels have been nearly all unheated, but I seem to have weathered it all right.
>
> I have said I am having June, July and August off and don't want to go back on that, as I have already turned down so much work, and I think it is wise to go carefully for this year. I am having Gerald exclusively now to save as much effort as possible and it would be a bit difficult to change over – much as I would adore you to play for me. The only thing might be recording – and I will ask Victor Olof when I see him – I have several dates to record, but all orchestral at the moment.
>
> I still have money of yours – I forget the exact amount as it is in my last year's diary – it's waiting for you any time you can get here.
>
> I have cancelled a trip to France, Switzerland and Germany because it was going to be too heavy (Feb and March) but I am perfectly all right. My

doctor wants me to stay in England as much as possible so that he can keep an eye on me. I go to Vienna in May to record *Das Lied* with Bruno Walter, but shall only be away just over a week. I am feeling fine and very perky, and I am fair, fat and forty (nearly). It would be wonderful to see you here – I just don't want to hold out hope of work and perhaps let you down *again*.

Have quite a few more masterpieces in oil – mostly Stilles Leben, of food and drink! Very photographic and not your style at all – but it *is* fun! Have been accompanying a lot for fun – Barbirolli on his cello, Evelyn, oboe and the doc. on fiddle – heavens!

Hope you are well. I'M FINE! God bless sweetie, Love Kaff.

On 3 February she sang in the first London performance of *Abraham and Isaac*, which took place at the Victoria and Albert Museum. This was followed the next day by a broadcast of the work, and on 8 February she flew to Belfast for a recital.

Upon her return she found the pain in her back unbearable and had to take to her bed for two days. This time her resilience failed her and she had to return to hospital as an outpatient, for a further course of treatment.

She was profoundly distressed when she received the news of the death, from cancer, of cellist Kathleen Moorhouse. Miss Moorhouse had undergone a mastectomy and although Kathleen had done her best to cheer her up, she had suffered deep depression afterwards. When Kathleen heard this news she went for a walk alone through the cold mists of Hampstead Heath. The only relief from the greyness came when she discovered a cluster of crocuses, their brilliant colours stabbing through the frozen earth. She looked at them for a while, and they seemed to bring her strength. Pulling herself together, she decided to do something positive. Leaving the Heath immediately, she went to the High Street and bought a book on gardening, determined to turn the few feet of barren earth at the back of her flat into a garden.

'Does it say how to grow things in concrete?' Bernie asked her sarcastically.

'It won't be concrete by the time I've finished with it,' Kathleen replied. 'You've got to give things a bit of a push to make them happen.'

Despite her back pains, she started work and eventually turned the dusty soil over and installed some bedding plants. The place began to look quite pretty.

In a surge of high spirits one day, as she gardened she burst into a thunderous rendition of 'Like as the Love-Lorn Turtle'. The noise brought out Mr Wilson the caretaker, who thought some louts had broken in.

On 2 March she wrote to Benita:

Haven't sung a note for ages but have been playing chamber music with John Barbirolli and his wife. I tinkle on the joanna. I love accompanying but ordinarily don't have much time.

My doctor still comes regularly, but really so that I will accompany him on his Strad., more than to examine me. I go to the hospital so that they can keep an eye on me and, apart from rheumatiz in my back, feel okeydoke.

I start working again on 25 March, so have a little time yet to be idle. I'm very lazy at heart.

Finishing her course of hospital treatment, Kathleen took Bernie to the theatre to celebrate. They saw Sir John Gielgud in *Much Ado About Nothing*. Later, Gielgud came to visit Kathleen and sat in her rocking chair, which accidentally scratched the paint on the living room wainscoating. She refused to have the paintwork retouched and proudly pointed out Sir John's marks to her visitors.

Kathleen was quite ready to wield a paintbrush herself. She was handy about the house, and could mend fuses, lubricate squeaking doors and fix rattling windows. The workings of the radio intrigued her, and if anything went wrong she would remove the back panel and try to put it right herself. She had a chiming doorbell and was infuriated when the chimes went out of tune. Out came the screwdriver and she adjusted it with the patience of a piano tuner.

She was at the Albert Hall on 30 March 1952, to take part in the *St Matthew Passion*. Despite the snow on the ground, she had a picnic in the park with Bernie, Winifred and Emmie in her lunch break. She was exhausted when she returned to Frognal Mansions that evening but explained that this was due to the twinges brought on by her rheumatism. By April, she said, her pain would have blown away like the March winds. 'I'm just rheumaticky,' she continued, as she tried in vain to untie her shoes, or rise from her chair.

She seemed little better by April, but her spirits had a boost when she received a gratifying letter from Newmark, telling her that their record of *Frauenliebe und Leben* had been awarded the Grand Prix du Disque. She replied to him:

I had no idea about the French award. Upon me soul! I always thought we were a bit of all right. Well, well. If I get a medal and you don't, I shall split it in half with me false denture and send it at once. Then, when I sing flat or you play a wrong note each half will jingle. Heigh ho! How very nice.

I have had six weeks off and have been very lazy. I had to have a bit more treatment on my back, and it's ached like heck this cold weather but is better again now, and I feel fine in misself. Started again last week with Sir Adrian Boult in the Brahms *Alto Rhap*, 'Che Faro' and 'Schlage doch, gewünschte Stunde', and had lovely notices – then the *St Matthew Passion* all day Sunday – a Brahms recital two nights ago on the radio, and on Sunday with the London Symphony Orchestra two newish works – *Four Poems of St Theresa* by Lennox Berkeley and 'The Enchantress' by Sir Arthur Bliss. Then Bernie and I go off to the north for lots of Hallé concerts with Barbirolli which I always adore – *Gerontius* – the *Messiah* and *Das Lied von der Erde*. Lucky Kaff.

On 30 April I have been asked to sing at a little private party for the Queen Mother and Princess Margaret and am tickled pink. They are evidently, and obviously, very sad and heartbroken by the death of the King, and it was suggested by one of their ladies that they had a little 'do' and I am told they have cheered up considerably at the idea – so ain't that nice. I won't have to sing 'Oh I wish I were a fascinating bitch' or anything too sad, but guess I can hit a happy medium. I *am* thrilled, – they're such dears.

Did I tell you Win had changed jobs from teaching to dress designing and is having the time of her life? It has taken twenty years off her, and I have never seen her look so perky. Good for her. I think it takes a lot of courage to give up a steady, pensionable job at her age don't you? I'm so pleased it has turned out so well, and she is getting more money to *learn* the job than she did as a headmistress. Such is life!

Bernie is angelic! She thinks of everything, and I am ruined – oh! I do enjoy it.

Gerald Moore tells me that Fischer-Dieskau is a superb singer – I certainly hope you will play for him e'er long.

It is lovely to know your bank balance is looking healthier – I still have twenty-three pounds five shillings of yours. I can always let you have it through Andre Mertens if you need it.

That's all for now, sweetie. I would let you know if there were any possibility of work here, but I am not very hopeful at the moment. It would be heavenly to see you.

Meanwhile look after yourself – bless you for lovely letters – and God bless.

On 9 April she and Bernie left for Manchester, where Kathleen was to sing in *The Dream of Gerontius* and *Messiah* with the Hallé, under Barbirolli. They stayed with the Barbirollis and Evelyn met them at the station with the car, as Sir John was conducting that night. Barbirolli had prepared a meal for them before his departure, and had left explicit instructions about its heating, adding in his note that all the ladies were to remain in bed the next morning until after he had brought them their breakfasts.

Kathleen seemed frail at the morning rehearsal for *The Dream of Gerontius* and confided to Bernie afterwards that she had a pain in her chest which made breathing difficult. She went to bed after lunch, making Bernie promise not to tell Barbirolli she was unwell. The performance was that night and as the reviewer from the *Daily Despatch* reported: 'Kathleen Ferrier's lovely voice was a joy to listen to.'

Amazingly, Barbirolli had come to *Messiah* late in life, conducting the first performance of his career just four months earlier, on 8 December, 1951. Kathleen had been due to sing in that performance but ill health had forced her to cancel. She had often mentioned to Barbirolli that the modern heavy scoring of 'O Thou That Tellest' prevented her from giving the light phrasing she felt essential for the aria, and that she was forced to 'pump it out'. On examination of the score, Barbirolli had agreed with her and restored the scoring to something nearer the original. And after that first performance Kathleen had written to him: 'I think Mr Handel will revolve in pride and peace tonight instead of whizzing round in bewilderment at the strange things done to his heart's outpouring!'

Both Kathleen and Barbirolli were exhausted at the end of the Manchester performance and Evelyn drove them home. As Kathleen walked to the car she slipped her arm through Barbirolli's and a spasm of pain shot through her chest, making her gasp. At that moment a fan took a snap with his camera. She said nothing to the man, but just muttered to Bernie, 'Every picture tells a story.'

Barbirolli had revived by the end of the journey, and back at the flat, he presented Kathleen with a huge, gold-wrapped Easter egg. He then set about preparing a roast duck for their supper. Kathleen, who was still tired, excused herself until the meal arrived, going to bed with two hot water bottles and a Codeine tablet. She felt better after her nap, and dressed for dinner, which was served by candlelight. To round off the meal, Barbirolli offered his vintage port. 'You do spoil me, love,' Kathleen told him.

Even so, when she returned to London after a couple of days, she left behind a worried Sir John. Winifred was equally concerned and discussed the situation with Bernie. Winifred had been warned that Kathleen would suffer side-effects after her mastectomy, but that had been a year ago and by now these should have diminished. Instead, far from improving, Kathleen's health was clearly deteriorating. Winifred believed that Kathleen should seek another medical opinion, but who best to persuade her? She would undoubtedly be unreceptive to the idea, as she had complete faith in her doctor.

Finally Barbirolli was deputed, and he agreed over the telephone to mention the subject to Kathleen in ten days' time, when she was to return to Manchester to perform *Das Lied von der Erde* with him.

Unfortunately, the waiting weighed so heavily on Bernie's mind, that she could not keep the secret. The result was one of the few occasions when Kathleen lost her temper, and she rounded on Bernie and Winifred, accusing them of interference. Her fury was based on the fear that if she sought a second opinion, Dr Hilton might refuse to continue to treat her. This fear was eventually dispelled and she gave in, consulting Sir Stanford Cade, an eminent surgeon who had had a certain success in the treatment of cancer patients with the administration of a bilateral adrenalectomy. But this was usually only given as a last resort, and Kathleen did not believe she had yet reached that stage.

Another method of treatment which she also investigated, and rejected, was the injection of androgenic hormones. As Dr K. A. Newton, Consultant to the Radiotherapy and Oncology Department of Westminster Hospital, points out 'This would have been totally inappropriate in Miss Ferrier's case, as it may well have altered the timbre and quality of her voice.'

Despite her attempt to restrict knowledge of her illness to friends, by now word had got out and she was inundated with well-meaning, but outlandish, remedies. These varied from a diet exclusively of onion juice to the wearing of certain colours and metals. Ultimately, she accepted the advice of University College Hospital, that further doses of radium would be the most hopeful and positive treatment.

April 22 was Kathleen's fortieth birthday. In order to take her mind off her illness, Barbirolli surprised her with a little party dominated by an enormous and magnificently iced birthday cake. One of his musicians in the Hallé owned a cake shop.

On 30 April 1952, she attended the party given by pianist Franz Osborn (a pupil of Schnabel) for the Queen Mother and Princess Margaret. Kathleen, who was an ardent royalist, was deeply honoured by the invitation. Gerald Moore was also at the party and he accompanied Kathleen while she sang. Normally, no singer would care to follow Kathleen and risk comparison but, displaying enormous spirit, Princess Margaret herself sang next. Kathleen was the first to lead the applause and said afterwards that the Princess was so good she could have earned her living on the stage. At one a.m. Scottish reels were played and Kathleen rounded off the evening by singing 'Annie Laurie'.

Due to the amount of therapy Kathleen now needed, she was worried she might be unable to travel to Vienna on 13 May to record her long-planned *Das Lied von der Erde* with Bruno Walter. She anxiously discussed this with Dr Hilton who, knowing how important the recording was to her, did not even try to dissuade her.

On the eve of Kathleen's departure, Barbirolli conducted her in a concert at the Free Trade Hall which was given in aid of the Hallé Pension Fund. Her programme consisted of the *Alto Rhapsody* and a group of songs which she had arranged herself for voice and string quartet, in which Barbirolli played the cello. They went down so well that two encores had to be given.

Next morning, 13 May, she was at London Airport with Bernie, to catch the plane for Vienna.

TWENTY

Victor Olof met Kathleen at the airport and drove her, through territory that was still Russian-occupied, to the Ambassador Hotel where she was staying. As she passed a group of Russian soldiers she muttered, 'Morning, boys, how are the salt mines?'

The hotel was palatial, and her suite magnificent in gilt and white. There were separate bedrooms for her and Bernie and a bathroom with a huge, sunken bath. A bank of buttons was supplied for the various room services, and she only resisted with difficulty the impulse to press the whole lot at once and see what happened.

As soon as she had unpacked, she told Bernie she was 'going to test the bed', and fell asleep at once. She slept soundly throughout the evening and night.

Rehearsals started the next morning, and it took a long time to balance Kathleen's voice with the orchestra. She had to sing a phrase then wait while this was tested, frequently having to repeat the phrase several times.

Recording started in earnest the following day, and Kathleen was in good form. By the evening, however, her back was troubling her. Olof took her and Bernie to a restaurant, and she delighted in the excellent food. She went to bed that night satisfied with her day's work, but still in pain. But pain was something she had learnt to live with by now.

One afternoon, when she was not needed at the studios, she took Bernie on a trip to Leopoldsburgh, where they had coffee and cakes in a little outdoor café. She told Bernie her pain was like toothache, almost worth having because it was so good when it stopped. The soprano, Hilde Gueden, took them to an early dinner. In Vienna Kathleen never stayed up late. Whatever the diversion, she was always back at the Ambassador for an early night, to be ready to face the rigours of the next day.

'I can still see Kathleen walking into the studio,' remembered Bernie. 'She'd be wearing a navy suit and her sensible shoes. She always gave a wave to the backroom boys, then took off her coat and got down to it. She was happy to do whatever was required and never showed signs of impatience.'

After six days of recording, Bruno Walter and Kathleen gave a morning performance of *Das Lied von der Erde* in Vienna. Just before they walked on to the rostrum, Bernie heard Walter reassuring his anxious soloist, 'No, there is nothing I have to tell you. Except this – don't stand up too soon.'

After the performance, Kathleen had to attend an official lunch at the British Embassy, so Bernie went for a walk. She returned at tea time to find Kathleen waiting for her in the restaurant, at a table laden with cakes and sandwiches, complaining she was starving and that she had not been fed enough at the Embassy.

The following day the tape of *Das Lied von der Erde* was spliced together and the cast assembled for the playback. Walter was calm. Julius Patzak, the tenor, was so still he seemed to be carved out of stone. Kathleen had a look of intense concentration. When the music finished there was a silence which no one seemed willing to break. 'Was it all right?' Kathleen eventually asked Walter. He could not speak, but the expression on his face answered the question.

Although *Das Lied von der Erde* was the major event, it was not the only item on the schedule. 'You haven't seen the last of me yet, boys!' Kathleen called to the engineers as she jubilantly left the studio. 'See you in the morning.' Recording in Vienna was expensive, and Decca was determined to gain as much material as possible from this historic gathering of artists. Three Mahler songs were also to be recorded. All settings of poems by Ruckert, these were 'Ich bin der Welt abhanden gekommen'; 'Ich atmet' einen Lindenduft' and 'Um Mitternacht'.

Kathleen went to bed early as usual, but had a relapse next morning. She usually telephoned Bernie as soon as she woke, and they discussed their breakfast menus together. This morning there was no call. Bernie went to Kathleen's room and found her ashen faced. 'I don't know if I'm going to make it,' she told her. Bernie could do nothing but stand helplessly at the foot of the bed. With a visible effort, Kathleen pulled herself together. In immense pain she clambered from her bed and dressed, sitting silently until her breakfast arrived, which she doggedly ate, convinced it would give her strength to help her through the day.

The first two songs were recorded relatively easily, but there was trouble with the third, 'Um Mitternacht', which was the most difficult of them all. The great crescendo at the end was causing technical problems, and for two hours, while Kathleen constantly repeated the same taxing phrase, the engineers fought to create an acceptable balance between voice and orchestra.

At length, the technical requirements were fulfilled but, by this time, Kathleen showed signs of strain and was dissatisfied with her performance. Time was running out and Olof dreaded that they might have to leave Vienna without a releasable version of the song.

Kathleen tried another take but was still unhappy. A third take had to be abandoned as her voice cracked. Olof called for a coffee break and Kathleen limped to a chair, her face white and drawn.

'I hope it's laced with sugar,' she commented, as Bernie handed her a cup of coffee. After ten minutes Olof called for the session to be resumed and, as Kathleen rose from her chair, she violently twisted her back and fell with a cry of pain. There was utter silence in the studio. Everyone believed this was the end of the session, and she could read the disappointment on the faces around her.

Screwing her eyes with the pain, and with her back hunched, she dragged herself in front of her microphone. Kathleen sang that song as she had never sung it before. Bruno Walter had tears running down his face, but his beat never wavered. The take was an artistic and technical triumph. 'That was hard,' murmured Kathleen as Bernie helped her back to her chair.

Bruno Walter travelled back to Zurich with them the next day. There they both changed planes for their respective flights, he to New York and she back to London. 'Take great care of yourself until I see you again,' she told him. It was their last meeting.

She rested for three days at home, until her next performance, which was in Newcastle, where she was to sing the Chausson with Barbirolli. 'I think the old Chausson's growing a bit now, isn't it?' she wrote to Barbirolli after the performance. 'I enjoyed it really for the first time last week, and now feel I am getting away from a *Messiah*-like sound.' Critic Ernest Bean likened her performance to 'living in sin with Kathleen'.

On 28 May, at the Festival Hall, and with Sargent conducting, she sang Britten's *Spring Symphony*, which *The Times* described as 'glowing with warmth'. But she was anything but warm at a subsequent Festival Hall appearance. Always susceptible to draughts, she felt achingly cold in her sleeveless gown. Seeing a young woman in the audience wearing a shawl, she stepped forward and asked if she could borrow it. The young woman delightedly handed it over and refused to accept its return after the performance.

On 8 June Kathleen wrote to Benita:

> Now I'm free till Edinburgh, 26 August. And it feels wonderful! I'm going to Aldburgh and Cornwall for a month. Whoooopee!
>
> I am feeling heaps better this last month with the warmer weather and the doctor's *very* pleased *mit mir*. But for twelve months, at least, I shan't be leaving this country, so that if I need more treatment I shall be on the spot, and I'm doing so well, it seems potty to overdo it, eh? So I shall work gently here, and give a little less to the government! There's great excitement at No 2 – Bernie's mamma arrived from New Zealand yesterday – by air – her first flight, and came off fresh as a flea – she is just trying to catch up on sleep now – not having had much for four nights – so Bernie's cup is very full – she hasn't seen her for four and a half years – S'long time, ain't it?

It had taken much persuasion on Kathleen's part to get Bernie to accept hospitality for her mother. But Kathleen was insistent, and clinched the argument by buying an extra divan, which she installed in the music room. Bernie could hardly refuse after that.

When Mrs Hammond arrived, Kathleen told her: 'Remember, this is your home for as long as you like. So do what you want.' Mrs Hammond stayed for six months.

Kathleen was in Aldburgh for the annual Festival run by Benjamin Britten and Peter Pears, and she saw a great deal of them.

Britten asked if she would take part in a special performance of *Abraham and Isaac* and, although she was on holiday, she agreed. Britten later recalled, in the BBC radio programme *A Voice is a Person*, 'Although very weak, and probably in considerable pain, she gave a performance of *such* radiance . . . she seemed to know more about Isaac than anyone has ever done, or perhaps, ever will.'

After her two weeks in Aldburgh she made her way to Cornwall for a further fortnight's holiday with Winifred, Bernie and Emmie. The weather was hot and she spent hours on the beach, protected by a sun hat. In the evenings she enjoyed a Pimms in the local pub, where she was sometimes joined by the author, Howard Spring, who lived nearby.

Other neighbours were Phyllis Sellick and Cyril Smith, who also came to visit. To Winifred and Emmie, Kathleen seemed much fitter, but to the Smiths, who had not seen her for a while, the deterioration in her health was frightening. Phyllis Sellick recalls:

> It was like some dreadful harbinger hovering over us. Kath was very brave and kept up appearances, joking and clowning as she always had done. But, now and then, if she thought no one was looking, the mask would drop and her face would become overshadowed. This would be gone in an instant as she recovered herself, and she'd pitch straight into the conversation.
>
> She was determined not to receive special attention for her illness. When we went to the beach together, she would leave early on some pretext. The truth was that the walk to the car park was so taxing for her, she could not make it without several rests on the way, and another rest when she got there. There was no way she wanted to be a burden to her friends.

When the time came to leave, Cyril Smith drove the four women in his Armstrong-Siddeley to Penzance station. Truro was nearer, but as the train started at Penzance, it was usually crowded by the time it got to Truro, and everyone wanted to be sure Kathleen found a seat.

Despite this well-organised plan, when the party arrived at Penzance, it was discovered that one of Kathleen's suitcases had been left at the hotel. Leaving the women at the station, Smith drove as fast as he could back to the hotel, picked up the case and raced to Truro station, just in time to heave it into Kathleen's compartment as the train moved away.

As the good weather seemed to be holding out, she accepted the invitation of some friends to accompany them to Glyndebourne, getting Bernie to pack some sandwiches and a thermos of coffee to contribute to the picnic. Their hostess collected them in a Rolls-Royce, and at supper time a hamper was unloaded by the chauffeur who distributed iced oysters and champagne.

'What's in our sandwiches?' Kathleen quietly asked Bernie.

'Bloater paste,' she replied. 'It was all we had.'

'Better let them rest in peace,' said Kathleen, helping herself to several slices of smoked salmon.

Another invitation she accepted was to spend the weekend at Burnet Pavitt's country home. As she and Bernie were taking their painting equipment with them, Kathleen hired a car and, having been that extravagant, went further and bought a new dress from Marks and Spencer. Winifred was now working at Marks and Spencer, so Kathleen supported the company. The new job was quite a change of direction for Winifred, and she had thought deeply before making the move. Kathleen had encouraged her by telling her, 'I'll always bail you out if anyone gives you the sack.'

While she was enjoying an aperitif in Pavitt's drawing room, two large dogs bounded through the open French windows, closely followed by a young man who turned out to be David Bowes Lyon, brother of the Queen Mother. He lived next door and as his niece, the Queen[1], was dining with him the following evening, he asked Kathleen if she would be gracious enough to sing for her.

'I'm sure the poor love would rather sit with her feet up than listen to me,' Kathleen muttered.

Reassured this was not the case, Kathleen then flew into a panic. She had nothing to wear. Expecting a quiet weekend, she had brought no evening clothes, and her two day dresses were woefully inadequate. So the recently-dismissed hired car was again summoned, and Bernie went back to Hampstead to fetch a suitable gown and a selection of music.

By ten the following evening everyone was ready. 'Are we all booted and spurred?' Kathleen asked. 'Then just aim for the royal standard.' They set off, through the garden and, en route, she bobbed a trial curtsey to a hollyhock.

Kathleen was presented to the Queen, who invited her to sit next to her. After some polite conversation Kathleen asked the Queen what music she would like to hear and it was suggested that, perhaps, some Handel might be nice. Kathleen had not brought any Handel, so the Queen, always tactful, made it clear that she would be pleased to hear anything of Kathleen's choice.

[1] Following the death of George VI, Queen Elizabeth had succeeded although she had not yet been crowned.

With Pavitt accompanying, she sang some Schubert and some folk songs. During the lively 'The Spanish Lady' one of the Queen's corgis leapt at Kathleen and noisily attacked her feet. The Queen stood up in consternation, but Kathleen started to laugh and this brought the recital to a close.

Champagne was served, during which the Queen asked after Kathleen's health. 'Just the odd ache, ma'am,' she replied. 'You have to expect these things.'

TWENTY-ONE

Arriving at Frognal Mansions for lunch one day, Barbirolli brought Kathleen a fish for the meal he intended to cook, and a box of hand-made petits fours. Then, over a glass of sherry, he asked her if she would like to sing in *Orfeo ed Euridice* in a new production, at Covent Garden, which he would conduct. He had persuaded David Webster, then General Administrator of Covent Garden, to mount the new production around Kathleen. This was a bold undertaking on Webster's part, and credit must be given, for he was well aware of the precariousness of Kathleen's health.

She was enraptured by the idea. The new production would be sung in English and retitled *Orpheus*. As Kathleen had only sung the part in Italian (with the exception of the aria 'What Is Life'), she would have to learn the English words. In a flurry of excitement she telephoned the publishers to send her the English version of the score. When it arrived, both she and Barbirolli were disappointed. Compared to the fluidity of the Italian, the English seemed stiff and ugly. They decided to rewrite it themselves. There was plenty of time as the production was not scheduled until February 1953, eight months ahead.

More immediately, she was to appear at the Edinburgh Festival that August, her sixth Festival appearance in succession. She took advantage of one of the few free days before her departure to take Bernie to see *South Pacific*. She viewed such outings as great treats and, as they went to a matinée, she ordered tea to be served in the interval. A cake enthusiast, she was very disappointed when all she got was a single slab of fruit cake. 'We should have come six months ago,' she told Bernie. 'The cake might have been fresh then.' On the way home she hummed the tunes from the show, pronouncing them as 'jolly good'.

Another day was spent ordering new carpet for Frognal Mansions – no mean undertaking as the hall alone was twenty-two yards long, the length of a cricket pitch. It arrived the next day, and so did the bill which was astronomical. As she could never enjoy anything new until she had paid for it, she wrote the cheque at once – only then could she sit back and enjoy the luxury.

On 10 August 1952, she wrote to Newmark:

It has been heavenly having all this time off – the first time in my life – I have even taken to gardening on my coal shed and have one hollyhock, five marigolds and six geraniums! fantastico! I am just warming up gently on mees-mees for Edinburgh in a fortnight's time, but have taken life very easily. Haven't been to the hospital since the middle of July, and it's been lovely to have a rest from it, and to feel well again – fingers crossed!

Bruno Walter was thrilled with the recording of *Das Lied* in Vienna, tenor Patzak – fine! Shall be singing with him again in Edinburgh (Patzak) – *Das Lied* (Concertgebouw, van Beinum), Liebeslieder Waltzes – *wish* you were playing in those – and *Gerontius* and *Messiah* with Barbirolli – so I'm looking forward to it.

It will be heavenly if you are over here next year – so far I am taking the summer months off again tho' I have been asked to do Erda at Bayreuth – but I think it is a wise policy and I pay the government less tax! Tommy Scherman wrote asking me to do two concerts in New York, but it seems a bit daft to go such a long way, much as I would love to.

The folk songs were made last year – I thought 'O Waly, Waly' was awful[1], especially when I did it later with Ben in recital. I'm relieved that you don't mind it.

You are an angel to send me such a heavenly present. Thank you very, very much. I haven't any of the Debussy songs, and I am having a wonderful time staggering through them. Bless you, love.

We were invited for a weekend to a friend's house some weeks ago and the young Queen was staying next door – and we were asked to sing for her – then chatted with her for about half-an-hour on all subjects – sweet poppet, she is. Wasn't that a lucky chance, eh?

She travelled to Edinburgh on 24 August, and stayed with the Maitlands once again. There were four days of rehearsals before her first performance, when she was to sing in *Das Lied von der Erde*. The day after her arrival she wrote to Benita:

I am having a peaceful evening while the family are out at *The Magic Flute*. It

---

[1] It is exquisite. Kathleen was always severe on her own recordings.

gives me a chance to practice and to catch up on some letters. It's a lousy day and it's good to have the curtains drawn against the stormy weather. Our holiday was very good . . . (but) it was rather nice to get home to the slopes of Hampstead again. Since then I have just lazed, and gardened quite a bit on our eight square yards on top of the coal bins!, seen a lot of my buddies, made several Yorkshire puddings with great success and, in fact, just thoroughly enjoyed being a *Hausfrau*. . . . Arrived here yesterday and my first concert, *Das Lied* is on 28th, *Liebeslieder Waltzes* 2nd Sept, *Gerontius* 5th and *Messiah* 6th, so I have plenty to think about. Am just concentrating on work and not going to any concerts or parties. Good girl, eh? Now I am fairly busy till December and must take an interest in singing again. It *does* interfere with my gardening! Had a week of invitations last week – funny how everything comes at once. Bayreuth, Scala, New York and now Stravinsky in Germany, turned them all down – *must* get my bulbs in!!!!

That same evening she wrote to Decca. She was keen to record the *B minor Mass* with Barbirolli, but he was an HMV artist and similar contractual problems had arisen to those which had complicated her work with Bruno Walter. Neither HMV nor Decca relented in this case, and Kathleen and Barbirolli never managed to record together.[1]

The press were unanimous in praise of her Edinburgh performance in *Das Lied von der Erde*. The reporter of the *Inverness Courier* noted, 'A young man beside me cheered vociferously at the end, shouting "bravo" over and over again and I heard him remark that the performance was a miracle.' The *Daily Despatch* stated, 'She is indeed a great singer – with the voice of a generation and intelligence and sensitivity to match.'

For her next Edinburgh appearance she was to sing two Brahms works which were new to her, the *Three Vocal Quartets with Piano* (Opus 40) and the *Liebeslieder Waltzes*. Her fellow artists were the Viennese soprano Irmgard Seefried; Julius Patzak, and Horst Gunter of the Hamburg State Opera, who deputised at the last moment for an indisposed Frederick Dalberg. The pianists were Clifford Curzon and Hans Gal.

The *Waltzes* were the hit of the evening,[2] the audience leaping to its

[1] The record of 'Poème de l'Amour et de la Mer', in which Kathleen is accompanied by Barbirolli is taken from a radio broadcast (Decca 414 095-1).

[2] The performance was recorded and is now available: Decca 417 634-1 (LP) and Decca 417 634-4 (cassette).

feet with shouts of 'bravo' and 'encore' at the end. Audience members on the extreme left of the auditorium had a bonus with a view of Kathleen and Seefried dancing with each other, believing they were out of sight in the wings.

Bernie felt that the *Liebesleider Waltzes* had stirred poignant memories for Kathleen, despite her gay behaviour during the performance and immediately afterwards. When she returned to the Maitlands she 'suddenly looked as if she had fallen from a great height. There was a sadness in her face as she pulled back the curtains and looked into the night. But after a bit, she drew the curtains and came back to the present. "Those were the days," she said, obviously following her train of thought. Then she added, enigmatically, "When we worked nights."' What significance could that, seemingly inexplicable, remark have contained? Perhaps she was simply shrugging off her sadness. That would have been a typical way to do so.

The following evening Kathleen gave a dinner party for the Maitlands. She put a great deal of thought into the menu and visited the manager of the restaurant no less than three times with changes. Barbirolli, who was among the guests would be arriving late as, on the night in question, he would be conducting the *Four Serious Songs*. This time, instead of Kathleen, the soloist was to be a twenty-seven-year-old German baritone who was already causing quite a stir – Dietrich Fischer-Dieskau. Kathleen was to appear with Barbirolli a few days later, in performances of *Messiah* and *The Dream of Gerontius*.

After Kathleen's performance in *Messiah*, *The Scotsman* suggested, 'She should be crowned the Festival Queen that she is.'

Before leaving Edinburgh, Kathleen was approached by Ian Hunter, one of the organisers, who asked her to return for the 1953 Festival. She readily agreed, but refused to sign a contract, telling Hunter she preferred to do this nearer the event, when she could be sure that her health would be up to it.

On the journey southwards, she gave concerts in Hereford, Sale and Carnforth. In Hereford she sang *The Dream of Gerontius*, in Sale she was with the Hallé, under Barbirolli, to sing the *Alto Rhapsody*, and in Carnforth she gave a recital. She enjoyed all of these, despite the linking train journeys during which she was frequently troubled by severe back pain.

On Bernie's birthday, Kathleen took her to dinner at Rules restaurant, Kathleen ordered six portions of vegetables each for them, acting on Dr Hilton's advice that plenty of solid food was good for her. 'We'll be rattling with vitamins,' she said with satisfaction. After the meal they went to see Jimmy Edwards in *London Laughs*.

She undertook a joint recital with Pears and Britten on 5 October, at the Victoria and Albert Museum. The press requested a photograph of the three of them grouped around one of Britten's scores. As no music was to hand, Kathleen took the telephone directory, which looked remarkably like a score when opened, and sang the name 'Smith', to give her mouth the right shape. The photograph was widely used in publicity.

On 21 October she wrote to Newmark:

I am still on me two feet, and apart from rheumatiz, doing very well. Singing here and there, not too much, paying much less income tax! and enjoying a bit of gardening in me spare time. Old age creeping on, eh? I am off to Dublin on Thursday to sing in *The Dream of Gerontius* with the Hallé and my favourite conductor – not Klemperer, but Barbirolli! It's the 100th anniversary of Cardinal Newman, who wrote the poem, and according to the priest, after the performance is over successfully, we're going to have some 'hoi jinks'!

Then on to Manchester to sing *Four Serious Songs* with the Hallé again – Sargent orchestration – then a recital in the new Festival Hall with Gerald – *Frauenliebe* and all sorts and sizes of things. Then *Kindertotenlieder* with Clemens Krauss – should have been Furtwängler but he is ill – and *Das Lied* with Krips – nice concerts, eh?

I had a letter from Paul Frankfurther asking if I had news of you, as he had written several times and had no reply. I didn't say perhaps you didn't *feel* like replying, but that I would write myself, and see if that had any effect! He is at Belsize Park Gardens, just in case you want to drop a line to the old burgher, Frankfurther. Okeydoke?

That October was particularly trying for Kathleen, as she began to get nuisance telephone calls at all hours of the day and night. A series of malicious tricks were also played on her: one evening, for example, just as she was leaving Frognal Mansions to sing at the Albert Hall, six chauffeur-driven Daimler limousines arrived in her name. A woman identifying herself as Bernie had ordered them over the telephone.

The climax came when she returned from a recital one evening to find her door barricaded by a dozen full dustbins. By now she had discovered who the perpetrators were and Gerald Moore, who fortunately was with her and could help remove the bins, persuaded her to take legal action.

A small group of women were responsible for the incidents. Initially fans, they had started calling on Kathleen backstage after performances. At first she had been courteous to them, even inviting them into the green room, but they became more demanding, wishing to take the relationship further. Kathleen always valued her privacy and, in any event, was usually exhausted after a performance. Eventually, she was obliged to bring things to a halt and refused to see them. The women felt snubbed and their spiteful actions were their revenge.

It was during this period of unpleasantness that she made her last recordings, a collection of Bach and Handel arias, in which she was accompanied by the London Philharmonic Orchestra under Sir Adrian Boult.

Bernie remembers Kathleen returning from the first session: 'I heard a taxi stop, and Kath came very slowly up the steps. She almost fell into the hall, bypassed the front room and collapsed on her bed. Not even her usual restorative – a cup of tea – revived her. All her vitality had gone into that recording.'

The Bach and Handel arias were made in mono. By 1960, however, stereo was making an impact on the record-buying public and Decca were inundated with requests for the record, which had always sold well, to be issued in stereo. A conversion process was devised, whereby the original accompaniment was taken out and a new, stereo accompaniment was recorded, the London Philharmonic Orchestra being reassembled with exactly the same combination of instruments as before. The track bearing Kathleen's voice was left untouched.[1] The stereo record was an enormous success, and Sir Adrian described his part in the proceedings as 'a great privilege'.

Towards the end of October, Kathleen had a booking in Antrim. Arriving at her hotel on a wild and rainy evening, she found a group of

[1] Decca SPA 531. These Bach and Handel arias are now available on compact disc but for this version Decca had to revert to the original tapes.

travellers assembled in the lounge, singing round the piano. Not knowing who she was, they asked her if she could sing. Answering she would try, she sang some folk songs, then joined the others in the choruses of their songs. It was not until the next day when the morning post arrived, that they learned of her identity.

At another hotel, where she was staying for a longer period, she was worried that she would disturb the other residents if she practised. The proprietor solved the problem for her by offering the garden shed, where he stored an old piano, as a rehearsal room. He also kept the chicken feed there, and Kathleen used a sack of this as a piano stool. The chickens wandered in and pecked around her feet but they did not interfere with her, nor she with them.

She sang for royalty again on 2 November, this time at a private performance in the morning at the Chapel Royal, Windsor. Her audience included the Queen Mother, the Queen and Princess Margaret. Kathleen sang 'How Lovely Art Thy Dwellings', in which she was joined by the high pure voices of the Windsor Cub Pack. After lunch with the royal party, she was to sing in *Messiah* at Windsor. Great consideration was shown to Kathleen after the meal when it was noticed how tired she was. A chair was placed for her at a discreet distance from the other guests, the royal family came for a brief chat, and then she was left in peace until it was time for the afternoon performance. She much appreciated those quiet moments before singing again.

Her next appearance was the Festival Hall recital, on 4 November, with Gerald Moore. This was very important to her for, although she had appeared at the Festival Hall some half a dozen times, in large works, this was to be her first recital (the Chausson/Moore evening had not been planned). That day she stayed in bed till lunch time, doing the *Daily Telegraph* crossword puzzle, then got up for a steak lunch. After that she returned to bed, telling Bernie, 'No carfuffle now, just wake me at three-thirty.' With that she went to sleep.

The papers were full of praise the next day, with the sole exception of the *Manchester Guardian*, whose critic, Neville Cardus, wrote:

During the *Frauenliebe und Leben* Miss Ferrier allowed distracting extra vocal appeals to interfere with our absorption in an art of song which had no need of anything so likely to breed mannerisms in what is known as 'expressionism'. Poetry is at once dispersed if the singer even unself-consciously takes an audience into her confidence and it came as almost a personal shock to me when this beloved artist, after a devout prelude with 'Seit ich ihn gesehen', an ardent if too familiar 'Er, der Herrlichste' began 'Ich kann's nicht fassen' in a toneless, breath-snatching way obviously directed at our sense of the dramatic, but at the expense of true song.

Miss Ferrier's precious endowment and her natural musical feeling are of themselves, and usually have been so far, capable of transmitting all that a composer has put into his notes. Smiles, or movement of the hand, and swayings of the head should never become habitual with any platform singer; they suggest so many underlinings of points made.

I was vastly relieved when Miss Ferrier was singing 'Du Ring an meinem Finger' with a quite wonderful raptness of musical tone, that she did not look intimately at her hands and show the ring to us. Such glorious singing as she gave us in the 'Schwestern' lyric might have persuaded us that only hyper-criticism would stay to make a note of expression.

Cardus's review of so important an event greatly upset her. There was an outcry in the musical world at his words, and he later defended himself by claiming that much heart-searching had taken place before he had written his critique:

After the concert I walked up and down the Embankment battling with my conscience. The human being in me wanted just to forget everything about the concert except the beautiful singing. The critic pointed out that irrelevancies and artificialities in a platform manner might easily cheapen style if not stopped in time.[1]

Concerned that his review had distressed her, Cardus wrote Kathleen a letter explaining his reasons for making his criticism. Her reply is dated

11 November 1952

My dear Neville,

It was kind of you to write, and I appreciate it very much. I know I use my hands and I am trying to get out of what is an unconscious gesture – one

[1] *Kathleen Ferrier, A Memoir.*

must be told these things, because it must be most irritating. I suppose it's hard to please everybody – for years I've been criticised for being a colourless, monotonous singer – 'this goiterous singer with the contralto hoot' [sic], said the *New Statesman* – so I have plodded on! I adore the *Frauenliebe* and I can see that girl growing up from a child to a woman – and these light songs are all the highlights of joy and sorrow. If someone I adored had just proposed to me, I should be breathless with excitement and unable to keep still; and if I had a child I should hug it till it yelled, so I can't help doing it this way, especially as I usually sing it to English audiences with little, or no knowledge of German. I probably underline more than I ordinarily would the changes of mood.

But I promise you I am never aware of the audience to the extent that I do anything to impress or wake 'em up! . . . I don't think you were 'unkind' – it's just made me think, and that doesn't do anybody any harm.

The general concensus of opinion is that Kathleen was generous in her response to an over-fastidious critic.

Kathleen gave a dinner party after her Festival Hall appearance and this so tired her that she had to spend the next few days in bed. 'Don't worry, I'm not poorly,' she tried to reassure Bernie. 'Just a lazy Kaff.' She blamed her aches on 'that ruddy draught at the Festival Hall.'

But she had to get up for a performance at Archway Hall and, during the interval, she complained to Bernie that her corset was hurting her back. 'Be a love, and let me have yours,' she asked her. So Bernie peeled off her clothes and gave her lighter undergarment to Kathleen. Kathleen's movements were so stiff that it took a long time to help her remove her clothes but when this had been achieved, and Kathleen was sitting down for a few moments to rest before putting on her dress again, there was a knock on the door. Gerald Moore had arrived with a party of friends who wanted to pay their respects.

Modesty was preserved by Bernie calling out that he was to wait outside, and not peep. It took quite a time to get Kathleen back into her dress, and they were not helped when laughter overtook her and she had to sit down again at the thought of the sight that had nearly met Gerald.

Two days later she was due to sing *Kindertotenlieder* at the Albert Hall, under Clemens Krauss. She awoke that morning with a severe pain in her jaw which almost prevented her from opening her mouth. 'I think

I've got tetanus,' she joked as she held a hot water bottle to her face. Bernie urged her to cancel but she would not hear of it.

Despite her discomfort, it seems to have been a brilliant performance. Certainly so in the opinion of the reviewer for the *Daily Express*, who wrote: 'All my life I have waited for this. This is the stuff dreams are made on.'

She returned to the Festival Hall on 23 November, for what turned out to be her last performance of *Das Lied von der Erde*. The London Symphony Orchestra was conducted by Josef Krips and Richard Lewis was the tenor. Later Krips wrote, 'When she sang "Abschied" we all, the orchestra and myself, were in tears.'

Once again Kathleen took to her bed until her next performance. She slept most of the time, with Rosie curled at her feet, and when she was awake she was studying the score of *Orpheus*.

Bernie could not bear to see Kathleen so ill and broke down in tears one morning. Kathleen would not permit that. 'Stop it,' she ordered. 'I'm all right today, and that's all that matters.' From then on Bernie sometimes cried in the privacy of her room, but she never again allowed herself to cry in front of Kathleen.

On 6 December, against everyone's better judgment, Kathleen left for a tour of *Messiah* in the Lake District. She was staying with Ena Mitchell, who was the soprano. In addition to *Messiah*, she was giving a recital in Carlisle, and the demand for seats was so overwhelming that hundreds were turned away disappointed.

With Bernie at her side, Kathleen limped around Carlisle, mainly to look at the antique shops. Bernie could not avoid noticing that the limp was getting worse. Risking Kathleen's wrath, she timidly suggested Kathleen seek the advice of a specialist when she returned to London. Kathleen dismissed the subject as 'too boring', but admitted her leg pained her. 'Why did it have to happen *now*, just when I'm going to do *Orpheus*?' she burst out. There was no answer to that.

Before Kathleen left, Ena arranged a farewell party for her. Her husband, Jack, proposed a toast to 'The same old Kath', and received the hoary response, 'Not so much of the "old"'. Kathleen then led the singing with an old music hall song, which contained the lyric 'We ain't

---

[1] 18 November 1952.

got much money, but we sure have fun'.

Britain was covered with snow as Kathleen travelled by train back to London. She wore her heavy travelling overcoat, under which was a thick dress that Winifred had made for her out of fleecy, woollen material; this had the advantage of a stole, which she could wrap right round herself.

A huge pile of Christmas cards awaited her when she opened the door to Frognal Mansions, plus some welcome food parcels from America. On 16 December, she wrote to Benita:

> I am still rheumaticky from the neck down. Makes me feel my age, ducks, so I am staying quietly by the fire and going to bed in the afternoons like an old lady.
>
> But I'm happy as a lark, specially as two weeks ago – can you keep it dead secret until New Year's Day – I had a letter from the Prime Minister asking if I would be willing to receive the honour of the CBE – if the Queen sanctioned it? Can a duck swim? I can't believe it can be true because these honours usually come after ninety years of singing, or some such. So, perhaps it won't come off, but won't it be exciting looking in the Honours' List on New Year's morning, eh?
>
> I haven't much work until I do *Orpheus* at Covent Garden in February. Have specially kept these bad travelling months free, and it's gorgeous to be home. Have one or two broadcasts, and the Christmas broadcast *Messiah*, but that's all.

The Christmas *Messiah* took place on 23 December and was to be the last time she appeared in Handel's great oratorio. She had served Handel well, and that particular broadcast has been described as 'quite wonderful'.

Christmas Day was spent at Emmie Tilletts, but Kathleen was as eager as a child for New Year's Day to arrive, when she would be officially created Commander of the British Empire. In anticipation of this, Barbirolli gave her a party on New Year's Eve. At the stroke of midnight he formally toasted Kathleen's elevation. It was a tired, but very elated CBE who slipped into bed that night.

A press photographer woke her at nine the next morning. Hastily preparing for him, she was glad he had got her up as she was giving her own New Year's party that evening, and had a lot to do. Her guests included Winifred, the Barbirollis, the Norman Allins, the Gerald Moores, the Hamish Hamilton's, the Maitlands, and old Lancastrian friends, Sir Benjamin and Lady Ormerod.

As the Frognal dining room could not possibly accommodate all these people, Kathleen hired a trestle table and converted her sitting room into a dining room for the evening. She wanted to provide a memorable meal, and planned to start the proceedings with smoked salmon. By six pm everything was ready, the salmon on its dish, garnished with parsley and surrounded by thinly-cut brown bread. She and Bernie gratefully sipped gin and tonic while awaiting their guests. Then, luckily, Bernie remembered she had not put out the pepper mill, for when she went into the converted dining room to do so she found Rosie on the table, paws in the smoked salmon dish, greedily munching.

Bernie's scream brought Kathleen who stood in the doorway with her hand over her mouth, appalled. Then her practical nature came to the rescue. 'Our Rosie's very clean,' she said, briskly rearranging the remainder of the salmon with a fork. 'We can't waste that food, it was 25/– a pound.' Kathleen did not keep many secrets from Barbirolli, but that was one.

TWENTY-TWO

The beginning of 1953 was mostly taken up with rehearsals for *Orpheus*, and these intensified as the opening night, 3 February, approached.

When she was not rehearsing, Kathleen spent most of her time resting in bed. She had learnt the role while lying in bed, making it a rule that she would learn twelve pages each morning as soon as she was awake. Bernie had strict instructions not to bring her even so much as a cup of tea until she had completed her quota. On rehearsal days Bernie would help her down the icy steps of Frognal Mansions and into a taxi. Merely to walk was now a difficulty.

Rehearsals started at about ten in the morning. 'Kath usually stayed in bed until the last moment,' Bernie says, 'and then the struggle began. Once dressed she then had to get down very steep steps and over frosty, slippery concrete and into the car. Pain in her legs and back made this difficult for her. At the other end the struggle was the same, and I am thankful it was not seen by people other than Sir John, for it would have broken their hearts. Sometimes Sir John came home with her, but he felt as I did that to appear at all upset was letting Kath down. However, as soon as she got on the stage an amazing thing happened – I always found it very hard to believe – she was able to move about as if she had never in her life had a pain or an ache.'

On 16 January she wrote to Benita:

> I'm writing this in bed, it being the most comfortable place, we've been having filthy weather and the slightest cold sets off me screwmatics. I think I must hibernate next winter. I am praying my aches will clear up and that I shan't have to limp through *Orpheus* because it looks as though it should be a lovely production. So keep your fingers crossed for me, won't you?
>
> My sister, uncle and I go to Buckingham Palace on 17 February for my decoration, and are all thrilled. I hope I can manage to curtsey.

Barbirolli was determined that Kathleen's *Orpheus* would be the finest ever produced, and he had secured the best possible production talent. The scenery and costumes were designed by Sophie Fedorovitch, and the producer-choreographer was Frederick Ashton, with the Sadler's Wells Company providing the ballet sequences. 'How on earth am I going to have the nerve to put my big feet amongst all those lovely girls?' Kathleen groaned when she saw them rehearsing. Sopranos Adele Leigh and Veronica Dunne sang Amor and Euridice.

Kathleen was lost in admiration for the artistry of Sadler's Wells' principal dancer, Svetlana Beriosova. So was Barbirolli, who came to Kathleen during an orchestral break, ascending the staircase in ecstasy, exclaiming 'Perfecto, perfecto!' He was so excited that he mistook his footing and tripped up the last four steps.

Sir Frederick Ashton recalled Kathleen's immense courage at rehearsals: 'She was terribly jolly throughout, and absolutely determined to do it. There was one terrible occasion when she got knocked down by the stage curtains. Those curtains are lead weighted and it was serious, everyone was worried. But she got up as though nothing had happened. There was never any fuss with her, she wasn't a bit like a prima-donna.'

Kathleen now visited the hospital daily and the treatment eased her pain: 'It's nice to have eine kleine pause,' she told her radiologist Gwen Hilton as she lay on the treatment table, about to be bombarded with radium. Fearing that her health might not last out the four performances, Barbirolli rang Dr Reggie Hilton, but the doctor could guarantee nothing. To have cancelled the production would have broken Kathleen's heart, so Barbirolli could only agree to continue and pray for the best.

Kathleen consulted laryngologist James Ivor Griffiths, about the effects of an oophorechtomy:[1]

'She asked my opinion about this operation with two points in mind,' states Griffiths, 'with regards to the effect on the general cancer and the effect on her voice. I told her that the long-term effect on the cancer would be negligible but that the effect on her voice might be disastrous. I had quite a bit of experience of the effects of hormones on the voice and I told her that it would at least alter the character of the voice. She

[1] An operation for the removal of the ovaries. It was thought (or hoped) that the removal of the ovarian hormones would inhibit the growth of breast cancer.

said she regarded her voice as a divine gift and would go to the grave with the voice as it had been given her. She had this overpowering desire to sing in *Orpheus* and said that she would go ahead. I then had a consultation with Sir John Barbirolli and Sir David Webster and I told them that I was doubtful whether she could complete the four performances. However, we decided to let her carry on.'

Friends still called regularly, and some brought little gifts. Elsie Suddaby always brought her some cream from the country, where she had a home. An admirer sent her a case of one-third-sized bottles of champagne, just enough for two glasses. She and Bernie would sip it at mid-day. 'Aren't we a couple of devils,' Kathleen would say to her.

Once, a friend called while she was sleeping, and went immediately away. When Bernie told her, she came in for a reprimand, 'I want to see *everyone*,' Kathleen told her. And Bernie had instructions to wake her if any other friends called in the future while she was asleep.

On the morning of the dress rehearsal, Kathleen wore the completed costume of Orpheus for the first time. Sophie Fedorovitch had designed a simple blue tunic with a white floating panel; the effect was both youthful and elegant.

A dress rehearsal is usually fraught with problems, but *Orpheus* seemed remarkably smooth-running. There was only one difficult moment, and this was during the Flames of Hell scene, when the fog gun, which created the swirls of sulphurous fog around Kathleen's feet, made so much noise that she was unable to hear the orchestra and lost her place. But the gun was soon more tactfully positioned.

Ruth Draper had been at the rehearsal, and wrote home:

Her voice is sublime, and her looks so beautiful. She suffers terrible lameness, she says, from rheumatism in her hips, but those who know the hideous fear that hangs over her are deeply anxious it may be something worse. She is superbly courageous, and her voice is more rich and beautiful than ever – and heart-breaking too.

The rehearsal finished at five pm, and Kathleen slept in the car on the way home. There was a two-day break before the first night and she spent this resting, only leaving the flat for treatment at University College Hospital.

She ate a good steak lunch on the day of the performance, and followed this by two hard-boiled eggs for tea. The food had to sustain her as she would not be eating again until nearly midnight.

The taxi which was to take her to the Opera House arrived at six pm and, helped by Bernie, she made her torturous descent of the steps of Frognal Mansions. At the theatre, she presented both Adele Leigh and Veronica Dunne good luck presents of Arpège perfume.

The performance went without a hitch. Critics were unanimous in praise of Kathleen:

Kathleen Ferrier's Orpheus is a wonderful achievement.

Observer

Certain passages touched the sublime.

Manchester Guardian

Her Orpheus confers unusual distinction on the current repertory.

Sunday Times

Kathleen Ferrier, an Orpheus whom, for dignity and nobility, it would be hard to match in the world.

New Statesman and Nation

A feature, by Richard Buckle in the *Observer* brought her particular pleasure. In it, he commented: 'None of the dancers moves with more expressive simplicity than Kathleen Ferrier, whose physical as well as vocal impersonation of Apollo's child is something I shall long remember.' If not her acting, then at least her stage movements, had been praised. It was a breakthrough.

The second performance of *Orpheus* was on 6 February, and she awoke that morning with a presentiment of disaster. 'I'm not going to make it,' she blurted out when Bernie brought her in her tea. The presentiment did not lessen throughout the day. 'She left for the theatre as if she were going to her own execution,' Bernie remembered. 'I only saw a small portion of the agony she was going through, for she maintained complete control of herself, but the weight of this premonition was just too much for her. I shudder, even now, to think of that day.'

At the theatre she was composed, but unusually sombre. 'Once you get started, you'll be all right,' Bernie tried to reassure her. 'You always are.' Kathleen did not answer. Frederick Ashton came to see if there was anything he could do, but she shook her head, thanking him for taking the trouble to ask and apologising for being a nuisance. Bernie wanted to stay in the wings during the performance in case she was needed, but Kathleen would not hear of it and pushed her towards the auditorium, telling her to enjoy herself.

Her voice was as glorious as ever, and it seemed at the interval that her presentiment had been groundless. In the second act, however, her fears were realised. As she went to move a searing pain lacerated her left thigh and the leg ceased to function, preventing her from moving to her correct stage position. She leant against some scenery and sang from there. Barbirolli knew at once that something terrible had happened, and went through his own personal torture in the pit, unable to help.

Adele Leigh was equally helpless. In her role of Amor, she was positioned on a platform suspended above the stage: 'It was one of the most awful evenings of my life,' she recalled. 'I could see something was dreadfully wrong with Kathleen, but I was unable to get to her to help, or do anything but pray.'

Veronica Dunne was able to be of more practical use. Disregarding her stage instructions, she went to Kathleen: 'I stood next to her, and while the orchestra was playing, she said to me, "Veronica, I can't stand the pain." I put out my hand, palm upwards, in the classical Greek manner, and she took it. By supporting her like that she was able to drag her leg along, and I helped her from the stage.'

While this real-life tragedy was taking place, the audience had no idea that anything was amiss. That seasoned professional, Dame Eva Turner, was watching the performance: 'There was no hint of any catastrophe,' she stated. 'We were just mesmerised by her beautiful singing.'

The opera, however, had not yet finished and there was still more for Kathleen to sing. She sat in the wings, but the pain made her vomit. When there was no option other than she miss her cue or continue to sing, she forced herself on to the stage for her closing music.

'All I could do was stand back, amazed,' said Veronica Dunne. 'Like the rest of us, I hadn't realised how ill she was until then. She had never mentioned it.'

James Ivor Griffiths had been standing in the wings, and continued: 'The moment the opera was over she practically collapsed, suffering agony. I gave her an injection of morphia and she recovered and returned to the stage to the tumultuous applause of the audience. Seeing Kathleen performing this extraordinary opera was one of the most poignant experiences I myself, as a doctor, ever had.'

Her dressing room was full of visitors who, not knowing how unwell she was, had come to offer congratulations. She chatted to everyone, and not until the last guest had gone did she ask Winifred, 'Get me a stretcher.'

Winifred wanted to take her straight to hospital but was over-ridden by Barbirolli who thought it best to get her home, where Bernie made her as comfortable as possible with hot water bottles and the electric blanket.

A portable X-ray machine was brought to Frognal Mansions next day, which revealed that Kathleen's femur had partially disintegrated and that a portion of bone had actually broken away from the shaft; accounting for the agonising stab of pain she had felt when on stage.

Immediate medical treatment was essential, and she was taken to University College Hospital. Once there, she was installed in her old room and welcomed by Sister Rhona Phillips, who had nursed her after her mastectomy. She told Bernie that her single ambition was to resume her career as soon as possible.

On 22 February, Ruth Draper wrote to Dorothea Draper:

I went to see Kathleen Ferrier this morning; she's in the hospital taking daily radio therapy. It's a terrifying outlook, but she is responding well, and her general health is fine, and her voice superb, but she had to cancel two of the four Orpheus performances and lots of concerts. She hopes to be at work again at Easter time. They 'call it' arthritis – but it's not – but one tries to keep the public from knowing. I got her a lovely wrapper, Shetland jacket, and shawl and bed cover, and she looked too beautiful – with flowers everywhere and she cheerful and sanguine and calm in her own mind. Perhaps it can be arrested – it was in her back, and that's stopped, now in her hip, and it's improved already.

The remaining performances of *Orpheus* were rescheduled for April, when Kathleen felt she would be sufficiently recovered to sing them. As the production had been specially mounted around her there had been no understudy.

On 27 February she wrote to Newmark from hospital.

For the first time I really felt it had been done as I could have wished with a most lovely ballet and fine chorus and, between you and me, I wasn't so bad meself!!

The first night was a wow and the very elegant audience shouted their heads off at the end. The second night was also going fine until I snipped a bit of bone in my hip during the second act and had to limp for the rest of the evening. It was an experience I don't ever want to have to repeat.

I could not walk the next day and had to be carried down our stairs at great risk to my life – do you remember our stairs? – by two perspiring, hefty, ambulancemen. And here I am in UCH once more, furious at letting Covent Garden down, furious at missing my investiture, but counting my blessings that I am in wonderful hands, with Bernie here to nurse me. Sir John's niece is also here, doing all my letters in shorthand for me, and I'm being thoroughly spoiled by everyone, but ain't it a budder? – I'm getting better each day but will probably be here another four or five weeks.

Much love to all my buddies, and passionate, lascivious love to you. Kaff.

On the same day she wrote to Benita:

... I don't feel a bit poorly, but I am not allowed, as yet, to stand on my legs, but I hope I'll be all right for some more performances [later]. I had to miss going to Buckingham Palace, but have heard a whisper that I may be pushed into one of these summer investitures. I do hope so, because I've got a new hat and coat!

As Kathleen had been forced to miss her investiture, Benjamin Ormerod brought her a piece of ribbon in CBE colours, and this was proudly pinned to her pillow. 'Swanking again,' Dame Eva Turner told her on one visit.

Bernie arrived each morning at eight thirty with the mail, and insisted on cooking Kathleen's breakfast herself in the little kitchen off the main ward. One of the letters which Bernie brought contained an offer from the cellist, Pablo Casals, for Kathleen to sing in the Casals Festival the following July. Very reluctantly this had to be turned down as she was committed to sing with Barbirolli and the Hallé that summer, on a tour of Rhodesia.[1]

In hospital, Kathleen had come to the sad conclusion that her leg would never again be completely sound, and that she would have to move from Frognal Mansions as the steps to the front door would now be too much for her.

Winifred and Bernie set about looking for alternative accommodation and came up with a flat in St John's Wood. 40 Hamilton Terrace, NW8, had a ground floor, containing a living room, bedroom and bathroom, and there were a further two bedrooms upstairs. Plans of its layout were drawn up for Kathleen, who was so excited she could not wait until she was discharged to view it. She inveigled a day's leave of absence from the hospital, on the proviso she hired an ambulance, and with Sister Phillips and her physiotherapist, Molly Turner looking after her, and seated in a wheelchair, she made the journey to her new home. The two ambulancemen said that never before had they heard such laughter in an ambulance.

It was a rainy day and the flat had been unoccupied for months, so she was seeing it in the worst possible circumstances. Nevertheless, she thought it ideal. And later, propped up in her hospital bed, with the sample books about her, she spent hours selecting wallpapers and furnishing fabrics.

On 14 March, the flat was legally hers and a few days later the removal van arrived at Frognal Mansions. Under Winifred's fierce eye the removal men carefully packed Kathleen's belongings. Winifred left with the van, and Bernie followed, with an indignant Rosie, in a taxi. They bade an affectionate goodbye to Mr Wilson on the way out.

That evening, Bernie gave a progress report to the anxious Kathleen. Assured that her possessions were safe, Kathleen then enquired, 'And what about my "Pink Pearl"?' The 'Pink Pearl' was a beloved rhododendron which Kathleen had planted in her garden at Frognal Mansions, and upon which she lavished attention. Bernie shame-

---

[1] Despite her resolution not to appear during the summer months (and her doctor's request that she stay in Britain), she had optimistically accepted the Rhodesian tour out of respect, and loyalty, to Barbirolli. The offer had been made before Barbirolli was fully aware of the severity of her illness.

facedly admitted she had forgotten all about it, but promised to retrieve it first thing in the morning. Armed with a spade and a sack she transported the plant to Hamilton Terrace, where it awaited the return of its owner.

The garden was wildly overgrown. In contrast to the freshly decorated flat, it looked like a jungle. Ruth Draper took matters in hand. As a house-warming present to Kathleen she hired four gardeners to clear the debris, turn the earth, instal bedding plants and mow the lawn. She further arranged that a gardner should call each week, at her expense, to keep it in order.

On 3 April, she wrote:
Dearest Benita,

I'm still in hospital but leaving in the morning – whoopee, whoopee – and going to a new home which, Bernie tells me, is looking lovely. I should have gone three days ago but caught a bug from somewhere and a temperature and a very greasy stomach, so had to stay – I was furious! Well, I'm quite all right now and looking forward to the morning. My legs are much better and I can take a few steps, but not too many, and for the moment will be whizzing round in a wheelchair.

On 4 April, the staff at UCH lined the corridor to say goodbye. Kathleen shook hands with each one and kissed most of them as well. Then, in a welter of suitcases, flowers and good luck gifts, she took the lift to the ground floor and her waiting taxi.

Winifred was waiting for her outside the flat, and handed Kathleen the front door key to open up for herself. As soon as she had done this she stood in the doorway with her eyes closed. 'I'm just making the excitement last', she said. 'I know it's going to be one of the biggest thrills of my life.'

The weather was glorious, and when she opened her eyes she saw the sun streaming through the French windows into the lounge. The garden looked magnificent and she spent most of that first day sitting in the sun, commenting on the wonderfully fresh air; in fact, she was not more than a mile from the Edgware Road. There were two sheds at the bottom of the garden, which she decided to call the tool house and the summer house.

She was able to take a few steps each day but spent most of the time in her wheelchair or, as the weather continued sunny, in her beautifully upholstered garden seat put there by her friends to welcome her back. She even achieved a mild tan. Every morning Bernie would wheel her from bedroom to bathroom and help her wash. As she was receiving home treatment for her leg most evenings, this prevented her taking a bath.

The Rhodesian tour had to be cancelled, as had her hoped-for *Orpheus* appearances, but she was anticipating resuming her career that September at the Edinburgh Festival.

On 5 April she was well enough to entertain a few friends for tea, and Ruth Draper, John Gielgud and the Hamish Hamiltons were there. Gielgud later wrote of the occasion in a Foreword to *The Letters of Ruth Draper*,[1] 'We all tried to behave quite naturally, talking and laughing as best we could, while Miss Ferrier, radiantly beautiful as she sat up to greet us, in a little pink jacket edged with white fur, held Ruth's hand and waved gallantly to us all as we bade her farewell.'

On 29 April, Bernie wrote to Benita:

Kath has gone ahead in leaps and bounds since she came out of hospital a month ago. And is now up and dressed and getting about entirely under her own steam. Has even made some very good sponge cakes. She is her usual bright, cheery self and we have a steady stream of people coming who all admit they come to be cheered up.

Kathleen would proudly tell visitors that her next door neighbour was none other than the famous soprano Maggie Teyte. Sometimes she added a little bob of the head when she mentioned Dame Maggie's name. One morning, she noticed an open window next door, and a ladder leaning against the wall near it. It looked suspiciously as though Dame Maggie had been visited by burglars. Bernie knocked at the door and could get no reply and she and Kathleen were worried some harm might have befallen her, so they rang for the police.

Two constables arrived almost immediately and, as they could gain no reply to their knocks either, they went round to the back of the house and tried knocking there. Finally, the more agile of the two mounted the ladder, climbed on to the roof and looked in through a skylight. There,

[1] Pub. Hamish Hamilton.

confronting him, was Dame Maggie, sitting in her bath, the radio playing, blithely unaware of the havoc outside. She had a dreadful shock when she saw the policeman peering down at her.

When all had been explained, however, she saw the funny side. She had employed a decorator who had left his ladder behind, to be collected later. The window was open to allow the fumes from the paint to escape.

During this enforced rest period Kathleen spent much of the time painting. She would proudly show her 'opuses' to her physiotherapist, Molly Turner, who came in the evenings. She even bought Miss Turner a set of paints to encourage her to start. Hearing of Kathleen's hobby, a charity asked if she would donate one of her paintings for auction. She gladly complied and was sent a copy of the catalogue. Her painting was listed under the heading Gifted Amateurs.

On her birthday Kathleen invited the Barbirollis to dinner. Mémé, Barbirolli's mother, prepared the food, and Sir John delivered it, together with several bottles of wine, and he also brought Kathleen's birthday present. When he had asked her what she would like she had replied a diamond tiara, and when she unwrapped her gift she found one glinting up at her – made from paste.

A few days after this, Kathleen casually mentioned to Bernie that she was going to treat her to a new bedspread, as she thought the existing one did not go with her bedroom carpet. The full implication of this did not register with Bernie at first, then it hit her. Bernie's bedroom was upstairs: if Kathleen had seen the bedspread then she had obviously climbed the stairs. It seemed she was getting better every day.

She felt strong enough to accept an invitation to dinner from Hamish Hamilton who lived nearby. The guest of honour was to be Princess Margaret. This would be the first time Kathleen had left the flat since moving in, and she was looking forward to the occasion.

Burnet Pavitt came to collect her, and drove her the few yards to Hamilton's home. For the first hour, Kathleen was in good form, convincing everyone that she was getting well and then, quite suddenly, her conversation dried up and she became quiet. In panic, she whispered to Pavitt, 'I'm going to be sick,' and he helped her to the bathroom. She was overcome with nausea and weakness, and Pavitt had to take her home, where Bernie put her to bed. 'I lost my dinner,' she told her. 'Poor Yvonne [Mrs Hamilton], what a washout I was to her tonight.'

The nausea attacks continued, but Kathleen was still determined to resume her career, and anxious that the public should not regard her as having retired. On 23 May 1953, the *West Somerset Free Press* published the following retraction:

> In our issue . . . for the 25 April 1953, in the course of a critique of a concert given by the Minehead Choral Society we referred to Miss Kathleen Ferrier, who was a soloist in a similar concert some years ago. It was inadvertantly stated that illness had ended Miss Ferrier's brilliant career and her golden voice. We are now informed that although Miss Ferrier has been ill her incapacity is purely temporary and will in no way affect her return to professional activity.

Yet, on 17 May Ruth Draper had written to Dorothea: 'My heart is heavy over lovely Kathleen. Her beauty and goodness and marvellous voice all to be sacrificed to this evil thing. She's so brave and keeps cheerful – and one only hopes for a miracle. They continue to try and hide the truth but all who love her know.'

For all her bravado, Kathleen was in fact losing ground. It seemed her recovery had peaked and she was now on a downward curve; she felt weak all the time, and was often unable to get out of bed. Sometimes she would make a valiant effort and struggle into her wheelchair, and Bernie would push her into the garden. Determined to be useful, she once mixed a cake from her bed.

She went to University College Hospital for an X-ray examination and, back home, burst into tears, convinced the news would be bad. The results came a few days later; she was to be re-admitted to hospital on 22 May for further treatment. She had been in her new home just seven weeks.

On the evening of 21 May, while Kathleen was sleeping, Winifred was in the lounge writing letters and Bernie was sitting in the garden. Unexpectedly, through the still air, came the sound of Kathleen's voice, singing 'Abschied' from *Das Lied von der Erde*.

Winifred rushed into the garden, and she and Bernie stood, motionless, listening. Kathleen's record of *Das Lied von der Erde* had been released that day, and was being played on the gramophone by Alan Blyth, who lived nearby. 'I found no pleasure in it,' states Bernie, 'only unbearable sadness and a feeling of finality. I threw myself into Win's arms and sobbed.'

TWENTY-THREE

Now, once again, Kathleen was back in her old room at UCH, with Rhona Phillips looking after her. Her condition deteriorated rapidly and by 2 June she was so ill it was thought she might not last the night.

But she rallied to such an extent that it was thought worthwhile to operate on her. 'Dr Eccles told me I must lose me ovaries', is the simple entry in her diary. 'Nae bother at all,' she said to Bernie. Kathleen did not tell Winifred about the operation for fear of upsetting her sister. Winifred simply thought Kathleen was having another difficult day when she was told she could not see her.

Strength gradually returned after the operation. She was a good patient, and obeyed her doctor's instructions, eating well and drinking pints of liquid.

The coronation of Queen Elizabeth took place while she was recuperating, and she hired a television set to watch the ceremony. Bernie was told to wake her should she nod off, as she did not want to miss one minute of it.

Pain still racked her at times, and she had to cancel the Edinburgh Festival performance where she had been due to appear, once again, with Bruno Walter. This was a bitter disappointment. On learning of the cancellation Bruno Walter wrote to Kathleen:

> I am sure you will realise the pain my heart feels, and I want you to know that I think of you daily with the deepest affection. Our last common work, the records of Mahler songs and *Das Lied von der Erde* belong in my mind to the most beautiful musical events of our time, and whoever hears them must respond with an upsurge of admiration and love for you.

A few days later the *Daily Telegraph* carried the announcement: 'As Dr Walter does not feel able to pick any substitute for Miss Ferrier, the recital has been cancelled.'

The cancellation was not altogether a surprise to Emmie Tillett.

Realising that Kathleen could not live much longer, she proposed to the Royal Philharmonic Society that it should award its Gold Medal to Kathleen with all possible expediency. The RPS Gold Medal is one of the highest honours that can be bestowed on a musician; previous recipients have included Gounod, Brahms, Paderewski, Kreisler, Casals, Henry Wood, Delius, Elgar, Beecham, Vaughan Williams, Rachmaninov, Sibelius, Richard Strauss, Prokofiev and Barbirolli.

At the next RPS committee meeting the proposal was unanimously accepted, and was publicly announced immediately afterwards. David Ritson-Smith, of the RPS, came to the hospital to present the award personally, but Kathleen had had a relapse so he left it with Bernie, who gave it to her when she felt better. 'Would you convey to the Committee of Management' she wrote, 'my humble and deeply grateful thanks for offering me the award. . . . I accept with a very full heart and a real knowledge of the supreme honour you do me.'

When Kathleen had consulted Sir Stanford Cade a year ago, he had mentioned the possibility of a 'last resort' operation. This was a bilateral adrenalectomy, a relatively new operation at the time, for the control of the endocrine milieu, important in many patients with breast cancer. By now Kathleen's cancer had metastasised to the skeleton, and she felt she had nothing to lose by having the operation. Sir Stanford did not guarantee complete recovery, but he gave an assurance that the pain would lessen. This, in itself, was inducement enough.

Sir Stanford had to operate at the Westminster Hospital, so Kathleen was transferred there. The operation took place on 27 July, and Kathleen pinned all her hopes and prayers on its success. She was allowed no visitors for a week afterwards, not even Bernie. After that time, as promised, the pain decreased. Visitors were pleasantly surprised by how well she looked.

'I shall have to be patient,' Kathleen told Winifred. 'The miracle has happened but it will be some time before I regain my strength.'[1]

But no miracle had taken place. As Dr Newton of Westminster Hospital states, 'The operation did not achieve the required result. I clearly recall Sir Stanford was enormously impressed at Miss Ferrier's courage during her painful illness.'

[1] *The Life of Kathleen Ferrier.*

Kathleen had an opal ring which Bernie had always admired. Saying it was now too big for her fingers, she gave it to Bernie telling her, 'Wear it for me, it's just wasting where it is.' Bernie had never possessed such an expensive piece of jewellery and one can only hope that Kathleen felt well rewarded for her generosity by Bernie's obvious pleasure as the ring glowed on her finger.

Barbirolli visited often, and she told him that she sometimes passed her time by going over the words of her repertoire. It annoyed her that she always got stuck at the same point in the Chausson. He commiserated, and told her that when he had been a cellist he had had the same problem with the *Bach Suites for Unaccompanied Cello*. She sang a few phrases of the Chausson for him and he was astounded that, despite her ravaged body, the voice was untouched, as beautiful as ever.

At the end of September she very tactfully explained to the staff of Westminster Hospital that she would like to be transferred back to University College Hospital. Not because she was in any way dissatisfied, but because she wanted to return to her friends – and she viewed the staff at UCH as friends.

'Nurses don't cry that easily,' states Bernie, 'but when I went into the little kitchen at UCH on the afternoon of our return, I found two of them crying their eyes out, as if their hearts would break. I did my best to comfort them, then made them go in to Kath and say hello. They came out all smiles, the tears were forgotten.'

Several old friends came to visit her. One was Joan Hammond, 'She looked radiant and laughed so much,' wrote Dame Joan.[1] One topic Dame Joan did not discuss with Kathleen was that she had deputised for her on several occasions, during Kathleen's illness. Occasionally managers had complained to Dame Joan of Kathleen's unreliability, perhaps not fully aware of the gravity of the disease. A seemingly casual remark along these lines could produce the unnerving phenomenon of the normally placid Australian in full operatic fury.

In fairness to the managers, it must be stated that there were extenuating circumstances for their remarks. Tickets for Kathleen's recitals were always sold out weeks in advance, and it was no easy task to find a substitute of Kathleen's calibre at short notice. If an audience

[1] *A Voice, a Life*, Joan Hammond, Gollancz.

had come to hear Kathleen Ferrier, it was understandably disappointed to be presented with an alternative artist. Money had often to be refunded at a substantial loss to the bookers. Joan Hammond, as a soprano, could offer a replacement, but for orchestral works a contralto was needed.

The previous year, due to their similarity of repertoire, Nancy Evans had often been called upon to deputise for Kathleen. Where broadcasts were concerned, both Nancy and the BBC conspired to protect Kathleen's morale: 'Kath had been booked to sing *Das Lied von der Erde* at the 1953 Proms,' recalled Nancy Evans. 'But the producer knew she was unwell and he couldn't take a chance. So two contracts were issued, one for Kath and one for me, for the same performance, so that if Kath could not make it they were not left high and dry, and I could step in at the last moment. I was asked to keep this an absolute secret as none of us wanted Kath to know, it would have been dreadful for her. She thought I was the deputy who came in at the last moment – that was what we wanted her to think.'

Nancy remembers visiting Kathleen after she had deputised for her at a performance of *The Dream of Gerontius*, which had been conducted by Barbirolli. Kathleen greeted her with a stern face, saying, 'I've had a letter from John, about your performance', then read out, 'I'm afraid I've got to tell you, Katie, that Nancy was awfully good.' She then kissed her. 'You'd think visiting her in hospital wouldn't be fun,' continued Nancy, 'but it was. Bernie was always there, and as soon as six o'clock came, Kath would say, "Right, Bernie, the bar's open." Bernie would pull back the curtains and there, on the window ledge, would be a line of bottles.'

For all her determinedly good spirits, Kathleen was fading. Once again visitors had to be restricted. Winifred and Bernie were with her night and day. 'The nightmare pain returned,' remembered Bernie. 'Days and nights seemed to be rolled into one. The doctors tried to persuade Kath to have an injection to ease the pain, but she refused, on the grounds that it would make her sleepy, and she would miss her meals and be unable to keep up her strength. She could barely move, but she could smile.' And she remembered Bernie's birthday. At seven that morning Rhona Phillips telephoned to congratulate Bernie on behalf of Kathleen, with the message that, as Kathleen had enjoyed a good night's sleep, there was no need to hurry in.

Bernie disregarded the last part of the message, and arrived at eight-thirty as usual. Sister Phillips intercepted her and explained that Kathleen had insisted she telephone, but the true reason Bernie had been asked not to hurry in, was because Kathleen was sleeping. She had, in reality, spent a bad night with hardly any sleep at all, and had had to accept an injection.

Bernie peeped in and found an envelope with her name on it propped on the locker. Inside was a cheque and a card signed 'With love from Kaff'.

For a few days Kathleen was desperately ill then, incredibly, her strength returned, and some of her friends were allowed to visit again.

Relieved at the improvement, Winifred took a break. She went for a week's holiday to the Lake District but had not been gone two days before a telephone call came from Bernie. Kathleen had had another relapse.

Winifred caught the next train back to London and arrived at the hospital at ten p.m.. She was greeted by a wan Kathleen who told her, 'You'll be getting me the sack, calling at this time of night.'

Six weeks later, Kathleen told Sister Phillips, 'Wouldn't it be lovely if I could just go to sleep and not wake up again.'

On 8 October 1953, her wish came true.

EPILOGUE

Kathleen's untimely death cast a pall not only over musical circles, but over much of Britain. People were stunned: the conspiracy of silence with which she had surrounded her illness had worked well – perhaps too well, as the public were unprepared for the end. But newspapers, radio and the few television sets there were in those days, soon acquainted people with the truth. To many, it seemed that they had suffered a personal loss. Barbirolli wrote that, in the three weeks following her death, countless people approached him, and their sentiments were always similar: 'I felt ill when I heard the news.'[1]

Celebrities who had been part of her life were swiftly sought out by reporters, to whom they readily gave quotes. 'She has no equal,' stated Britten; Sargent claimed her voice was 'of exceptional beauty, coupled with a woman of the greatest artistry, integrity and intelligence'. Bruno Walter added, 'She is irreplaceable', and listed the gramophone records they had made together as his proudest achievement. Later, a reporter suggested to him that, perhaps, the 'cult' of Kathleen Ferrier was exaggerated. Walter simply shook his head and answered, 'She is for keeps'. Musician Peter Feuchtwanger recalls an occasion, in 1956, when he was attending a Bruno Walter orchestral rehearsal. A journalist asked Walter for his greatest musical experiences, to which he answered, 'To have known Kathleen Ferrier and Gustav Mahler, in that order.'

In accordance with her wishes, Kathleen was cremated at Golders Green Crematorium, as her father had been two years previously. The service was private, attended only by close friends and relatives. A bed filled with roses named after her was planted in the Garden of Remembrance. According to the handbook of the National Rose Society, the Kathleen Ferrier Rose is deep salmon pink with lighter shades, semi-double, opening to two and a half inches, in small clusters on erect stems, fragrant, free flowering and very vigorous.

[1] *Radio Times*, 30 October 1953.

Public recognition of her life, and her life's work was given on Tuesday 24 November 1953 at Southwark Cathedral, where she had so often sung in oratorio. The service was presided over by her old friend Cuthbert Bardsley, then Bishop of Croydon. About three hundred people had been invited. Bardsley recalls: 'I woke up that morning feeling that I had better get to the Cathedral early as I anticipated rather more than three hundred would turn up, but I was utterly unprepared for the crowds that were there, the streets were nearly jammed.'

More than a thousand were eventually fitted into the cathedral, many standing in the aisles or at the back. Winifred, Bernie, Roy Henderson and Dr Hutchinson were there. Shopgirls, clerks, nurses and housewives mingled with celebrities such as John Barbirolli, Arthur Bliss, Astra Desmond, Benjamin Britten and Peter Pears, Joyce Grenfell, Myra Hess, Gerald Moore, Laurence Olivier and Vivien Leigh, Gladys Ripley and Elsie Suddaby.

During his address, Bardsley told the congregation: 'Her exuberant love of life had communicated itself through everything she sang. She seemed to bring into this world a radiance from another world.' He added, 'Born among the warm hearts of the North Country, her mysticism found expression in a genuine compassionate caring for her fellow men. She wore herself out on their behalf, travelling long hours in crowded railway carriages, sleeping in badly-heated hotels, endeavouring to answer every human appeal for help. She knew she was a steward of a great and glorious possession, and was determined to use it to bring happiness into the lives of millions.'

All of this was true, but he could have further added that her greatest happiness was in singing to an audience and that she was rewarded by the appreciation and, indeed, love that she received in return. To Kathleen it was no self-sacrifice but a fulfilment, a labour of love.

Throughout the following months there were several memorial services, notably one with the Hallé orchestra under Barbirolli, at the Free Trade Hall, Manchester. The music chosen was not that with which Kathleen would normally have been associated, but Fauré's *Requiem* was appropriate.

The Etruscan Choral Society, under the administration of her old friend Harry Vincent, also paid tribute to Kathleen. Vincent chose a suitably varied programme of music which he felt she would have enjoyed. This included the Wilbye madrigal, 'The Lady Oriana', and Renee's 'Italian Salad', which burlesques Rossini opera. But the evening ended solemnly, when two songs were sung in memory of Kathleen, 'O Lovely Heart' and 'How Very Dear She Was', the latter solely with male voices.

The British Council in Paris remembered Kathleen with an evening of gramophone records. *The Gramophone* for December 1953, covered the event:

> The recital was attended by the most celebrated musicians in Paris, all of whom had come to pay homage to the greatest, and best loved, of all British artists. Pierre Bernac, [who had coached her French pronunciation for the Chausson], spoke most movingly of Kathleen and at the end of his vivid and intimate address there was scarcely a dry eye in the concert room. The French Foreign Office, the British, American, Dutch and Italian Embassies were represented.

Kathleen's estate totalled £15,134, not a fortune for a world-famous singer, even by the standards of the day. In hospital, Kathleen had said that when she was better she would give a concert for the funds of the radiotherapy department of University College Hospital where she had been treated with such concern. But this had never been possible. So, in October 1953, an appeal was launched by Barbirolli, Laurence Olivier, Myra Hess, Benjamin Ormerod and Bruno Walter for funds to establish a cancer fund in her name.

Donations came in from all over the world from choral societies, gramophone societies, music clubs and thousands of individuals. Sometimes these were sizable amounts but, according to the *News Chronicle* for 30 April 1954, 'much of it (was) in shilling postal orders from anons. A Huddersfield pensioner sent two £5 notes in a battered envelope. A woman in the teashop sent £1.' It seemed people wanted to do everything they could to repay Kathleen for the joy her singing had given them.

A concert was given by the Hallé at the Royal Festival Hall to launch the Kathleen Ferrier Cancer Research Fund, for which Bruno Walter flew over from America to share the conducting with Barbirolli. Neither conductor accepted a fee. Walter chose Schubert's *Unfinished Symphony* and the Prelude to Wagner's *Parsifal*, while Barbirolli conducted Elgar's *Enigma Variations* (Kathleen had loved the work and Barbirolli had memories of conducting the piece while Kathleen stood in the wings listening, flashing him a smile if she caught his eye) and ended the evening with the Prelude to *Dream of Gerontius*. There were no singers at the concert and only the ghost of a song. Barbirolli also conducted the orchestra for Purcell's 'When I am Laid in Earth' which Kathleen had often sung. That night a solitary cor anglais played the singer's part.

There was a final tribute at that concert, which was unexpected and completely spontaneous. Almost before the last note of Elgar's great theme had died away the members of the orchestra all got to their feet and stood with bowed heads. The audience too, at first hesitantly, stood and bowed their heads. The *News Chronicle* of 8 May 1954, reports: 'For two minutes there was utter silence, there was not a cough, not a rustle. Barbirolli set down his baton and left the platform; his orchestra followed him. Quietly, the great audience dispersed.'

James Thomas, of the *News Chronicle*, eloquently ended his report of the concert, 'It was Dr Walter, leaning from his rostrum during the playing of the Schubert symphony, who perhaps brought the concert closest to song. He whispered to his violins: "Sing, here you must sing." And the violins sang, for there was no one else to sing last night at London's Festival Hall.'

Despite the solemnity, there was nothing morbid about the occasion; rather, it was a night of fond memories. Later, in the *Nursing Times* of 22 May 1954, Sister Rhona Phillips, who had done so much during Kathleen's stays in hospital, contributed some of her own recollections: 'She was a most wonderful person . . . a gay patient, facing the future with happy stoicism . . . her happy nature and her courage filled those of us who cared for her with joy and wonder; she was an inspiration to us all.' Sensible Sister Phillips followed her piece with the address of the Cancer Fund. That fund is still in existence. There is a plaque to Kathleen in the waiting room of the radiology department of UCH and in 1987 the Kathleen Ferrier Chair of Clinical Oncology was created at UCH and Middlesex School of Medicine. Professor Souhami gave the Inaugural Lecture on 24 November 1987.

Another fund was started also, as the result of a letter to *The Times*, which suggested a scholarship be founded to perpetuate Kathleen's memory. Administered by the Royal Philharmonic Society, the Kathleen Ferrier Memorial Scholarship Fund was set up, open to singers of all voices and both sexes who are either British born, or holders of British, Commonwealth or Republic of Ireland passports. An annual competition decides the winners, who must be over twenty-one but younger than twenty-six.

The scholarship competition, which usually takes place in April, near Kathleen's birthday, is held at the Wigmore Hall where, as a young hopeful, she auditioned for John Tillett. There are now additional prizes, including one from Decca International. Considerable prestige accompanies the prizes and several international singers are past recipients.

In the autumn of 1954 a book entitled *Kathleen Ferrier, A Memoir* was published by Hamish Hamilton. Edited by Neville Cardus, the memoir contains a chapter by Cardus himself plus chapters from Roy Henderson, Benjamin Britten, Barbirolli, Bruno Walter and Gerald Moore, all of whom donated their royalties to the scholarship fund. Winifred is of the opinion that, 'Of all the tributes paid to Kathleen since her death, the memoir would have pleased her the most. That these great musicians should have written so enthusiastically about her would have filled her with astonishment and delight.'

Generously illustrated, the memoir received good reviews and went into several editions, the *Daily Mail* commenting:

The word 'love' dominates everywhere . . . and Gerald Moore makes clear why . . . 'Where Kathleen is concerned,' he declares. 'lukewarm feelings did not exist. She was surrounded by the love that her personality and her gifts deserved.' He quotes a friend, 'Any man who does not acknowledge that Kathleen Ferrier is the most wonderful woman in the world has something wrong with him.' Moore remarks, 'It was not a case, let me add, of 100 men and a girl, for though we men loved her, our wives loved her themselves.'

In addition to his contribution to the memoir, Barbirolli also paid tribute to her at the 1954 Edinburgh Festival where he dedicated a performance of the Verdi *Requiem* to her, to 'commemorate her association with the Festival'. It was a work she loved.

In 1955, Winifred's biography, *The Life of Kathleen Ferrier*, was published, also by Hamish Hamilton. Winifred had been shattered by her sister's death and the book was written only after a great deal of heart-searching. But the writing of it acted as a panacea; 'by poring over memories and committing them to paper, the grief became easier to bear.' The book was translated into Dutch, Danish and, later, German.

An astounding number of recordings turned up from various sources, after Kathleen's death. They are still being discovered and, at time of writing, Decca have just released a version of *Kindertotenlieder* which Kathleen sang with the Concertgebouw, under Klemperer, at a live concert at the Holland Festival, which was broadcast on 12 July 1951 – the same concert at which she had sung the Mahler *Resurrection* symphony which Decca had issued, in record and cassette form, to great acclaim in 1982. Kathleen's interpretation of *Kindertotenlieder* with Klemperer is quite different from the earlier version she recorded with Bruno Walter in 1949 (re-issued by HMV in 1972 and now on compact disc). Kathleen was always happier singing to a live audience, rather than performing in the more controlled conditions of a recording studio. As *Sunday Telegraph* journalist, Caroline Faulder, put it: 'Fortunately for posterity, some of the magic she created every time she walked on to a concert platform has been captured on record.'

The first of the previously unknown recordings to be unearthed was the broadcast recital from Norway. This came about through a visit made to Winifred, in 1956, by Ella Arntsen of Norsk Rikstringkasting, who was planning a radio programme on Kathleen. During the conversation, Winifred mentioned a postcard she had received from Kathleen, saying that she was going to sing a song in Norwegian. When Ms Arntsen returned to Oslo she located the radio recording, and found the song to be Jensen's 'Altar', which Kathleen had specially learnt for the occasion. It was part of a whole recorded recital which included songs by Purcell, Handel and Wolf. The programme director of Norsk Rikstringkasting, Thorstein Diesen, eventually presented the recorded recital to Winifred, 'as a gift for your own personal use'. Finally, Decca issued it as an LP.

The record of Kathleen's lieder recital with Bruno Walter was made from a BBC broadcast from the Edinburgh Festival in 1949, and issued by Decca in 1975. For all the differences of opinion about Walter's playing, there is no doubt that he inspired Kathleen as could no other pianist. Her singing of the *Frauenliebe und Leben* was described as full of radiance, passion and tenderness – everything that Schumann could have desired.

Another exciting Ferrier find was the complete recording of the 1951 live performance of *Orfeo ed Euridice* that she gave in Amsterdam. This had been broadcast at the time, but it did not occur to anyone that a recording of the broadcast might still exist. It was only through sheer luck, in 1976, that record producer Klaas A. Postuma found a tape of the broadcast performance in the archives of the Dutch Broadcasting Corporation. Despite the fact that, as this was a live performance, there were various extraneous noises from the audience and that members of the ballet sound as though they might have been wearing heavy boots, when EMI released the recording, it was viewed by many as the musical event of the year. Everyone who was eligible for royalties donated them to the Kathleen Ferrier Memorial Scholarship Fund.

The recording of Chausson's *Poème de l'Amour et de la Mer* was issued by Decca in 1985. The original was on privately-made 78 rpm discs from a BBC broadcast which was well below the technical standards of today. Consequently it was difficult to decide whether to issue the recording. Some people, including Gerald Moore, thought not. On the other hand, it was the only record of Kathleen singing in French, and singing with Barbirolli. On the whole, the record was enthusiastically welcomed, and perhaps her performance of this work is an indication of the direction Kathleen's career might have taken had she lived.

Some critics consider the 'Poème' to be Chausson's finest work. Wagnerian in its harmonies, yet with the delicacy of Massenet, it is unique. 'This music needs both richness of voice and strength of interpretative impulse to bring it off,' stated *Ovation* magazine. 'Kathleen Ferrier is astounding. She brings to life the anguish of the final part as vividly as the limpid beauty of the opening. In Sir John Barbirolli she has a partner, not a mere accompanist, and despite the rather faded sonics this is a recording to treasure.'

The other side of the record contains Brahms's *Four Serious Songs*, sung in English. These were written originally for piano accompaniment. Malcolm Sargent, however, had transcribed them for orchestra, during the bedside vigil of his terminally-ill daughter. This increased the emotion Kathleen felt for the songs, and her performance is further enhanced in this recording by the fact that it is performed in front of a live audience. 'This recording qualifies as a classic,' *Ovation* continued. 'The latent tragedy in the first songs and the shining optimism and faith of the last, are captured by the Ferrier voice (and Ferrier heart) in a way that other singers have not been able to approach.' The royalties from the Chausson go to the Kathleen Ferrier Cancer Research Fund and those from the *Serious Songs* to the Malcolm Sargent Cancer Fund for Children.

There was one great disappointment. The November 1953 edition of *The Gramophone* carried the news:

The Decca Record Company regret to announce that Decca LXT 2789 (works by Britten, Purcell and Morely) . . . will not now be issued. When the details of the May release were first compiled, it appeared possible to have the record ready at least shortly after the release date. Miss Kathleen Ferrier's continued illness made this impossible, and the record had still not been made when the tragic news of her death became known last month.

In 1952 Britten, Peter Pears and Kathleen had given a series of concerts in aid of the English Opera Group. Their programme consisted of solos and duets (including the comic song 'The Deaf Woman's Courtship', which Kathleen performed, to much mirth, in a feeble and cracked voice). To complete the programme, Britten had written a canticle for the three of them, *Abraham and Isaac*, and he was anxious to put this on record. Several dates had been fixed to do this at Decca studios, but had to be cancelled because of Kathleen's illness. Finally, the Decca engineers arranged to set up their equipment in her bedroom at Hamilton Terrace, to record there. Lord Harewood, who visited Kathleen at the time, remembers how 'optimistic' she had been about these plans, but again her health broke down, and the project was never completed.

After her death, there seemed to Britten to be just one other possibility of having the piece on record. A broadcast had been made of a concert in which the canticle had been performed, and the BBC readily granted permission to Decca to issue this as a record. Then the blow fell. The recording of the broadcast had been inadvertently destroyed. In *Kathleen Ferrier, A Memoir*, Britten later wrote: 'There are many beautiful performances of hers recorded for our delight but it is my own special, selfish grief that none of my own music is among them.'

Apart from a few arrangements of folk songs, all that exists of Kathleen singing Britten, as far as we know, is the private recording of *The Rape of Lucretia*, highlights of which were issued on the Educ Media record.

On 7 October 1954, the people of Lancashire paid homage to Kathleen in yet another memorial service, presided over by Barbirolli and the Hallé. It was a drizzly evening, but this did not dampen the spirits of the 3,000-strong audience who waited for the doors of King George's Hall, Blackburn, to open. Reporter Margaret Roberts later wrote in the *News Chronicle* that she felt like an eavesdropper, 'such was the intimacy of the conversation', as people chatted about their personal memories of Kathleen.

The occasion was the Lancashire unveiling of a bronze head of Kathleen, the work of Australian sculptor Arthur J. Fleischmann. The work had originally been unveiled in London at the National Society's 21st exhibition of painting, drawing, engraving and sculpture, which opened at the Royal Institute Galleries in Piccadilly on 12 February 1954. It had subsequently been acquired by Blackburn Corporation.

It was a fine civic occasion, of the kind Kathleen would have appreciated. The Mayor of Blackburn was present, as were Winifred and Barbirolli's mother, Mémé, who at eighty had travelled from London for the occasion. Sir Benjamin Ormerod gave the address, remarking that it was 'in this very hall' that he had first heard Kathleen sing; it was in *Messiah* on Boxing Day, 1943. He recalled parties where she had sung, not just from her concert repertoire, but amusing rhymes she had made up herself. Barbirolli had been present on one occasion, and had lent Ormerod his propelling pencil with which to conduct. He also recalled visiting her in hospital and how 'I always came away more cheerful than I went, marvelling at her fortitude'.

In May of 1967, Winifred sold Kathleen's personal musical scores for the benefit of the Scholarship Fund. They were bought for the Blackburn Library, Museum and Art Gallery. There was, however, one piece of music they failed to acquire, and this was the manuscript for *Abraham and Isaac*, upon which Britten had written, 'For Kath and Peter'. It had been bought by a private dealer, Clifford Maggs of the antiquarian booksellers Maggs Brothers, who obtained it on behalf of one of their overseas clients. Such, however, was the desire of Blackburn Corporation to possess the music, that Maggs Brothers allowed them to have it.

To complete this collection, Winifred then sent to Blackburn Kathleen's CBE medal and ribbon and the Gold Medal of the Royal Philharmonic Society. In 1986, a sheltered housing complex was opened in Blackburn and named after Kathleen. These medals were displayed at the official opening ceremony as were many records and memorabilia.

The Tennessee Williams poems were sent to Winifred by Peter Feuchtwanger and artist Michael Garady. They had come into their possession on 3 October 1978 when Williams was in London and visiting Garady's studio for a painting lesson – Williams found painting relaxing.

As they painted, the two men were listening to Kathleen's recording of *Kindertotenlieder* (Bruno Walter) and Williams had not heard her before. 'I think her voice was difficult for him at first,' recalls Garady. 'The impact was strange and he became very quiet and docile, but it was a good atmosphere for painting.'

In the evening Feuchtwanger joined them and, continues Garady, 'The day culminated in a special, warm atmosphere. I played a record of Kathleen singing "He Was Despised" and that was when her voice really reached him, he understood the words, it was in English. "We don't have anything like that in America," Tennessee said, and he was the last person in the world to be sentimental.'

Garady played more of Kathleen's records and it was obvious Williams was becoming very moved. '"Dedication to art is a great thing," I remember him saying,' recalls Garady. 'I told him that if he really loved her singing he should write a poem about her for posterity, "But what can I write about that heavenly voice? One feels so inadequate in front of such a voice?" he replied.'

'He sat down and wrote a poem. We tried for half a dozen but he wrote just the two. They took about an hour. Kathleen's records were playing all the way through, the "Abschied", Bach and Handel.'

Almost thirty-five years after her death, interest in Kathleen and her work is still strong. Winifred maintains a considerable correspondence with Ferrier fans all over the world, many of whom regard her as a personal friend, the last link with their heroine. 'It is very moving to meet those who still remember her,' says Winifred, 'their faces light up when they talk about her. Some write, regretting they were too young to have heard her in person but who love the records. Students and schoolgirls choose to prepare projects about her and write for information or photographs. Many send cards regularly on her birthday. Nadia Boulanger wrote every year, until her death. A nun, Sister Mary Teresa Joseph of St Edward's Convent of Mercy, London, who taught in a school, made a collection among the children every year for the Cancer Fund. There are houses in schools named after her, and so it continues.'

So it does. She was one of the subjects chosen by contestant Paul Campion in a 1983 series *Mastermind* television programme, and at a recent Edinburgh Festival a cantata was performed which was based on incidents from her career.

Attempts have been made to make a film about Kathleen's life, but these have been firmly resisted by the resolute Winifred. 'Hers was not a Mimi story and to have made an interesting film would have meant distorting it, something that Kathleen would have hated. Besides, Gerald Moore, Benjamin Britten and Barbirolli would probably have taken a poor view of actors playing their parts.' Winifred also concedes, 'Kathleen was a lot easier than me in her private life, she could be very easy going; but musically she never compromised.'

Barbirolli wrote that Kathleen's singing contained 'all the bloom and tender ache of spring'. She sang movingly because she was a great artist and not, as has often been stated, because she imbued the music with her own tragedy. Kathleen was a fighter and fought right to the end. Singing was life's blood to her and, unlike some professionals, she often sang from pure joy or for fun. Kathleen could always be relied upon to sing at a party, it was no chore to her. Towards the end of her life she wrote to Barbirolli, after she had spent a couple of days with him and Evelyn: 'It has been a memorable and lovely few days, and I have saved some heather and rose petals of my posy to keep and gloat over in my old age.' It was not a brave façade, it was something she believed to be true. She believed she would live to an old age – Winifred is convinced that it was only after her final operation that she accepted the inevitable.

In assessing Kathleen's life it would be unbalanced to place cancer in the leading role. From 1951 onwards she sang better than she had ever sung before and made her most important records. When she was on stage there was never any indication that anything was wrong with her; all that transmitted itself to the audience was delight in what she was doing. The only exception was the last *Orpheus* and even then most of the audience were unaware of the true circumstances.

Most singers spend five or six years studying at college, but Kathleen did not have that luxury. She did it the hard way, learning while she worked, and despite leaving school early and having little knowledge of foreign languages she climbed to the very top. Several singers are still remembered long after their deaths, but few so positively.

Bruno Walter said she should be remembered in a major key, and that is certainly how those who were close to her remember her. It is what she would have wanted.

DISCOGRAPHY

DECCA

BRAHMS

Brahms Recital
Vier ernste Gesänge Op.121 (a); Sapphische Ode Op.94/4; Botschaft–Wehe,
Lüftchen Op.47/1 (b); Gestillte Sehnsucht Op.91/1; Geistliches Wiegenlied
Op.91/2 (c); Rhapsody for Contralto, Male Chorus & Orchestra (d)
(a) Newmark (pno); (b) Spurr (pno); (c) Gilbert (vla), Spurr (pno); (d) LPO &
Choir/Krauss
ACL 306 (LP)

GLUCK

Orfeo ed Euridice (abridged)
Ayars, Vlachopoulos/SPO/Stiedry
417 182–1 DM (LP) 417 182–4 DM (MC)

MAHLER

Das Lied von der Erde
Patzak/WP/Walter
414 194–2 DH (CD) 414 194–1 DM (LP) 414 194–4 DM (MC)

Symphony No. 2 *Resurrection*
Vincent/CO & Chorus/Klemperer
D264D 2 (2LP)

COLLECTIONS

Kathleen Ferrier Collection
Contains the following LPs (side order in this set varies from that of the individual LPs):
ACL 306–310; 414 194–1 DM; 414 623–1 DG plus: **Mahler: 3 Rückert-Lieder; Jensen: Altar AKF 1 (7LP)**

RECITALS

Arias
J.S. BACH: My Master and My Lord . . . Grief for sin; Ah! now is my Saviour gone; Have mercy, Lord, on me; O Gracious God! . . . If my tears be unavailing; Ah Golgotha! . . . See the Saviour's outstretched hands (Matthäuspassion) (a); Handel: Art thou troubled? (Rodelinda: Dove sei, amato bene?); Frondi tenere . . . Ombra mai fu (Serse); Gluck: What is life to me without thee? (Orfeo ed Euridice: Che farò senza Euridice? (b); Mendelssohn: Woe unto them; O rest in the Lord (Elijah) (c)
(a) Bach Choir/ JO/Jacques; (b) LSO/Sargent; (c) BNO/Neel
ACL 308 (LP)

Bach & Handel Arias
J.S. Bach: Qui sedes (Mass in B); Grief for sin (Matthäuspassion); All is fulfilled (Johannespassion); Agnus Dei (Mass in B); Handel: Return O God of Hosts (Samson): O Thou that tellest good tidings to Zion (Messiah), Father of Heaven (Judas Maccabaeus); He was despised (Messiah) LPO/Boult
414 623–2 DH (CD) 414 623–1 DG (LP) 414 623–4 DG (MC)

Brahms: Liebeslieder-Walzer Op.52/1–18;
Neue Liebeslieder-Walzer Op. 65/15 Mahler: Kindertotenlieder; Seefried/ Patzak, Günter/Curzon, Gál; CO/Klemperer*
417 634–1 DM (LP) 417 634–4 DM (MC)

A Broadcast Recital of English Songs
Purcell: Mad Bess of Bedlam ('From silent shades'); Hark! The echoing air (The Fairy Queen); Handel: Like as the love-lorn turtle (Atalanta); How changed the vision (Admeto) (a); Stanford: The Fairy Lough; A soft day; Parry: Love is a bable; Vaughan Williams: Silent noon; Bridge: Go not, happy

day; Warlock: Sleep; Pretty ring-time; Traditional: Come you not from Newcastle (arr. Britten); Kitty my Love (arr. Hughes) (b)
(a) Spurr (pno); (b) Stone (pno)
ACL 310 (LP)

Chausson: Poème de l'amour et de la mer (a);
J.S. Bach: Vergiß mein nicht; Ach, daß nicht die letzte Stunde (b); Brahms (arr.Sargent): Vier ernste Gesänge (in English) (c)
(a) HO/Barbirolli; (b) Silver; (c) BBC SO/Sargent
414 095–1 DH (LP) 414 095–4 DH (MC)

Grandi Voci: Schubert, Brahms & Schumann
Speech by Kathleen Ferrier: 'What the Edinburgh Festival has meant to me'; Schubert: Die junge Nonne D828; Der Vollmond strahlt auf Bergeshöh'n (Romance from Rosamunde D797); Du liebst mich nicht! D756; Der Tod und das Mädchen D531; Suleika l D720; Du bist die Ruh' D776; Brahms: Immer leiser wird mein Schlummer Op.105/2; Der Tod, das ist die kühle Nacht Op.96/1; Botschaft–Wehe, Lüftchen Op. 47/1; Von ewiger Liebe–Dunkel, wie dunkel Op. 43/1; Schumann: Frauenliebe und Leben: Walter (piano)
414 611–2 DH (CD) 414 611–1 DG (LP) 414 611–4 DG (MC)

Lieder Recital
Schumann: Frauenliebe und Leben; Volksliedchen Op. 51/2; Widmung Op. 25/1 (a); Schubert: Gretchen am Spinnrade D118; Die junge Nonne D828; An die Musik D547; Der Musensohn D764; Wolf: Verborgenheit; Der Gärtner; Auf ein altes Bild; Auf einer Wanderung (b)
(a) Newmark (pno); (b) Spurr (pno)
ACL 307 (LP)

Mahler & Brahms Recital
Mahler: Rückert-Lieder–Ich atmet' einen Linden Duft; Ich bin der Welt abhanden gekommen; Um Mitternacht (a); Brahms: Rhapsody for Contralto, Male Chorus & Orchestra (b); Gestillte Sehnsucht Op. 91/1; Geistliches Wiegenlied Op. 91/2 (c); Vier ernste Gesänge Op. 121 (d)
(a) WP/Walter; (b) LPO & Choir/Krauss; (c) Gilbert (vla), Spurr (pno); (d) Newmark (pno)
421 299–2 DH (CD)

Pergolesi: Stabat Mater (a);
J.S. Bach: Have mercy, Lord, on me (Matthäuspassion) (b); Cantata BWV 11 Praise our God (c)

262

(a) Taylor/Nottingham Oriana Choir/BNSO/Henderson; (b) NSO/
Sargent; (c) Mitchell, Herbert, Parsons/ Cantata Singers/JO/ Jacques
417 466–1 DM (LP) 417 466–4 DM (MC)

Song Recital

Ma Bonny Lad (arr. Whittaker); The Keel Row (arr. Whittaker); Blow the
Wind Southerly (arr. Whittaker); I Have a Bonnet Trimmed with Blue (arr.
Hughes); My Boy Willie (arr. Sharp); I Know Where I'm Going (Hughes/
Gray); The Fidgety Bairn* (arr. Roberton); I Will Walk with my Love (arr.
Hughes); Ca' the Yowes* (arr. Jacobson); O Waly, Waly (arr. Britten);
Willow, Willow (arr. Warlock); The Stuttering Lovers (arr. Hughes); Now
Sleeps the Crimson Petal (Quilter); The Fair House of Joy (Quilter); To
Daisies (Quilter); Over the Mountains (Quilter); Have You Seen but a Whyte
Lillie Grow? (arr. Grew); Ye Banks and Braes (arr. Quilter); Drink to Me
Only (arr. Quilter); Down by the Sally Gardens (arr. Hughes); The Lover's
Curse (arr. Hughes)
Spurr (pno); Newmark* (pno)
417 192–2 DH (CD) ACL 309 (LP) KACC 309 (MC)

The World of Kathleen Ferrier

Blow the Wind Southerly (arr. Whittaker); The Keel Row (arr. Whittaker)
(a); Ma Bonny Lad (arr. Whittaker) (a); Bridge: Go Not, Happy day (b);
Come you not from Newcastle (arr. Britten) (b); Kitty my Love (arr. Hughes)
(b); Schubert: An die Musik D547 (a); Der Musensohn D764 (a); Brahms:
Sapphische Op. 94/4 (a); Jensen: Altar (a); Mahler: Um Mitternacht
(Rückert-Lieder) (c); Handel: Art thou troubled? (Dove sei, amato bene?) (d);
Gluck: Orfeo ed Euridice – Che puro ciel! (e); What is life to me without thee?
(Che farò senza Euridice?) (d); J.S. Bach: Have mercy, Lord, on me
(Matthäuspassion) (f); Handel: He was despised (Messiah) (g); Silent Night
(arr. Fagan) (h)
(a) Spurr (pno); (b) Stone (pno); (c) WP/Walter; (d) LSO/Sargent; (e) SPO/
Stiedry; (f) JO/Jacques; (g) LPO/Boult; (h) BNSO/Neel
PA 172 (LP) KCSP 172 (MC)

EMI

Arias

Gluck: What is life to me without thee? (Orfeo ed Euridice). Brahms:

Constancy, Feinsliebchen. Elgar: My Work is done (The Dream of Gerontius). Moore (pno).
HLM 7145 (LP)

Mahler: Kindertotenlieder (complete cycle) (a) Purcell: Sound the trumpet, Let us wander, (Shepherd, Leave decoying) (b) Mendelssohn: I would that my love, Greeting (b) (c) Handel: Spring is coming, (Come to me, soothing sleep) (b) Greene: O praise the Lord, I will lay me down in peace (b) (a) VPO/Walter (b) Moore (pno) (c) Baillie
HLM 7002 (CD)

GLUCK

Orfeo ed Euridice (complete live performance)
Netherlands Opera Orchestra and Chorus/Bruck/Koeman/Duval
RLS 725

ADDITIONAL RECORDINGS

KATHLEEN FERRIER: *The Singer and the Person*
REGL 368 LP

Introduced by Sir Peter Pears with tributes from Gerald Moore, Roy Henderson, Benjamin Britten, Bruno Walter, etc, and a selection of songs.
ZCF 368 MC

Accompanist not named, nor place where the concert was given, produced by Rodolphe, registered in Italy, contains a few songs not otherwise recorded. The best is 'Lasciatem morire' from *Arriana* by Monteverdi. Quality of recording rather poor.
RPK 22407

Danacord Records of Denmark produced a disc called 'Two Immortal Concerts', on one side, Brahms's *Alto Rhapsody* with the Danish Radio Male Chorus and the Danish Radio Symphony Orchestra conducted by Fritz Busch from a live concert on 6 October 1949. The other side is of Furtwängler conducting Beethoven's *Fifth Symphony*.
DACO 114

The Rape of Lucretia by Benjamin Britten. Excerpts taken from a live performance in 1946, produced by Educational Media Associates, P.O. Box 921, Berkeley, CA94701, USA, with Peter Pears, Joan Cross, Otakar Kraus, Edmund Donleavy, Owen Brannigan, Margaret Richie, Anna Pollak, the English Opera Group Orchestra conducted by Benjamin Britten.
IGI 369

Live recording produced in Italy of J. S. Bach's *Passio secundum Matthaeum* performed on 9 June 1950 in Vienna with the Wiener Symphoniker and Wiener Singverein conducted by Herbert von Karajan with Irmgard Seefried, Walther Ludwig, etc.
FO 1046

Beethoven's *Ninth Symphony* with the London Symphony Orchestra conducted by Bruno Walter with Isobel Baillie, Heddle Nash and William Parsons on 13 November 1947 in the Royal Albert Hall. Produced by the Bruno Walter Society in USA. Recording quality poor.
BWS 742

BBC Broadcast on 12 January 1953, not available as recording, and there unlikely to be in the forseeable future: Ferguson's *Discovery* (Fire Songs); Wordsworth's 'Red Skies', 'The Wind', Clouds; Rubra's Psalm No 6 'O Lord, Rebuke Me Not', Psalm No 23 'The Lord is my Shepherd' and Psalm No 150 'Praise Ye the Lord' Lush (pno).

There is a private recording of Kathleen affectionately burlesquing certain songs at a party during her second American tour. She sings five items. The first is 'Annie Laurie'; three others are parodies of Annie Chadwick's concert repertoire, 'Will o' the Wisp', 'The Antelope Song' and 'Sing Joyous Bird', the latter in piercing, not to say biting, soprano. The last song is 'The Floral Dance', which Tom Barker, Annie's husband, used to sing. She accompanies herself on the piano in all items. Annie heard the recording and told Win she 'loved it'.

INDEX

270

Hallé Orchestra, 9, 13, 41, 42, 81,
167, 176, 193, 205, 206, 208, 219,
220, 235, 247, 248, 254
Hamilton, Hamish, 238
Hamilton, Yvonne, 239
Hammond, Bernadine, xiv–xv, 67fn,
164–5, et seq.
Hammond, Joan, 52, 66, 243–4
Handel: *Messiah*, 9, 33, 41–2, 49,
64–5, 66, 79, 81–2, 139, 149, 205,
206, 219, 222, 225, 226, 254; at
Westminster Abbey, 57; *Ottone*, 77
Hanley, 41
Harewood, Lord, 89, 92, 189–90,
253
Hark Forrard variety show, 34–5
Harrison, Julius, 8
Harrison, Tom, 43–5, 55
Haydn: *Nelson Mass*, 191
Head, Michael, 42
Heifitz, Jascha, 135
Heinitz, Thomas, 73
Henderson, Roy, xiii, xv, 28, 50, 61,
62, 63, 65, 74, 84, 93, 101, 104,
108, 118, 166, 179, 199, 247, 250;
coaching by, 51–2, 53–4, 56, 68,
73, 78
Herbert, William, 182
Hess, Dame Myra, 51, 151–2, 180,
183, 192–3, 247, 248
Hetherington, Wyn, 33, 39
Hill, Granville, 12, 48, 66
Hill, Ralph, 100
Hilton, Dr Gwen, 190–1, 229
Hilton, Dr Reginald, 179, 180, 183,
186, 187, 188, 190, 194, 207, 208,
220, 229
Hodgson, Albert, 16
Holland, appearances in, 91, 116–
17, 118, 140–2, 168–9, 171–2,
188–90
Holliday, Jack, 28–9
Holliday, Judy, 158
Hooke, Emilie, 101

Hunter, Ian, 219
Hutchinson, Dr J.E., 33, 35, 36–8,
40, 41, 54, 247; singing lessons
with, 37–8, 40, 41, 62

Ibbs and Tillett (agents), 43, 45, 49,
57, 63, 65, 101
illness and treatment, 179–85, 190–
1, 196, 203, 207–8, 229–30, 233–6,
239–45

Jacques, Reginald, 52, 57, 79, 96,
100
Jacobson, Maurice, 29, 41, 42, 51,
56, 61, 64, 69, 70, 82, 166
Jacobson, Michael, 69–70
Jacobson, Susannah, 51, 69, 164,
166
James, Ifor, 150
Jarred, Mary, 63
Jewett, Paddy, 101, 133, 139, 153,
159, 160, 176
Johnson, Roy, 93–4
Jones, Roderick, 80
Jones, Trefor, 33
Joseph, Sister Mary Teresa, 256

Karajan, Herbert von, 3, 144, 165,
197
Kathleen Ferrier, A Memoir, 73fn, 90,
100, 184–5, 193, 201, 223, 250,
254
Kathleen Ferrier Cancer Research
Fund, 178, 248, 249, 253, 256
Kathleen Ferrier Memorial
Scholarship Fund, 172, 250, 252,
255
Kingdom, The, 65
Kirkby-Lunn, Louise, 37
Kisch, Eve, 40, 41
Kleiber, Erich, 164
Klemperer, Otto, 169, 174, 177,
189–90, 194, 251
Koshetz, Nina, 53